Praise for

The Compounders

"This is an excellent summary of a too-little-known phenomenon—the extraordinary long-term returns for a small group of publicly traded Swedish serial acquirers. The authors' thoughtful, analytical approach brings this story to light with great verve. As someone once said—a turbocharged hedgehog of a book."

—WILLIAM N. THORNDIKE, JR.
Author of *The Outsiders*; founder and managing director of Housatonic Partners

"A wise book, rare in its genuine focus on the essential principles of long-term compounding and wealth creation. Learn all you need to know to invest successfully in these compelling business models. No doubt this will be an invaluable guide for all investors. The historical deep dives into these winners serve as perfect templates to help investors find the next generation of 100-baggers."

—CHRISTOPHER MAYER
Portfolio manager and co-founder, Woodlock House Family Capital; author of *100 Baggers*

"*The Compounders* is an insightful exploration of the rare companies that consistently reinvest and deliver durable, long-term returns. It captures the strategies, cultures, and leadership qualities that set such firms apart. For anyone seeking to understand how disciplined capital allocation and decentralized decision-making can create lasting value, this book offers both inspiration and instruction."

—LAWRENCE A. CUNNINGHAM
Director, John L. Weinberg Center for Corporate Governance, University of Delaware; editor and publisher, *The Essays of Warren Buffett*

"A classic in the field of long-term investing. Highly rewarding and insightful reading that deepens your understanding of what truly drives value creation in companies over time."

—ADAM GERGE
Managing director, AEMG Capital; co-founder, Didner & Gerge Fonder AB

"The authors do a phenomenal job retelling the stories and strategies of a select group of compounding machines in Sweden. It is a must read if you love studying outperformance in the public markets."

—IAN J. CASSEL
CIO IFCM MicroCap Fund LP and founder of MicroCapClub

"The blueprint for turning small acquisitions into generational wealth—the proven, counterintuitive strategies behind the world's greatest compounding machines."

—TOBIAS CARLISLE
Portfolio Manager, Acquirers Funds®

"This is an excellent book that will make you look at conglomerates in a new light."

—MATTHEW PARTRIDGE
Moneyweek

The Compounders

From Small Acquisitions to Giant Shareholder Returns

9 Case Studies of Extraordinary Shareholder Value Creation

Oddbjørn Dybvad
Kjetil Nyland
Adnan Hadžiefendić

First published in 2025 by The Book Press.

Paperback ISBN: 978-1-917943-03-1
eBook ISBN: 978-1-917943-04-8

V 1.3

thebookpress.co

THE BOOK PRESS

Contents

Introduction

"Compound interest is the eighth wonder of the world. He who understands it, earns it; he who doesn't, pays it."
—Attributed to Albert Einstein[1]

IN 1976, WHEN shareholding was still relatively uncommon for the broader public, an ordinary woman in Sweden made a decision that would change her life in ways no one could have imagined. With a small amount of savings, she entered the bank to purchase shares in a little-known and recently listed company. However, even though this company was relatively obscure and new to the market, it had a long corporate history of 70 years, marked by a deep passion for engineering.

Year after year, she showed up at the company's annual general meetings, sitting quietly and listening intently. She didn't draw any attention to herself. Instead, she observed, learned, and held on to every share she owned. Through decades of market highs and lows, when others sold in fear or chased quick profits, she remained calm and stayed the course. She didn't focus on short-term price movements.

As the years turned into decades, her patience paid off in ways few could comprehend. What began as a modest investment snowballed into a fortune. She became a millionaire many times over simply by holding all that company's shares and its spin-offs for nearly 50 years.

The authors of this book learned of this woman's story when visiting the company she had invested in many decades later. Over time, the company had got to know her from her steady attendance at the AGMs. The woman, a regular shareholder with no public recognition, had quietly accomplished what most investors could only dream of.

It wasn't about luck. It resulted from unwavering belief, calm in the face of uncertainty, and discipline to focus on the long term. We were fortunate enough to later run into her at an AGM ourselves. Curious, we asked how she had decided to hold on to her shares for all those years. She seemed surprised by the question. Her answer was simple: "You don't sell great companies." Her journey serves as a reminder that extraordinary wealth isn't always built through bold moves, constant activity, or unique insights. Sometimes, it's built by simply staying the course and trusting in the power of time.

The company she had bought shares in? Bergman & Beving. Along with two of its spin-offs—Addtech and Lagercrantz—it is one of nine extraordinary firms you will meet in the pages ahead. A $1,000 investment in 1976 would have increased to $7.5 million today—excluding all dividends received. It is far from the only company in this book to have delivered such outstanding returns.

Just as this ordinary woman quietly allowed her wealth to compound for decades, a remarkable subset of companies has mastered the art of compounding wealth while flying under the radar. Their approach is, of course, more active: these are builders and acquirers par excellence. But they don't chase headlines or dazzle with flashy marketing. Instead, they relentlessly focus on creating long-term shareholder value. And they let time do the heavy lifting. Surprisingly, no book has yet told their story. We aim to change that.

Buy low, sell high the saying goes. But in fact the most astounding investment returns come from *buying well and selling never.* Nowhere is this more in evidence than in a small but intriguing universe of companies that seem to have perfected the art. Buyers and builders of other firms—with a strikingly keen eye for value—their structure and strategy combine to not only enable but accelerate the key drivers of business value compounding. In short: the amount of capital available for reinvestment, the return generated on that capital, and (the ultimate force multiplier) the duration over which these factors can be sustained.

Strikingly, they give a face to frugality. They don't have fancy offices or make showy investor presentations. Some of their headquarters are so small they seat just three people; during our visits, their CEOs have sometimes made our coffee. Some of these companies don't even display their names on the doors, and the leaders rarely make headlines or position themselves as heroes. Instead, they shine a light on the people within their decentralized cultures, crediting them with their enduring successes.

These acquisition-driven compounders operate with a simple and profoundly effective philosophy: decentralization. Push daily decision-making as close to the customer as possible, give extraordinary customer service, empower people with responsibility, accountability, and shareholder-friendly incentives, and give them ample room to grow. Pair this with an obsession and passion for delivering exceptional customer value and rewarding great performance, and people go the extra mile.

Such decentralization is reflected in their nimbleness when it comes to changing economic conditions. They have the flexibility to continuously pursue new opportunities for profitable growth. Take Lagercrantz's adroit navigation of the risk of commoditization when, loaded down with useless stock, it switched from product distribution to acquiring and developing niche product companies. Indeed, the knack of steering clear of assets at risk of becoming commoditized is common among these compounders. Instead, they direct capital towards recurring-like revenue and mission-critical products in small niches that generate strong cash flows. Take Mark Leonard and Constellation Software's focus on software developers that power chicken coops, manage cemeteries, or control traffic lights. In effect, Leonard identified a pond where the acquisition-driven compounder model allowed his company to fish on its own, while others went hunting for whales (often getting capsized in the process); the haul enjoyed by his shareholders as a result has been considerable. Another CEO featured in this book devised a recipe for generating a return of more than 100 times initial capital over 20 years. There are many more fascinating examples like this ahead; this book brings them together and explores them in depth.

The results speak for themselves. Over the past 35 years, $10,000 invested in these companies would have grown to an astonishing $8.7m—a compounded annual growth rate of 22%. They've outperformed all major indices, often by a significant margin. The questions naturally arise: How do they do it? What makes these companies so extraordinary? And most importantly, how can investors identify such long-term winners?

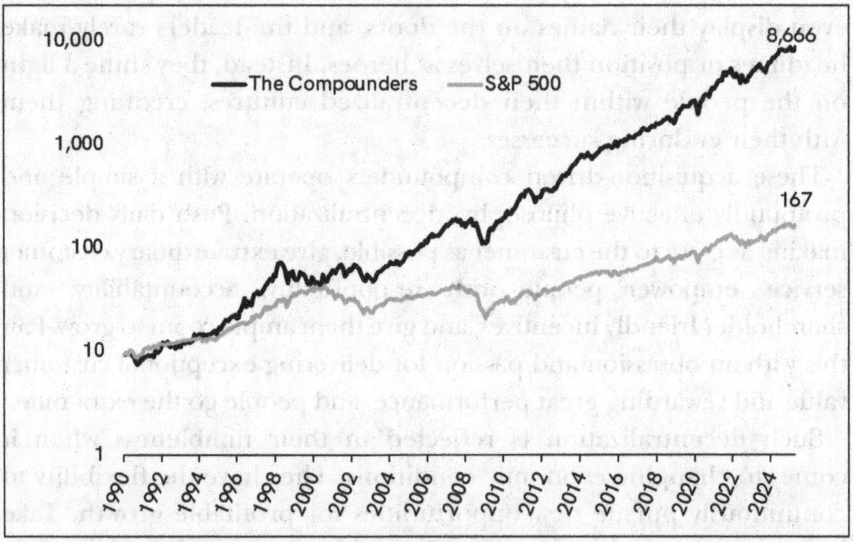

This book aims to answer those questions. Over almost two decades of research, and through significant firsthand experience, we have identified every characteristic that defines these firms and drives their success. This book will share them all, drawing on a wealth of real examples. They can best be summed up by two core principles:

1. **High-performing, decentralized cultures.** These nine companies foster meritocracy and empower local decision-makers to drive profitable earnings growth over multiple decades. Their performance is reinforced by substantial insider ownership and cash flow-based incentives that closely align leadership with long-term shareholder value.
2. **Durable reinvestment engines:** Management teams with an investor mindset. These companies are able to repeatedly allocate incremental capital in a disciplined manner to the highest-return opportunities because they are free from industry, geographic, or legacy constraints. In most cases, this means both organic investments and acquisitions of predominantly family-owned niche businesses.

Our many years of studying these companies has shown that those who embrace these principles tend to maintain remarkable returns on incremental capital—turning money into more money with amazing efficiency—and deliver strong earnings growth over decades. For shareholders, the result is nothing short of exceptional: multi-bagger returns and the opportunity to ride a phenomenal wave of success.

Why are we the ones telling this story? We have spent over two decades studying, analyzing, engaging with, and investing in acquisition-driven compounders. We've had countless conversations and interactions with companies, CEOs, directors, and employees, gaining a deep understanding of what makes these companies such interesting long-term investments.

As professionals, we've of course sought to share our knowledge with these firms over the years—but always found ourselves learning from them in surprising and profound ways. We have found our knowledge of investing compounded, as it were, through such interactions. Their unique practices and surprising insights have enriched our perspectives, and this book is our way of sharing those lessons and stories with a broader audience. This book is for investors looking to uncover their next long-term winners, as much as it is for executives and leaders eager to understand the critical aspects of compounding—as well as anyone curious about what it takes to create enduring value.

We owe a debt of gratitude to the many individuals who have shared their insights and experiences with us—employees and former employees, investors, analysts, and more. And to you, our reader, for trusting us with your time. We hope the unique attributes of acquisition-driven compounders inspire you.

In *The Compounders* we unveil the stories of nine remarkable acquisition-driven compounders that have richly rewarded those who believed in their potential and stayed invested. This book is designed to take you on a journey through the principles, strategies, and stories that define each of these successful companies.

We start by exploring the powerful nature of compounding, before taking a high-level overview of the key factors that have driven the success of the world's most successful compounders. You will notice that five of them hail from one country: so we also spend one chapter exploring the fascinating question of "Why Sweden?" Four of these names may be familiar to anyone with an investing background: Addtech, Lagercrantz, Indutrade, and Lifco. Known as "the big four," these companies have consistently delivered extraordinary results far outpacing the broader market and their peers. In fact, their performance has been so extraordinary that their returns have put them in the top 3% of the best-performing shares in Sweden (and the top 1% in the Nordics) since they were listed.

They have revolutionized the Swedish business landscape with their decentralized philosophies, and pioneered the practice of frequent acquisitions of small, family-owned niched companies. But their stories, as you will see with all of the compounders, goes beyond numbers.

The numbers, though, are impressive. Of the companies you will meet in this book, these are their total shareholder returns (including reinvested dividends) since being publicly listed:

- Lifco: 21-bagger—33% CAGR since IPO in 2014.
- Indutrade: 50-bagger—22% CAGR since IPO in 2005.
- Bergman & Beving (including spin-offs): 7,500-bagger—20% CAGR since IPO in 1976.
- Lagercrantz: 120-bagger—23% CAGR since IPO in 2001.
- Addtech: 210-bagger—26% CAGR since IPO in 2001.
- Constellation Software: 375-bagger—37% CAGR since IPO in 2006.
- Heico: 1,100-bagger—22% CAGR since 1990.
- AMETEK: 175-bagger—16% CAGR since 1990.
- Judges Scientific: 115-bagger—24% CAGR since IPO in 2003.

This book reveals the strategies that propelled these companies to the top, the leadership that steered them, and the lessons their journeys hold for businesses worldwide. By understanding their playbooks, you'll discover how these companies grew—and how you can apply their principles to your own endeavors.

1

The Power of Compounding

PICTURE YOURSELF AT a crossroads, faced with two options:

1. Take $1m in cash today.
2. Start with a single penny that doubles in value every day for 31 days.

Most people wouldn't hesitate—they'd choose the $1m and walk away. How could a humble penny compete with such a windfall? But here's the twist: by day 31, that penny, doubling daily, will have grown to an astonishing $21.5m.

Let's break down the penny's growth through compounding:

- Day 5: The penny is worth 32 cents.
- Day 10: It reaches $10.
- Day 14: It surpasses $100.
- Day 24: It exceeds $100,000.

At this stage, the growth becomes truly fascinating as the compounding curve steepens exponentially:

- Day 27: The penny grows to over $1m, outpacing the initial $1m cash option.
- Day 29: It climbs to more than $5m.
- Day 30: It exceeds $10m.
- Day 31: The penny skyrockets to $21.5m.

During just the last four days of the 31-day period, that penny's value soars by an additional $20m. The key insight here is that wealth creation is heavily back-loaded: early growth appears almost laughably small, but over time, momentum takes hold, and results become extraordinary. This is the power of compounding—wealth grows exponentially over time.

Yet this phenomenon is far more than a math trick; it lies at the heart of wealth creation and long-term investing. Throughout history, some of the greatest fortunes have emerged from the principle of compounding, and its lessons remain as relevant today as ever.

Time discovers truth

Owning businesses with compounding characteristics is like harnessing the principles behind that penny doubling. The companies profiled in this book have sustained a rare ability to drive growth by reinvesting their cash flow at high rates of return, turning time into a superpower. And, in the long game, time is everything.

Yet here's the challenge: our brains aren't wired to fully grasp exponential growth. We are creatures of immediacy, drawn to what is visible and tangible in the present. The allure of $1m today often blinds us to the transformative power of a penny that compounds. We see the first few days of growth—slow, almost imperceptible—and dismiss it.

But compounding rewards patience. It's not about the early days. It's about staying the course long enough for that curve to steepen and for the compounding magic to unfold.

Earnings on the earnings

While the term "compounding" is often thrown around, its true essence is rooted in something profound. When a business reinvests its profits effectively, it generates returns not only on the capital it started with but also on the additional capital it earned along the way. Over time, this creates a self-reinforcing loop—a growth cycle that builds exponentially.

But let's take a step back. What does compounding really mean in the context of a business?

For a business to grow its earnings over time, it must reinvest some portion of its cash flow back into the business. This reinvestment could take many forms: hiring more employees, building new facilities, researching innovative products, or acquiring other businesses. This highlights an important fact: earnings growth isn't free in the long run. It takes capital.

At its core, compounding earnings growth means sustained, exponential earnings growth over time. To achieve this, a business must do more than grow—it must reinvest its earnings at high rates of return, year after year. It's not just about generating profits; it's about redeploying those profits effectively to create earnings on the earnings.

Let's break this down into the three essential ingredients of compounding:

1. Reinvestment rate

A company's reinvestment rate is the portion of its operating cash flow reinvested back into the business. The formula is simple:

$$\text{Reinvestment Rate} = \frac{(\text{Organic Capex} + \text{Acquisitions})}{\text{Operating Cash Flow}}$$

The reinvestment rate tells us how much of the cash generated by the business is being plowed back into growth. The higher the rate (assuming effective use), the greater the potential for compounding.

The acquisition-driven compounders featured in this book have consistently reinvested more than 80% of their cash flows, meaning that out of every $100 earned, more than $80 has been plowed back into the business. A compelling example is the Swedish company Lifco. Since its IPO in 2014, Lifco has reinvested 85% of its cash flow at an average return on capital of more than 20%. This steady and disciplined approach to reinvestment has resulted in a remarkable 21-fold increase in shareholder wealth since IPO. Companies like

Lifco succeed because they have large "reinvestment opportunity sets" and are not constrained to a single industry, customer segment, or geography. These opportunities allow them to channel significant capital into both organic growth (expanding their existing business) and inorganic growth (acquiring other businesses).

2. Return on invested capital (ROIC)

Reinvestment alone isn't enough. A company must also allocate its capital efficiently. That's where return on invested capital (ROIC) comes in.

$$\text{ROIC} = \frac{\text{Net Operating Profit After Tax (NOPAT)}}{\text{Invested Capital}}$$

The higher the ROIC, the more effectively the company generates returns from its investments. For compounding to occur, incremental ROIC—the return on newly invested capital—must remain high (and higher than cost of capital) over time.

Constellation Software, the Canadian vertical software market compounder, has maintained high double-digit ROIC since its IPO in 2006. This disciplined allocation of capital has allowed the company to compound shareholder wealth by an incredible 375 times in less than 20 years.

3. Duration

The final ingredient in the compounding equation is time. Time is what allows compounding to reach its full potential. The longer a business can reinvest capital at high rates of return, the greater the exponential growth.

But time is also fragile. Disruptions to a company's operating environment or market saturation can shorten the compounding process. For companies with deep, untapped markets and enduring competitive advantages, duration becomes their secret weapon. A compelling example from this book is Heico, the American aerospace spare parts manufacturer in a highly fragmented market that has compounded wealth a staggering 1100 times over 40 years.

Imagine two businesses:

- The first business generates a 20% return on incremental capital, reinvests 75% of its earnings, and therefore compounds at an effective rate of 15%. Over five years, it doubles its capital, but it runs out of opportunities thereafter.
- The second business also generates a 20% return and reinvests 75%, compounding at the same effective rate of 15%. However, unlike the first, this business has plenty of reinvestment opportunities, allowing it to sustain its growth for 20 years. Over two decades, this business grows its capital 15 times over.

The difference is stark. Only the second unlocks the full potential of compounding. Time is the ultimate force multiplier.

In reality, an investor's return is influenced not only by the underlying business's compounding abilities but also by the expectations (multiples) embedded in the stock price and the change over the holding period. In other words, your future return depends not just on how the business performs, but also on how much optimism (or pessimism) is baked into the price you pay today (reflected in the multiple of earnings you pay)—and how that sentiment changes while you hold the stock (reflected in changes to that multiple over the years). However: mathematically, the higher the compounding rate and the longer the holding period, the less significant the impact of multiple changes on investor returns. Essentially, over the long run you get the investment returns that mirror the underlying company's earnings growth. After all, the multiple is a one-off; earnings growth, assuming the necessary foundational elements are in place, continues to compound over time.

The danger of leakage (dividends)

Not all businesses are built to compound. Many companies consume a lot of cash just to stay in neutral, which means there is no cash left to reinvest for growth. Other businesses choose to distribute a significant portion of their cash flow as dividends, limiting the capital available for reinvestment. For example, the average company in the S&P 500 pays out roughly half its earnings as dividends.

While dividend payments are not inherently bad—they are often preferable to low-return reinvestments—this "leakage" reduces the compounding rate. A company that reinvests 75% of its earnings will grow much faster than one that reinvests only 50%. Again, time acts as a force multiplier of this.

To illustrate, consider two companies, both generating a 20% return on incremental capital:

- Company A reinvests 75% of its earnings, compounding at an effective rate of 15%. Over 20 years, this company delivers a return of 15 times the original investment.
- Company B reinvests only 50% of its earnings, compounding at a lower effective rate of 10%. Over the same period, this company delivers a return of just 6.7 times the original investment.

The difference is profound. The key driver isn't just the return on capital—it's the reinvestment rate. The higher the reinvestment rate, the more powerful the compounding effect.

Key concepts

When it comes to understanding the performance of the compounders in this book, several key metrics will recur. Readers from the investment world will be familiar with these, but the firms in this book have much to teach a wider audience—so here is a quick breakdown of how they work.

CAGR

CAGR stands for compound annual growth rate. In plain terms it answers the question: If this company grew steadily each year, what average yearly rate would get you from the starting point to the end? Growth may be bumpy: CAGR smooths it out as if it were growing at the same pace and therefore makes it easier to compare growth between companies over time.

ROCE

ROCE means return on capital employed. It tells you how much profit a company makes for every dollar it uses to run the business. A higher

ROCE typically means a firm is run effectively and allocates capital wisely.

EBITA

EBITA is earnings before interest, taxes and amortization. It shows how much profit a company is making from its core operations, before taking into account things like debt costs, taxes, and some acquisition-related non-cash accounting adjustments.

These concepts help capture what is going on beneath the hood of these remarkable companies. But what defines these compounders, and leads to the outperformance captured by these metrics? It all starts with rejecting a well-worn script, as we'll see in the next chapter.

2

Acquisition-Driven Compounders

IN THE WORLD of mergers and acquisitions, the story is often one of failure. The "winner's curse" has become almost a rite of passage for companies seduced by grandiose promises of synergy. The corporate graveyard is filled with deals that eroded shareholder value instead of creating it, their lofty ambitions collapsing under the weight of misaligned expectations and inflated price tags.

Acquisition-driven compounders reject this script. They don't play by the rules of the traditional M&A playbook, which prices large, high-profile deals that require armies of consultants and are built on integration plans that look good on paper but falter in execution. Instead, these compounders focus on smaller, private-market acquisitions, each a deliberate step forward.

The world's best compounders featured in this book seldom define themselves solely by acquisitions. Instead, they are company builders. They think and act beyond transactions. In addition to a successful private acquisition strategy, they build the right culture for organic expansion, fostered by a strong "cash culture," embodying a deeper sense of purpose beyond mere deal-making. These compounders often evolved from industrial and engineering backgrounds, viewing the business landscape through the eyes of entrepreneurs in the trenches rather than as executives looking to make quick profits through rapid deal-making. While they have all eventually shifted to a growth strategy that includes acquisitive expansion, their foundations often rest on a heritage of industrial value creation.

They have proceeded not in haste but methodically, building brick by brick while instilling a strong entrepreneurial mindset through trial and error.

The dual engines of growth

If compounding had a soul mate, it would be the group of compounders in this book. Their power lies in their ability to perfect two engines of growth: organic reinvestments and programmatic acquisitions of small private companies. These dual engines provide a unique level of capital deployment that single-engine companies, relying only on organic growth, can rarely match. Unlike companies tethered to a single industry or market, they operate across a broad landscape, unconstrained by sector or geography. The global SME (small and medium-sized enterprise) market is their playground, offering a virtually endless runway of opportunities. Additionally, what truly sets compounders apart is their ability to sustain this growth over the long term. After all, the force that does so much of the heavy lifting in the end is duration: the power of time.

Organic growth is the foundation for growth—a company reinvesting its cash flow into profitably expanding its existing operations. The limitations of organic growth are well-documented: even the most innovative companies eventually face the challenge of finding a "new leg of growth", and organic growth is inevitably finite; profits can only be usefully reinvested so much. That's where acquisitions come in. When organic growth slows, the acquisition engine picks up the slack, ensuring a balanced and sustainable trajectory. Done right, they unlock extraordinary reinvestment levels and, more importantly, the duration of the compounding rate. These acquisitions are not random or opportunistic. They are small, targeted, and systematic, often involving years of discipline and patient relationship-building with potential targets.

Compounders rarely rely on brokers or intermediaries to source deals. Instead, they cultivate their pipelines of opportunities, engaging directly with small, profitable businesses that meet their strict return requirements. When the entrepreneurs are ready to sell, the deals are often quick, efficient, and free of the bureaucratic overhead that characterizes larger M&A transactions. This disciplined approach allows compounders to grow step by step, steadily compounding value over time.

The private markets offer fertile ground for compounders, teeming with structural inefficiencies that these companies are uniquely positioned to capitalize on. Unlike the public market, which is characterized by abundant information and liquidity, the private market suffers from a lack of transparency and liquidity. Moreover, smaller private deals typically require a significant illiquidity discount compared to the more accessible, click-and-buy nature of public markets. Smaller businesses also often rely on a few key individuals and a limited number of customers and suppliers. Additionally, compounders typically target deals with lower sales thresholds, which are less attractive to search funds and private equity.

This creates disparities in valuation multiples between public and private companies. Compounders thrive in this environment, using their free cash flow to acquire smaller private businesses at attractive multiples—often significantly lower than their own valuation as publicly listed companies.

Another defining feature of the compounders is their approach to the businesses they acquire. The companies are not stripped down or flipped for profit, as in traditional private equity. Instead, the compounders offer a permanent home for entrepreneurs, allowing their businesses to continue operating independently and flourish while benefiting from the resources and support of a larger parent company.

This philosophy resonates with entrepreneurs who have poured their lives into building their businesses and want to see them thrive long after they step away. For the compounders, it's not just about financial metrics; it's about nurturing the long-term potential of the businesses they acquire.

Roots of resilience

In the rugged wilderness of Africa, the *Ficus abutilifolia* performs a quiet miracle. Its roots, driven by an unyielding quest for sustenance, can split open massive rocks and burrow as deep as 60 meters into the earth. This remarkable tree doesn't just stand against the forces of wind and time—it thrives even when its branches are pruned or sections are cut away. It owes its resilience to an extraordinary root system, a deep and expansive network that safeguards the tree's survival for centuries. No matter how tall or majestic, the tree's growth would be fleeting, fragile, and ultimately doomed without such roots.

This image of the African rock tree provides a fitting metaphor for businesses that endure and excel through decades of growth and change. While investors often focus on the length of a tree and its leaves—skyrocketing revenues, expanding markets, and growing dominance—what truly defines a company's longevity lies beneath the surface. The unseen systems, like a tree's roots, sustain enduring growth. And just as a tree with shallow roots is vulnerable to a sudden storm, so is a company overly reliant on a single product, customer, or favorable economic tailwind.

In business and nature, compounding works both ways. A small but overlooked risk can grow into a catastrophe, much like a crack in a dam that slowly expands until it bursts. No matter how remote, every risk becomes inevitable when given enough time. Companies must avoid the "blowups" that can uproot their foundation to truly thrive over the long term.

This approach contrasts sharply with the allure of companies that seem to defy gravity. Our fascination with the compounders often stems from their ability to deploy capital at high returns over long periods. Their success, however, isn't driven solely by their acquisitions. It's rooted in the stability, the diversity, and the systems they cultivate beneath the surface.

The best of two worlds

To harness the power of compounding, companies need to manage both risk and return:

1. **Fundamental downside protection:** A well-diversified foundation, like a resilient tree's deep and wide roots, is essential to mitigate risks. It means favoring companies with internal diversification—businesses that don't rely on a single product line, customer, or market.

2. **Sustainable growth opportunities:** The branches and leaves of a company, representing reinvestment and growth, must grow wide and strong. This is achieved by deploying capital effectively, often through multiple small acquisitions that expand the company's reach without overexposing it to single-point risks.

For example, Lifco, one of the Swedish compounders featured in this book, has over 250 companies operating across diverse niches and geographies. This not only makes it resilient to changing conditions but also positions the company for long-term compounding. Its CEO, Per Waldemarson, often points out that "if we were forced to only buy companies in our dental division, we would not been able to grow as much or profitably as we have done." Its organizational structure mirrors the intricate root systems found in nature, spreading risk while enabling continuous growth.

Revisiting the penny-doubling example, we saw that the true magic of compounding—when the growth curve becomes steep—occurred in the final days. Out of the $21.5m created in 31 days, 20.1m was added in the last four.

To reach the critical compounding phase, a business must survive and thrive during its early stages, which is why having a strong foundation (the sprawling roots of the tree) is essential. This means offering a diverse range of products to a wide variety of customers across multiple end-markets. Achieving exponential growth—what some call reaching "the second half of the chessboard"—requires more than just aiming for the highest returns. It demands avoiding catastrophic losses at all costs. By steering clear of single-exposure risks and prioritizing long-term resilience, firms position themselves to thrive in the fullness of time. This book is not about the rockets; it's a story of long-lasting growth. Like the *Ficus abutilifolia*, the companies you'll meet ahead are those with roots deep enough to weather any storm and branches strong enough to reach for the sky.

Such diversification is also the basis of the dual engines of growth: by not being confined to a single market, and balancing organic growth with acquisitions, the businesses can effectively leverage both growth drivers.

This combination enables a compounder to enter the steep

compounding phase, reaching the days when compounding delivers its back-loaded benefits.

Additionally, there is one last crucial factor, the "secret sauce" that brings all these elements together, ensuring sustained and exponential growth: culture.

Above-average entrepreneurship

What distinguishes a mere "serial acquirer," mostly focused on deal-making, from a compounder is a strong decentralized culture combined with a long industrial heritage that has forged a powerful cash culture. The compounders track cash flow, not just revenue; spending is treated like it's coming out of someone's pocket; teams are rewarded for collecting payments, controlling costs and avoiding waste; and investments are judged by how quickly they pay back in cash.

This runs through each group as a kind of operating system. It fosters an efficient internal capital market, where the return on capital and entrepreneurship thrive, which has the added benefit of healthy organic growth. Management makes sure capital flows to the best opportunities. Take Addtech as an example: each business area is incentivized to grow—both organically and through acquisitions—but must also compete for internal capital. Similarly to Warren Buffett at Berkshire Hathaway, the CEO Niklas Stenberg acts as the overarching capital allocator, ensuring that the capital flows to the highest-return opportunities. This pushes business areas to sharpen their cases, only presenting their best opportunities.

This ecosystem allows new companies to maintain their entrepreneurial spirit while integrating into a system that encourages healthy competition. The emphasis on cash flow, a self-funded growth model, and a clear understanding of the levers to pull for value creation underscores the importance of balance in achieving long-term success.

The compounders excel not just by focusing on acquisitions but also by building businesses with a purpose, supported by a legacy of industrial value creation and a commitment to operational excellence. Moreover, as David Barber (founder of Halma and earlier long-time CEO) outlines: acquisitions financed through internally generated funds and assessed via a rational investment framework based on cash flow—akin to the methodology used for calculating expected returns from organic projects and their associated cash flow economics—should be considered equivalent to organic growth for these companies. In other words, if a company uses its own cash to buy another business—and evaluates that purchase the same way it would judge any internal project—then that acquisition should count like growth from within.

Yearly gatherings and ongoing sharing of best practices on pricing, working capital, sales, business acumen, and numerous other topics help generate organic uplift—an important contributor to overall profit growth. Simple profit goals related to cash flow conversion and predictability teach everyone that sales growth must be balanced with the cost of deploying capital. Furthermore, among the best, we often see a well-developed pricing culture and a keen awareness of what contributes to cash flow growth and what does not (e.g. discounts). Hence, one typically finds value-based pricing replacing the legacy of cost-plus pricing after onboarding new companies. Moreover, testing and failing are also allowed, supported by the confidence boost that comes with being part of a larger unit. The aim is to maintain entrepreneurial drive while prioritizing cash flow and a self-funded growth cadence; striking the right balance is paramount and a key differentiator. Tapping into this ecosystem and internal capital market is where 1+1 becomes 3.

This highlights what sets the compounders apart: a robust cash culture meticulously honed through persistent trial and error. While acquisitions are within reach for many, the true challenge emerges in the careful nurturing of acquired companies and cultivating a robust internal cash culture. Smart incentives and cultivating a collaborative culture with opportunities and a well-functioning internal capital market—while still balancing entrepreneurial drive and enabling natural synergies—are what drives founders in the underlying subsidiaries to stay beyond their earn-out periods.

The emphasis on a self-funding business model ultimately translates to a low-risk growth model by inherently limiting the pace of growth. Only so much cash flow in a given year is available to finance growth, either organic or acquisitions, in a self-funding manner. This ensures that the growth is sustainable. In effect, the built-in features of a self-funding model avoid reliance on equity raises and excessive leverage, and emphasize the importance of capital efficiency in generating cash.

This is why the compounders put enormous effort into developing a deep-seated "cash culture," which often becomes a multi-year mindset shift in acquired companies.

Avoiding overpaying for acquisitions is crucial. Paying a 10× multiple for a private company, compared to 5×, is the difference between 10% ROIC and 20% ROIC assuming 100% cash conversion. The higher the price paid, the greater the need for cash conversion to support self-financing growth. If you overpay, the deal has to work a lot harder to pay for itself.

Consequently, common pitfalls that often lead to failure in acquisition-driven companies—such as overly rapid acquisition pace and overextended balance sheets—are naturally avoided. A deeply nurtured cash culture and simple profit goals sustained over decades—like the focus on profit over working capital (P/WC) that Bergman & Beving, Addtech, and Lagercrantz religiously adhere to—is essential for the model to work. It is the true differentiator between transactional players chasing "deals" and the compounders. The latter take a low-risk approach to growth and master the art of "building"—not just "buying." These risk-mitigating characteristics built into the self-funding model explain why many of the compounders in this book boast multi-decade track records of uninterrupted compounding.

The beauty of small markets

A common thread across all nine companies in this book is the love of small markets, not crowded big markets promising lofty growth. There are several reasons for this.

Niche businesses in smaller markets are generally under the radars of deep-pocketed private equity players, who usually pursue larger markets with growthier prospects. Less competition for acquisitions usually means more attractive prices and higher shareholder returns.

A case in point: Brokk, a subsidiary of Lifco, a company we will meet later in this book, is dominating the market for small autonomously run demolition robots. With a market share of 70% in a \$250m–\$300m market, the company enjoys high margins above 30% and high returns on operating capital.

Another company we will visit in the book, AMETEK, focuses on markets averaging \$200m–300m in size, capturing a 25–30% share in each. Individually, these markets may seem insignificant, but collectively they create a powerful, decentralized portfolio built for resilience. AMETEK's playbook is simple: dominate small, defensible markets. Be the #1 or #2 player. This strategy delivers extraordinary resilience in regulated sectors, where stakes are high and disruption is low. Their highly engineered, mission-critical, and essential products become cornerstones for their customers.

Buyers who value a company's heritage and long-term fit can often "buy right" rather than having to outbid aggressive competitors.

Owning a collection of companies that dominate their respective niche markets—paired with strong, established customer relationships—positions the compounders as price setters rather than price takers. Small markets inherently discourage new entrants, as limited profit potential often fails to justify substantial investments. This leads to a favorable market structure with only a few competitors, sometimes as few as two, fostering more rational and less aggressive competition. Consequently, dominating these niche markets provides a dual advantage: it promotes rational competition among the incumbents while deterring new ones from entering.

Moreover, the niche businesses that the compounders focus on typically operate in the "hinterland" of the value chain. These are products and services that often go unnoticed by the end customer. Rather than selling directly to end customers, they concentrate on business-to-business (B2B) transactions, such as providing specialized machinery, components, or processes integrated into final products or services. Because they often deliver mission-critical, customized offerings at relatively low cost—like Heico's critical spare parts for the aviation industry—they can create a lock-in effect that fosters high customer retention and pricing power.

Another defining characteristic is their focus on flow products or consumables that link directly to customers' operating expenses rather than capital expenditures. This approach increases predictability and reduces dependence on cyclical spending. These companies focus on selling products that customers need to use regularly—like parts, supplies, or tools that show up in their day-to-day running costs—not big one-off purchases. Additionally, these businesses benefit from a favorable working capital mix—inventory levels are kept low, payments are often quick or upfront—and much of their production is typically outsourced, which minimizes capital requirements.

The kinds of companies the compounders target also benefit from close relationships with their customers. Their offerings are often tailored through deep collaboration with clients.

Another strength lies in the reinvestment engine such businesses create. Because they are often asset-light, with only a small total addressable market, they have minimal need for large organic growth investments. They're lean businesses in niche markets, so they can grow without using much of the cash they generate. A decentralized acquirer can bundle these companies together, becoming more diversified with every addition and collectively fueling the reinvestment engine at the group level. The profits can be reinvested across the group, targeted at wherever the greatest future growth may come from. While each niche may pose unique risks, spreading them across different end markets also makes the overall portfolio more resilient.

From a group standpoint, predictability is important; ongoing self-financed acquisitions rely on it. If they can't be sure the cash will have no other use, using it externally becomes fraught with risk. Smaller markets bring this certainty. Thanks to their relatively limited growth potential, they provide little incentive to new entrants and, as said, duopoly-like dynamics are not uncommon, ensuring limited competition, pricing power and strong cash flow generation.

Growing big by staying small

The compounders are master investors in private markets. Their DNA reveals a deeply ingrained preference for decentralization. This is no accident. In fact, it's essential—and inevitable. An entrepreneurial culture and close customer relationships facilitate scaling while maintaining a small-business mindset. Without granting autonomy to each business unit or platform, the acquisition process at the holding company level would inevitably slow down. Bringing multiple new private companies on board annually could overwhelm management. It would be easy to get bogged down by excessive integration efforts and micromanagement. Therefore, decentralized decision-making isn't merely a preference for conglomerates; it's a prerequisite for scaling and retaining the agility of a speedboat within a tankship-sized group. Without this, for instance, Constellation Software would not have been able to scale its organization to conduct over 100 acquisitions annually.

A thriving entrepreneurial culture involves treating individuals within business units as true owners, affording them substantial autonomy. This approach nurtures a sense of ownership and entrepreneurship, often compensating indirectly for any potential loss of synergies and efficiency gains.

Furthermore, small, niche businesses inherently require close customer relationships. Decentralized decision-making, leveraging local insights, positions these nimble businesses to make the best decisions regarding marketing, products, customers, and suppliers. Collecting these niche businesses at scale necessitates maintaining decentralization and proximity to customers. This often sets the compounders apart—they understand that growing big requires staying small. They strike a clear balance between maintaining an entrepreneurial spirit and the temptation to reap synergies, encouraging founders of subsidiary companies to stay engaged well beyond their initial earn-out periods.

In the 2014 annual report of Berkshire Hathaway, Warren Buffett reflected on the less-than-favorable reputation of conglomerates among investors and explained why Berkshire represented a departure from this perception. He discussed the business climate for conglomerates during the 1960s, when they became popular through questionable accounting practices, promotion, and leadership strategies aimed at inflating stock prices. CEOs of that era financed acquisitions of lower-quality, lower P/E ratio companies by issuing shares. Then, they utilized "pooling" accounting to artificially boost per-share earnings, presenting this as a testament to their management prowess. These practices, they argued, warranted high or rising P/E ratios, with the promise of continued earnings growth through the continuation of such strategies.

Buffett contrasted this with Berkshire, emphasizing how the conglomerate structure can enhance the rational allocation of capital: it lets capital flow to wherever it will earn the best return. For Buffett, the conglomerate structure, "if used judiciously, is an ideal structure for maximizing long-term capital growth."

Internal capital allocation often falls short of rational allocation due to structural constraints and natural biases. A company exposed to a single market or industry easily overlooks more rational choices for allocating capital. Indeed they may be forced to overlook such options. They can lack the flexibility to reallocate funds to other businesses and markets, or they can be artificially constrained by notions of commitment and consistency.

CEOs can also prove a stumbling block. Not all are the right fit for the task of capital redeployment. The CEO, who fulfills both the operator and capital allocator roles, can simply have too narrow a perspective—it is hard to step outside a single-focused business and assess available options rationally. This is why separating the capital allocation responsibility at the HQ level, and decentralizing operations throughout business units, works so well for the companies featured in this book. The compounders are often industry-agnostic. They can evaluate risk and reward across a broad spectrum of industries and pursue acquisitions outside their core competencies. They have no biases from a narrow focus.

The flexibility provided by separating the holding company level (where capital allocation occurs) from the operating company level (where operations are managed) allows the compounders to iterate, course-correct and change, often dramatically, in pursuit of creating shareholder value. The flexibility enabled by these structures calls to mind the philosophical puzzle of "The Ship of Theseus."[2] The hero Theseus's ship underwent a gradual replacement of all its timbers: at what point, if at all, did it cease to remain the same ship? Many of the compounders in this book have undergone similar transformations. The conglomerate model—with the right ingredients—facilitates renewal and favors pivots.

Leadership brewed from within

Entrepreneurs and owners who have a personal stake in the success of their companies play a vital role in creating and developing top-performing businesses. A crucial aspect of investment analysis therefore lies in examining management, ownership, and succession planning.

The leaders of the companies featured in this book all demonstrate exceptional investment acumen. They are remarkably able to maintain a "small business feel" within their organizations, free from excessive bureaucracy. They foster an entrepreneurial spirit and maintain rapid response times while carefully embracing calculated risk-taking. These executives operate with an informal approach, yet they are deeply process-oriented, consistently seeking improvements and focusing relentlessly on cost management.

Substantial evidence supports the notion that companies with founders actively involved in key roles—such as CEO, chairman, board member, or owner—tend to outperform their peers. As noted by Chris Zook in the *Harvard Business Review*, three fundamental practices, collectively known as the "founder mentality," characterize these superior founder-led companies. Notably, the founder-led decentralized approach is a recurring feature among the companies highlighted in this book. Owners, with their vested interests, tend to behave differently from employees. If you own your car, you treat it differently than a rental.

This heightened ownership mentality makes them prioritize long-term value creation over short-term profitability. This focus, in turn, safeguards against management decisions driven by empire-building ambitions or short-term financial strategies that might prove suboptimal. Therefore, high insider ownership is a vital investment criterion that bolsters the assurance of sustained value creation over time.

Also, the compounders in this book exhibit a profound "sense of purpose." They frequently challenge industry norms and prioritize the needs of underserved customers. Secondly, they possess a "frontline obsession." This means they elevate and empower their frontline employees, recognizing them as heroes within the organization. This approach contributes to a culture where frontline staff have significant influence.

Additionally, the ownership structures and succession planning strategies of these compounders confer a distinct competitive advantage. Many of these businesses are family-owned or have a substantial ownership stake held by their management teams. Long-term incentive plans play a crucial role in shaping their corporate cultures, which balance preserving the original (often frugal) ethos and fostering entrepreneurship, prudent risk-taking, and growth initiatives. Investment requirements and long-term incentive plans, complete with appropriate lock-up periods, should never be overlooked. These companies prioritize continuity while embracing a harmonious blend of tradition and change.

Corporate leadership is often described as a revolving door, with CEOs cycling in and out every three to five years or so. At AMETEK and Indutrade, two companies featured in this book, however, leadership has a much different rhythm. Over the last 58 years, AMETEK has had just four CEOs, and Indutrade, since its foundation 47 years ago, currently employs only its third CEO. This remarkable consistency reflects more than careful succession planning—it embodies a philosophy of internal growth and cultural continuity. Each of AMETEK's leaders has been deeply rooted in the company before stepping into the top role, while Indutrade's strong culture and long-term owners have allowed the company to hire externally. The largest shareholder of Indutrade is referred to as the "king of long-termism" in Swedish media.

Long tenures aren't just common; they are expected. Most business unit managers are promoted from within, fostering a leadership culture that combines deep technical expertise with an understanding of their long-term strategies.

Insiders, comprising senior management, board members, and significant private owners (often families), bring a long-term perspective—understanding their businesses deeply, prioritizing durability, and thinking in terms of decades rather than financial quarters. They translate this perspective into action through their representation on the board, the composition of the management team, and the strategic direction they chart for the company. Insider ownership is a strategic edge that empowers these companies to act in the best interests of their long-term shareholders. When senior management holds a significant stake in the company, their commitment can be akin to owning it outright.

Institutional investors are often perceived as more favorable from a governance standpoint. However, they frequently adopt a short-term perspective and seldom seek board seats. By contrast, private owners typically adopt a multi-generational viewpoint toward their ownership stakes and are inclined to secure board representation to safeguard a long-term perspective within the boardroom. Typically, the parent company acts as the chair of the board in subsidiaries, where they both support and challenge the founders who continue to run the business. Important topics highlighted in the boardrooms are succession planning, profit growth, and cash generation. Many also challenge the original founder on pricing, with greater willingness to increase prices.

CEOs who align with a company's core values and share a unified strategic vision tend to generate more value for shareholders than those who perceive the position merely as a stepping stone in their career or as a lucrative job opportunity. As seen below, the tenure of current CEOs at the compounders spans an average of 13 years. In most instances, new CEOs are recruited among these companies from internal ranks, and they have, on average, been within their organizations for 21 years. Such "forever CEOs" are important cultural carriers. Over the years—often over decades—they create a culture that mirrors their vision and personality. They walk the talk. A prime example of a "forever CEO" within the compounders is Mark Leonard at Constellation Software, who remains the CEO 30 years after he founded the company.

Figure 2.1: CEOs of the compounders

Company name	Founded	Name	Joined	CEO since	CEO end	CEO tenure, years	Company tenure, years
Bergman & Beving	1906	Arvid Bergman / Fritz Bevin	1906	Shared roles			
		Knut Stenberg	1924	1947	1964	17	40
		Carl T. Säve	1957	1964	1980	16	23
		Pär Stenberg	1960	1980	1990	10	30
		Anders Börjesson	1979	1990	2001	11	22
		Stefan Wigren	2001	2001	2012	11	11
		Ulf Lilius	2004	2012	2017	5	13
		Pontus Boman	2007	2017	2021	3	13
		Magnus Söderlind	2021	2021		4	4
Addtech	2001	Roger Bergqvist	1991	2001	2008	6	17
		Johan Olov Sjö	2003	2008	2018	10	15
		Niklas Stenberg	2005	2018		6	20
Lagercrantz Group	2001	Jan Friis	2001	2001	2006	4	4
		Per Ikov	2001	2004	2006	1	4
		Jörgen Wigh	2006	2006		19	19
Lifco	1998	Fredrik Karlsson	1998	1998	2019	21	21
		Per Waldemarson	2006	2019		6	19
Indutrade	1978	Gunnar Tindberg	1978	1978	2004	26	26
		Johnny Alvarsson	2004	2004	2017	13	13
		Bo Annvik	2017	2017		8	8
Constellation Softwa	1995	Mark Leonard	1995	1995		30	30
Heico	1990	Laurans Mendelsson	1990	1990		35	35
Judges Scientific	2006	David Cicurel	2005	2005		20	20
Ametek	1930	Dr. John H. Lux	1966	1966	1990	24	24
		Walter Blankley	1960	1990	1999	9	39
		Frank S. Hermance	1989	1999	2016	17	27
		David A. Zapico	1989	2016		9	36
Average						13	21

The compounders adhere to an internal recruitment policy for the position of CEO, prioritizing the promotion of existing talent over the hiring of external candidates. Within these organizations, the board diligently maintains a well-structured succession plan for the CEO role, actively cultivating multiple internal candidates for future leadership positions. This strategic approach affords the board the advantage of selecting a CEO with an intimate understanding of the company's culture, norms, and strategic direction. Consequently, it mitigates the risk associated with CEO turnover and offers shareholders greater continuity.

In these compounders, the CEO assumes the role of a custodian of the company's strategic DNA, a blueprint carefully established and nurtured by the board over time. Should a CEO decide to step down, the board can draw from a pool of capable internal candidates, ensuring a seamless transition for shareholders. As we will see later, the cases of Per Waldemarson, who ascended to the CEO position at Lifco from within the organization, and Niklas Stenberg, CEO of Addtech who made a similar journey, exemplifies the successful implementation of this internal candidate strategy.

These CEOs understand a company's culture and ethos, consistently generating long-term shareholder value. They maintain a steadfast long-term perspective, often eschewing providing short-term profit guidance to the market. In many respects, these CEOs can be regarded as mavericks, resolute in their determination to chart their course for running the business, indifferent to conventional wisdom.

Some investors argue that management plays a negligible role. We've witnessed firsthand that the swiftest path to dismantling a great company is to appointment inept individuals to leadership positions. Our unwavering conviction is that success ultimately hinges on the caliber of individuals at the helm. In this respect, as in so many others, the compounders do not disappoint.

3

A Swedish Model

The Unique Home of Many Compounders

Sweden constitutes just 0.13% of the world's population but three times that as a percentage of world GDP. The country has produced some of the world's most outstanding businesses, and among these are numerous successful acquisition-driven compounders.

Why is Sweden home to so many acquisition-driven compounders?

Sweden's ability to nurture companies that thrive through acquisitions is no coincidence—it is a story shaped by history, innovation, and an entrepreneurial spirit that has persisted for generations.

The country's rich industrial heritage dates back to the mid-19th century, with pioneers like Atlas Copco, Electrolux, SKF, Sandvik, Ericsson, Alfa Laval and Asea laying the groundwork for modern Swedish industry. Despite being relatively small and geographically isolated, Sweden quickly embraced innovation and globalization to unlock its growth potential. By the mid-20th century, many of its industrial giants had begun expanding internationally, often through acquisitions.

Successful companies like Electrolux and Atlas Copco, supported by the Wallenberg family, led this development, using acquisitions as a tool to grow. Their success inspired a new wave of entrepreneurial and engineering trading firms, such as Bergman & Beving and Indutrade, to follow. Sweden's landscape of small and medium-sized, often family-owned, businesses provided fertile ground for this strategy. Acquirers realized the value of uniting like-minded entrepreneurs, pooling their knowledge, and sharing best practices to create stronger, more competitive companies.

With deep industrial expertise, these firms understood the value of the companies they sought to acquire, particularly their ability to generate stable cash flows. This cash flow became a powerful engine for reinvestment, fueling further acquisitions and growth. Their approach was distinct: they maintained the autonomy and entrepreneurial spirit of the businesses they acquired while utilizing internal expertise and effectively allocating both resources and capital to grow profitably.

In the 1970s and 1980s, with their decentralized philosophies and entrepreneurial mindset, Swedish acquisition-driven compounders cultivated a reputation as preferred buyers for family-owned trading companies in a world where centralization, synergies and bureaucracy were dominant. Their shared language with entrepreneurs, and commitment to preserving local independence, made them natural partners. By reinvesting profits wisely and in a disciplined way, and nurturing decentralized management, they established a model of acquisition-driven growth that continues to thrive.

Sweden, notably, is a global leader in interpersonal trust and consistently ranks high on international indices for ease of doing business, global innovation, perceptions of corruption, and human development. This high-trust environment provides a solid foundation. Acquisition-driven compounders have excelled by demonstrating the practical value of their business models and by preserving the entrepreneurial spirit of the companies they acquire. They have fostered enduring relationships between buyers and sellers.

Transparency further reinforces this trust. Sweden's open society and easy access to data creates an environment of transparency.

Publicly available information extends beyond company numbers. Sweden is a country so transparent that Swedes can even access details about the cars people drive or the pets they own. Annual reports for all Swedish companies are also accessible to the public, providing a clear view of financial health and minimizing unpleasant surprises.

Another key to Sweden's success lies in the simplicity and efficiency of its business practices. Companies specializing in small private acquisitions have perfected a simplified approach to deal-making. Over time, they have developed non-bureaucratic, concise, and standardized transaction practices, reducing complexity and ensuring deals are executed with minimal friction.

This combination of trust, transparency, and efficiency has created a thriving ecosystem for acquisition-driven compounders—one where both entrepreneurs and acquirers can flourish.

The rise of the decentralized philosophy

The 1970s witnessed the rise of a decentralized governance philosophy influenced by two successful CEOs: Hans Werthén, former CEO and chairman of Electrolux, and Jan Wallander, former CEO of Handelsbanken.

They were pioneers of a governance model that rejected the rigid, centralized hierarchies dominating much of the corporate world at the time. Instead, they introduced a decentralized philosophy rooted in local entrepreneurship and autonomy—a framework that would become a cornerstone of Swedish business practices. The success of these companies inspired other Swedish companies to adopt similar models.

Hans Werthén, who served as CEO of Electrolux from 1967 to 1974 and as chairman from 1974 to 1991, was a pioneer of this philosophy. Under his leadership, Electrolux underwent nothing short of a cultural revolution. He dismantled bureaucratic structures and implemented a decentralized framework that empowered local decision-making close to customers.

Werthén's influence extended beyond decentralization. Known for his frugality and disdain for unnecessary bureaucracy, his values left a lasting mark on companies like Lifco, one of the compounders profiled in this book. His principles continue to inspire businesses, proving that empowering local teams can drive innovation, efficiency, and long-term success.

When Hans Werthén stepped in as CEO of Electrolux in 1967, he inherited a company mired in bureaucracy and dominated by a hierarchical, fear-based management style. Determined to turn things around, Werthén wasted no time.

One of his first actions was symbolic, and controversial: he sold Electrolux's luxurious office in Stockholm's central business district and relocated to a more modest location on the city's outskirts. This move set the tone for what was to come. Werthén streamlined operations, cutting unnecessary staff and trimming excess at every level. He held firmly to the belief that traditional corporate tools like budgets and forecasts were overvalued, famously remarking that "forecasts are only interesting when you look at them in the rearview mirror." Unnecessary internal meetings were also reduced to a minimum.

Werthén's philosophy reshaped Electrolux and influenced generations of corporate leaders. Under his guidance, the company became a de facto business school for executives, training them in the principles of meritocracy and the relentless pursuit of returns on capital. Leadership at Electrolux wasn't about abstract principles but measurable outcomes. Shareholder value and cash generation were the ultimate priorities. The leadership was so focused on this that former employees recalled management stating, "It is poetry to hear the managing directors talk about return on assets."

While concepts like "corporate culture" and "delegation" were never explicitly discussed or pronounced, they were deeply embedded in the DNA of Electrolux. Leaders were empowered to make decisions without micromanagement or rigid oversight. Leif Johansson, then the 28-year-old head of Husqvarna's motorcycle division (an Electrolux subsidiary at the time) and later CEO of Volvo Group, vividly recalls this culture of autonomy. When he once called headquarters for advice on restructuring production units, the response was clear and concise: "We have hired you with a high salary—make your own decisions!"[3]

Werthén's approach wasn't just about cutting costs or decentralizing decision-making, it was about instilling a culture of responsibility, and a sharp focus on results. His legacy continues to echo across Swedish business, as a model of how distinct leadership and a lean philosophy can drive extraordinary outcomes. During Hans Werthéns leadership,

Electrolux increased sales and earnings by 80×, an impressive compounded annual growth rate (CAGR) of 20% over two and half decades.

Dr. Jan Wallander, the long-standing CEO of Svenska Handelsbanken, also stands tall among great Swedish business leaders. His transformative journey with Svenska Handelsbanken turned the bank into one of the world's most consistently successful banks at the end of the century, and redefined the essence of effective management.

Bold and unconventional decisions marked Wallander's journey at Handelsbanken, starting in the 1970s. Facing resistance to decentralization, he understood the immense challenge of overhauling entrenched structures. "Bringing about decentralization is a very time-consuming process. One has to begin with oneself," he remarked. Over five years, he meticulously transformed Handelsbanken into a decentralized organization, proving that patience and conviction could pave the way for lasting change.

Wallander's philosophy was simple yet profound: "Decentralization is a management philosophy that can release the full potential of people in any corporation because it is in accordance with human nature, not against it. People are the only sustainable competitive advantage."

He abandoned the practice of traditional bank management when he took over as a CEO. Annual plans and budgets were tossed aside, breaking free from the fixed performance contracts that stifled innovation. Branch employees were bestowed with independent lending authority, embracing autonomy and responsibility. Despite initial skepticism, Handelsbanken's credit risks diminished as decisions were made closer to customers, and the bank abandoned centralized risk assessments.

Dr. Wallander's mantra was clear—decentralize, empower, and trust the frontline. Headquarters' role shifted from control to being a service provider for the front line, emphasizing a customer-centric approach. The head office saw a 33% reduction in employees; their perception of superiority over branch staff was decisively broken. Local branch offices became primary profit centers, challenging the traditional pyramid structure. The marketing department saw a drastic reduction from 40 to just one person, emphasizing efficiency over bureaucracy.

A transparent steering system ensured every branch's performance was visible, fostering healthy competition. Wallander introduced an incentive system that was aligned with the shareholders. He called it "The Octagon," a long-term profit-sharing system that prioritized better profitability and return on capital over the company's competitors while aligning incentives with sustainable success. This collective incentive system has created numerous millionaires among regular loyal Handelsbanken employees.

The philosophies of Hans Werthén and Jan Wallander have left an indelible mark on Swedish businesses. The decentralized management approach has proven its resilience and effectiveness from Electrolux to Svenska Handelsbanken. Building such a culture takes time, but its benefits—autonomy, agility, and empowered decision-making—offer a powerful competitive edge in today's rapidly changing world.

For over 150 years, Sweden has cultivated a strong industrial heritage, pioneering innovations that have shaped industries worldwide. Within this tradition lies a distinct group of companies that have mastered the art of profitable growth by acquiring small, family-owned businesses—and letting them continue to run their business with a lot of autonomy. These companies are ecosystems where high performance is rewarded and thrives on shared knowledge, wisdom, and collaboration.

These firms are less like rigid corporations and more like dynamic, decentralized cities—thriving because of their multidimensional nature. Each business under the umbrella operates with independence, yet contributes to the shared strength of the whole, much like diverse neighborhoods that form the fabric of a great metropolis. Bureaucracy is replaced by empowerment, and hierarchies give way to autonomy and accountability. Success comes from fostering strong local leadership, nurturing each unit's unique strengths, aligning incentives with shareholders, and rewarding results.

In these organizations, growth is not fueled by reckless spending or big deals that make the headlines but by a disciplined self-financing approach. These companies maintain an unrelenting focus on long-term value creation through small acquisitions that may seem immaterial on their own, but when aggregated, become incredibly powerful. Internal competition is a healthy catalyst, pushing teams to go above and beyond. The result is a stunning track record of shareholder returns, including one Swedish compounder that has delivered a 7,500× return over nearly five decades, entirely generated by compounding its cash flow.

This is the story of Sweden's acquisition-driven compounders—a tale of resilience, course correction, innovation, and the power of a decentralized culture. In the chapters ahead, we'll uncover the principles and strategies that have propelled these companies and explore how their unique cultures and self-funded ethos continue to drive extraordinary performance.

4

From Dental to a Smörgåsbord of Niche Businesses

Lifco

IN NORSE MYTHOLOGY, no weapon was more renowned or powerful than Thor's hammer. Forged by the masterful hands of the dwarf Brokk, the hammer was a tool of unparalleled strength, capable of feats that no other weapon could achieve.

The high-performing Swedish conglomerate Lifco has its own equivalent of this legendary hammer. As a company with a market cap of $18bn, Lifco embodies excellence in a variety of specialized industries. One of its shining examples is a small yet immensely powerful demolition robot, much like Thor's hammer itself. This demolition robot has been named Brokk, a fitting tribute to the dwarf blacksmith. Just as Thor's hammer could strike where others failed, the Brokk demolition robot can reach and dismantle areas where no other machine can; nuclear facilities, tunnels, mines, explosive areas and other hard-to-reach places. Brokk, the subsidiary of Lifco, dominates the global small demolition robot market with an impressive 70% market share in a niche industry valued at $250m. The company's stronghold is not just in its innovative technology but also in its ability to expand its operations internationally while growing margins to exceed 30%.

The example of Brokk perfectly reflects Lifco's strategy of acquiring and nurturing companies that excel in niche markets with high pricing power. Brokk has, under Lifco's leadership, expanded geographically and increased sales and profits, primarily organically, more than tenfold.

Lifco's journey from a small dental products distributor to a diversified industrial conglomerate with a collection (in Sweden referred to as "Smörgåsbord") of highly niched businesses is a remarkable tale of intelligent and disciplined capital allocation. Backed by the prominent industrialist Carl Bennet and led by the talented CEOs Fredrik Karlsson and Per Waldemarson, Lifco has compounded earnings at an astonishing rate of above 14% since 2006, with its stock price appreciating 21× since its IPO in 2014, widely outperforming the overall market which during the same period appreciated 110% (2.1×). This Swedish acquisition-driven compounder operates with a lean, decentralized structure, empowering over 250 portfolio companies to thrive independently while adhering to strict financial discipline.

Lifco is an industrial compounder with $2.7bn in sales, with an operating margin of 23%. The company's ability to consistently deliver value to its shareholders is evident in its extraordinary free cash flow per share growth, which has compounded at an annual rate of 21% since IPO, richly rewarding those who have invested in its success. As the largest shareholder, Carl Bennet controls 68.9% of the voting rights and 50.2% of the capital. His long-standing reputation for building and nurturing Swedish industrial companies is a cornerstone of Lifco's success. Alongside Bennet, former CEO Fredrik Karlsson played a transformative role in building Lifco into its success.

Under Karlsson's leadership as the CEO from 1998 to 2019, the company was marked by exceptional operational and acquisition skills with a unique aversion to bureaucracy. During his tenure, Fredrik Karlsson compounded earnings by an astounding 100×, representing a 25% CAGR. In 2019, Per Waldemarson succeeded Karlsson as CEO, having already spent over a decade with the company since joining in 2006. Under Waldemarson's leadership, Lifco has continued its trajectory, maintaining its disciplined approach to capital allocation and its focus on cash flow generation and high returns on capital. The company's stock price has consistently outperformed the broader market, reflecting both the solid foundation built by Karlsson and continued strategic execution under Waldemarson.

In this chapter we will discover how this company turned careful acquisitions and decentralized management into an industrial success story.

Figure 4.1: Share price performance of Lifco since 2014

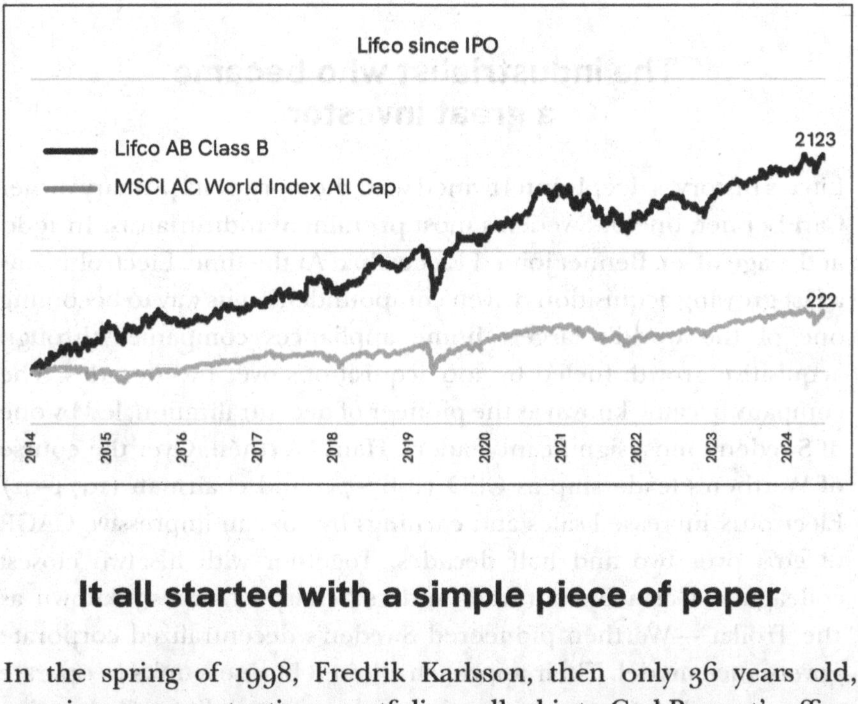

It all started with a simple piece of paper

In the spring of 1998, Fredrik Karlsson, then only 36 years old, carrying an unpretentious portfolio, walked into Carl Bennet's office in Gothenburg, Sweden. What transpired over a single hour would alter the trajectory of Lifco forever. Fredrik Karlsson pulled out one piece of paper—the numbers of his previous successful restructuring of a business. By the time Karlsson left Bennet's office, he had become the new CEO of Lifco.

It was a meeting of minds; Bennet and Karlsson shared a razor-sharp focus on performance and profitability. They were aligned in their vision for how to build and grow a great company. Their shared philosophy created the foundation for a partnership that would yield extraordinary results. When the stars align, great stories unfold, and Lifco's story is one of those rare ones that exceed even the most ambitious expectations.

Under Karlsson's leadership and Bennet's strategic guidance, Lifco would go on to deliver returns that most can only dream about. The meeting in that small office in Gothenburg would become a defining chapter in the company's history.

To fully understand Lifco, its operating model, and its relentless focus on generating high returns through simplicity and a performance-driven culture, we must take a step back and explore its history.

The industrialist who became a great investor

Lifco's history is deeply intertwined with the story of its primary owner, Carl Bennet, one of Sweden's most prominent industrialists. In 1980, at the age of 29, Bennet joined Electrolux. At the time, Electrolux was a fast-growing acquisition-driven compounder, on its way to becoming one of the world's largest home appliances companies through acquisitive growth fueled by 200 acquisitions over two decades. The company became known as the pioneer of decentralization, led by one of Sweden's most significant leaders, Hans Werthén. Over the course of Werthén's leadership as CEO (1967–74) and chairman (1974–91), Electrolux increased sales and earnings by 80×, an impressive CAGR of 20% over two and half decades. Together with his two closest colleagues, Gösta Bystedt and Anders Scharp—famously known as "the Troika"—Werthén pioneered Sweden's decentralized corporate governance model. Their approach allowed business units to operate autonomously, fostering innovation and accountability while keeping focus on overall profitability.

Werthén's leadership in Electrolux provided a compelling example of success for Carl Bennet. The autonomy given to local managers fostered a culture of ownership and efficiency that resonated deeply. Bennet fully embraced it as a guiding model.

When Hans Werthén assumed leadership of Electrolux in 1967, the company, like most corporations of the time, was highly centralized and burdened by layers of bureaucracy. Its corporate headquarters was vast, and control was concentrated at the top, creating inefficiencies and slow decision-making. Werthén saw an opportunity for radical change, and set out to completely remake the company's governance structure. What he implemented was nothing short of radical: a decentralized management approach that was virtually unheard of at the time. Under Werthén's vision, operational decision-making was pushed out to local management teams, giving them autonomy, almost to the point of abdication, to run their respective divisions with greater flexibility and speed. The new system was anchored by simple KPIs, focusing on profitability, strong cash generation, and minimal bureaucracy. Werthén believed that simplicity was the key to success, making it a cornerstone of what would come to be known as the "Lux-culture."

One of Werthén's first moves was symbolic of what he intended to do at Electrolux. He sold the company's prestigious offices in central Stockholm, and relocated to a more modest base on the city's outskirts. Lean replaced luxury, with only a handful of staff remaining at head office. The previous corporate environment, where closed office doors and long lines of employees awaiting instructions were the norm, was transformed into one of openness and accessibility. With most decision-makers operating at the local level, the once-bustling headquarters stood virtually empty. Werthén stripped Electrolux of all unnecessary bureaucracy and empowered managers across the organization to act decisively, fostering a culture of accountability and performance. This decentralized governance model streamlined operations and unleashed the potential for rapid growth.

When Carl Bennet joined Electrolux, he stepped into the role of head of export for its Commercial Kitchen division. It didn't take long for Bennet to distinguish himself within the organization. His sharp business acumen and leadership skills pushed him rapidly up the corporate ladder, and by 1983, he was appointed CEO of his division. This appointment came when his former boss, Rune Andersson, moved on to lead Trelleborg, another prominent Swedish industrial firm.

During their time at Electrolux, Carl Bennet and Rune Andersson developed a solid professional and personal bond, discovering that they shared a common mindset and worked well together. When Andersson took on the role of CEO at Trelleborg, Bennet, recognizing Rune's skills, purchased 1% of Trelleborg's shares and was at the time Trelleborg's largest private investor. Over the next few years, this investment yielded a remarkable return of 3,000% (31×), driven by the company's outstanding performance. This provided Bennet and Andersson with the capital they needed for a historical transaction that would shape Carl Bennet's history as an industrialist and a long-term investor.

In 1989, Bennet, only 38 years old, together with Andersson made history when they acquired Getinge, a struggling medical division within Electrolux. What made this transaction particularly significant was that it marked the first time Electrolux had sold one of its divisions to former employees, underscoring the unique business acumen the duo had developed under the mentorship of Hans Werthén. Both Bennet and Andersson had been schooled in Werthén's decentralized management style and disciplined approach to capital allocation, and this transaction reflected their ability to seize opportunities. Within just a year, Bennet and Andersson successfully turned Getinge around. One of the key reasons for their achievement was that Getinge, then a small and nearly forgotten part of Electrolux, had not raised its prices in nearly a decade. Bennet and Andersson saw untapped potential and were confident in their ability to revive the business—even in the face of skepticism from a senior Electrolux executive who remarked, "Good luck with Getinge."[4] This success demonstrated their skill as great operators and capital allocators—and it was where Bennet realized the true power of pricing. Bennet and Andersson were not just leaders capable of turning around a struggling company and unlocking its potential, but were also seemingly great investors—something Carl Bennet had also demonstrated when he purchased Trelleborg shares.

Today, Carl Bennet's continued ownership of Getinge is a testament to his long-term investment philosophy. What began as an opportunistic acquisition in 1989 has evolved into a multi-decade-long commitment, reflecting Bennet's belief in the value of patient, sustained ownership.

Lifco is formed

Building on the lessons they had learned during their time at Electrolux, Carl Bennet and Rune Andersson led Getinge through a period of growth, primarily through acquisitions. With Bennet serving as CEO and Andersson as chairman, the duo steered the company toward rapid expansion. In 1993, they decided to take the company public, listing Getinge on the Swedish stock exchange. Continuing along its acquisitive path, Getinge made an important acquisition in 1995 by acquiring LIC Care AB, the Swedish country councils central purchasing entity for medical equipment and services. The acquisition was driven by the belief that LIC Care's products would complement Getinge's existing portfolio and create synergies. However, these expected synergies did not materialize. Recognizing this, Bennet decided to allow LIC Care to evolve as an independent company. Rather than forcing the business to fit within Getinge's existing structure, he saw greater potential in distributing it to Getinge's shareholders. In 1998, LIC Care became a stand-alone company and subsequently changed its name to Lifco.

In 1998, Lifco was a modest, mid-single-digit margin company primarily focused on dental distribution and health and self-care products. Despite its potential, the company's performance lagged, and Carl Bennet, already experienced in successful turnarounds at Getinge, recognized the need for energetic leadership to lead Lifco toward profitability. Just as Hans Werthén had changed Electrolux and Bennet had transformed Getinge, Bennet knew that Lifco required a performance-driven CEO capable of replicating that success. The search for the right leader resulted in the appointment of Fredrik Karlsson as CEO. With a degree from the Stockholm School of Economics and experience as a consultant at the prestigious Boston Consulting Group, Karlsson had already proven his capabilities in a previous role as CEO of Mercatura, a German private equity-owned company manufacturing workwear. Karlsson executed a successful turnaround at Mercatura, improving the company's profit margin from zero to 10% in under five years. When Mercatura was eventually sold to another German firm, Karlsson returned to Sweden in search of new opportunities.

Fredrik Karlsson's first two years as the CEO of a public company were anything but smooth. Lifco did not perform well, and Karlsson was forced to take difficult but necessary restructuring steps, something the stock market did not appreciate. Simultaneously, the market for non-IT companies was tough. By 2000, Carl Bennet decided to take Lifco private in hopes of developing it more effectively away from the pressures of the public market. From his first day as CEO, Fredrik Karlsson had a single goal: to improve Lifco's profitability.

Figure 4.2: Lifco's history

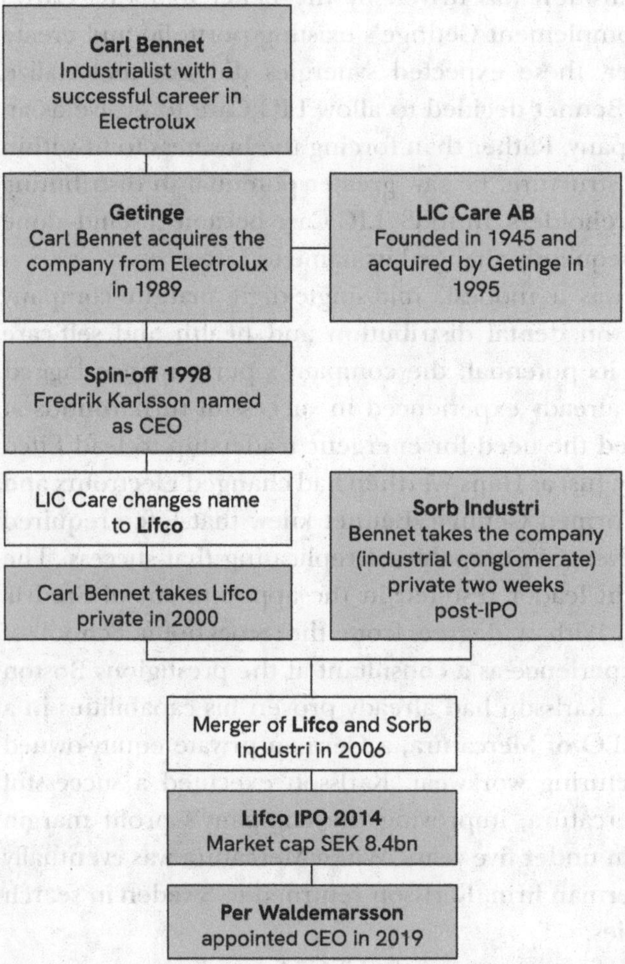

Restructuring, and realization of the power of autonomy

From the outset, Fredrik Karlsson embraced Carl Bennet's philosophy. Inspired by Bennet, one of his first actions in Lifco was delegating responsibility downwards in the organization. Instead of micromanaging, he went from believing he needed to do everything himself to giving others responsibility and not interfering with their daily work. This belief and his unconventional and extreme focus on profitability and cash flow generation led to him selling Lifco's non-performing healthcare and self-care business, shrinking the company by 40%. Simultaneously, he focused on restructuring the dental business, which he deemed had much higher entry barriers and profitability potential as it was Sweden's leading dental distribution business. Karlsson's operational excellence quickly began to show results, and by 2002, only four years after taking over the company, Lifco boasted operating margins of 8%, a significant increase from 2% in 1998. During this period, Fredrik managed to triple Lifco's profits despite shrinking the company by nearly half.

Fredrik Karlsson's successful restructuring of Lifco impressed Carl Bennet and led Bennet to appoint Karlsson as the CEO of Sorb Industri in 2001. Sorb Industri was a small Swedish industrial conglomerate containing various businesses, and among those was Brokk. Just as Carl Bennet had opportunistically acquired Getinge, he also proved his investor skills and business acumen when he acquired Sorb in 1998. The company had been a public company for just two weeks when Bennet pulled together a buy-out. The acquisition of Sorb Industri came to lay the foundation for Lifco's diversification beyond the dental industry.

As CEO of Sorb Industri, Fredrik Karlsson once again demonstrated his business excellence. When he took over Sorb, it owned a saw manufacturing business with severe losses. Karlsson's first move was to shut down the head office and push out the responsibility to each operating company. "There was a head office with seven guys, and no one felt responsibility for the operating companies. Previously, they flew private jet between the units," Karlsson later remarked. This epitomizes what Lifco's culture is still about today—strip away everything that does not create shareholder value, and focus on accountability through managerial ownership. In 2006, Sorb Industri merged with Lifco, transforming it from a dental company to a more diversified industrial group.

If you do not dare, you do not succeed

After successfully restructuring Lifco's dental division and turning around the sawmill business within Sorb Industri, Fredrik Karlsson faced a new challenge: finding growth opportunities for the new combined Lifco. In 2006, he decided that the best way to create shareholder value was to embark on a growth path based on accretive acquisitions. When he became CEO of Lifco in 1998, he had limited acquisition experience. His main task was to restructure the business and improve profitability. Although the initial years were dominated by sizable operational restructuring, he soon learned the skill of delegating responsibility down the organization, an idea that originated from Carl Bennet. This decentralized approach became a cornerstone of Lifco's growth and success.

Fredrik Karlsson, however, had developed a nose for identifying great business deals and great people early on, and he demonstrated this in 2007. Despite a limited acquisition track record, he made a bold move when he acquired Kinshofer Group, a German tools and attachment business for the construction industry. It remains Lifco's second-largest acquisition by sales and one of the most successful in its history. Despite Lifco's typical reluctance to buy from private equity, Fredrik saw exceptional potential in Kinshofer and pursued the deal. His mantra was simple: despite limited experience, never let a good deal go to waste. The acquisition of Kinshofer and Brokk formed Lifco's new business area, Demolition & Tools. Since then, Kinshofer has grown from $60m to $400m through organic growth and add-on acquisitions. Importantly, the company maintained its leadership team. Lifco's ability to seize opportunities like this underscores the company's disciplined yet opportunistic approach to growth.

Between 2006 and Lifco's IPO in 2014, Fredrik Karlsson led the company through a period of strong growth, completing 23 acquisitions across its three business areas. The acquisitions and organic improvements helped Lifco achieve an impressive 13% annual sales growth and an EBITA CAGR of 17%. During this time, EBITA margins expanded from 10% in 2006 to 14% by 2014.

In 2000, when Carl Bennet decided to delist Lifco, he entrusted Fredrik Karlsson with the freedom to shape the company under private ownership. This move allowed Karlsson the time and autonomy to develop Lifco into its current form. Bennet's decision to keep Lifco private for 14 years before relisting gave the company the flexibility to evolve and build a track record without pressure from public markets.

Today, Lifco operates across three business areas: Dental, Demolition & Tools, and System Solutions. Dental mainly comprises distribution of dental products as well as proprietary dental consumables in mainly the Nordics and Northern Europe. Demolition & Tools serves the global construction and demolition industry, and offers specialized remote-controlled machines and various tools and attachments. System Solutions is Lifco's diverse division, encompassing a variety of niche businesses operating across multiple industries, end markets, and geographies, reflecting Lifco's broadening scope and commitment to value creation through targeted acquisitions.

The year 2006 marked another important milestone in Lifco's history with the hiring of its current CEO, Per Waldemarson. After earning his degree from the Stockholm School of Economics and completing an academic scholarship at the University of Virginia, Per Waldemarson began his career in consulting at Bain & Co. However, he quickly realized that consulting wasn't a long-term fit for him, and applied for a role as an investment manager at Lifco. At the time, Lifco's headquarters essentially consisted of only Fredrik Karlsson. Karlsson quickly saw potential in Waldemarson, just as Bennet had seen potential in him eight years earlier. Recognizing the importance of hands-on operational experience, Karlsson appointed Waldemarson as CEO of Brokk, one of Lifco's best-performing companies. Over the next few years, Waldemarson quickly advanced and became head of Lifco's dental division, which accounted for half of the company's profits. In addition to his leadership roles, Waldemarson became Karlsson's right hand and fully embraced Lifco's unique company culture.

Underscoring Waldemarson's importance for Lifco, when Karlsson was once asked who would play his role in a movie about Lifco, his answer was immediate: "Per Waldemarson."

Since going public, Lifco has relied primarily on cash flow from operations to fund new acquisitions, without issuing any additional shares to fuel growth. Lifco maintains a conservative debt structure, with its outstanding bonds secured at highly favorable terms and the debt-ratios being lower than at the time of IPO. The strength of Lifco's cash flow generation is evident in its performance. Since its IPO, the company has grown free cash flow per share by 21% annually while continuing to pay dividends. Lifco's cash flow generation has been so strong that, within a decade, the total dividends distributed have equaled 80% of its market capitalization at the time of the IPO.

100× return and unexpected exit

In early 2019, following a bonus disagreement with Carl Bennet, Fredrik Karlsson had to leave Lifco. On that very day, the 7th of February 2019, one of our team members had scheduled a regular meeting at 9 a.m. with Karlsson in his office at the World Trade Center in Stockholm. On our way up in the elevator to the office, a press release appeared in our email inbox. It stated that "Lifco's Board of Directors has today taken the decision to terminate Fredrik Karlsson's position as CEO since the Board of Directors and Fredrik Karlsson have not succeeded in reaching an agreement about his future remuneration." Imagine our shock. Needless to say, the meeting did not unfold as expected.

Following the press release on that cold and rainy February day, Lifco's share price fell sharply by around 10%. As our team member sat in Karlsson's office that morning, Karlsson picked up his phone and called his broker with one clear instruction: buy Lifco shares. He knew that the company he had built was so strong that it would continue to thrive under the new leadership of Per Waldemarson, appointed by Bennet as CEO on the same day.

By the time Fredrik Karlsson left, he had achieved an impressive 25% annual earnings growth since 1998, effectively compounding Lifco's earnings 100 times. Under Waldemarson's leadership, Lifco has continued to thrive, underscoring the robust corporate culture and business principles Karlsson instilled over his 21 years with the company.

Discipline and focus on returns

Lifco has a successful history of deploying capital at high returns both via acquisitions and organically. The company maintains a disciplined acquisition strategy of buying small businesses. Since going public, only one acquisition has been larger than $50m in terms of sales. Each acquisition has typically comprised a low single-digit percentage of sales, with a clear limit of paying no more than eight times the operating profit (EBITA) for acquisitions. Historically, Lifco's acquisition multiples have consistently stayed below this threshold, largely because Lifco has continuously acquired smaller companies at lower prices. This disciplined approach is also supported by Lifco's broad acquisition strategy, which avoids limiting itself to specific industries or overpaying simply to fuel growth.

Lifco's capital allocation strategy is simple. The company focuses on acquiring and managing asset-light businesses, avoiding unnecessary spending on large, fancy headquarters or bloated corporate overhead. Lifco's approach is to invest in small, market-leading niche companies, often family-owned, with strong financial performance and strong cash flow profiles. The company prioritizes quality, seeking to own businesses that are leaders in their sectors, and further enhances the competitive position of those businesses by helping them become even more niched in their markets. Lifco's ideal acquisition candidate is one where it can make the acquired company even more specialized, turning already high margins even higher, resulting in outstanding returns on capital. At Lifco, managers aren't just encouraged to specialize and improve profitability—they're only rewarded when they grow profits organically. No bonuses are tied to acquired growth. This sharpens the focus across the organization, and ensures consistently high performance among its companies. It also encourages discipline in the acquisition process and incentivizes group managers to propose acquisitions of high quality. If they don't manage to improve performance of the companies they acquire, it will in turn impact their bonuses.

An excellent example of this is Brokk, Lifco's demolition robot business. Brokk has consistently stayed niche, continuously improving and differentiating its products and offerings, which over time has cemented a market-leading position. Lifco's model demonstrates that their companies can increase profitability despite lower volumes by concentrating on their most valuable products. This strategy of only going for quality and the best possible returns epitomizes the whole company.

Over time, Karlsson achieved operational excellence and honed exceptional capital allocation skills that played a pivotal role in Lifco's transformation. With the company generating strong cash flows, he developed a systematic approach to acquiring smaller, niche industrial companies that demonstrated strong profitability. This disciplined acquisition strategy resulted in a fantastic compounding effect.

In summary, Lifco seeks to find companies with:

- stable operations
- a leader within their niche

- an attractive position in the value chain without being dependent on specific suppliers or customers
- no or limited exposure to technology risk
- documented profitability
- appetite for high quality businesses.

Recognizing that these companies could be acquired at attractive prices, Lifco embarked on a series of acquisitions, adding nearly 140 companies to its portfolio since 2006. As Lifco's dental division held a dominant market position in the Nordics and already owned some of the industry's best companies, Karlsson realized that pursuing further growth in this area could lead to overpaying for lower-quality assets.

Instead of chasing growth in its core division for its own sake, Lifco took an opportunistic approach. It began acquiring niche, family-owned companies with long histories and strong financial performance in various sectors, leading to the formation of the System Solutions division. A compelling example of this, and one of its first acquisitions, was Zetterströms Rostfria, a family-owned manufacturer of pressure vessels, heat exchangers, skids, and thermos channels for the pharmaceutical industry, founded in 1974 by entrepreneur Alf Zetterström. When Lifco acquired the company in 2007 it had managed to grow sales by 8% and profits by 10% annually for the ten preceding years.

This acquisition positioned Lifco as the buyer of choice. Despite interest from several private equity firms, the previous owner chose to sell to Lifco, expressing strong confidence in its principal owner: "It's easy to trust Carl Bennet—he understands business." He added, "Now I can walk into the local grocery store without feeling ashamed of who I sold to."[5] That sentiment is something we often hear from entrepreneurs. Since the acquisition, Zetterströms Rostfria has significantly grown both sales and profitability.

Where many companies might have focused solely on expanding their core business, Lifco's strategy was grounded in maximizing shareholder value through intelligent, value-driven deals. By staying disciplined and flexible, they consistently made acquisitions that delivered the highest possible return rather than pursuing growth at any cost.

With a clear focus on shareholder value, Lifco's distinctive and unconventional approach to capital allocation has proven highly effective. The company expanded its acquisition strategy internationally to achieve the best possible returns. During an era of low interest rates, when aggressive acquirers crowded the private market in Sweden, Lifco shifted its focus to less competitive markets such as the UK, Germany, Italy, and the Benelux region. This international expansion has been a significant success, and Lifco has been able to acquire companies of at least the same quality in terms of operating margins at the same prices. In the last five years, 70–80% of the acquisitions conducted have been outside the Nordics (compared with less than half before IPO in 2014), without acquisition multiples increasing. Waldemarson has effectively proved that Lifco's decentralized and performance-driven model is attractive to entrepreneurs in other countries as well.

The company's adaptability to changing market conditions has also affected how it structures its acquisition deals. Around 2018, Lifco began experimenting with letting sellers retain an ownership in their businesses. This approach aligned the interests of Lifco and the original owners. Lifco observed that companies where entrepreneurs retained ownership performed better post-acquisition, and expanded the use of this model, further enhancing post-acquisition performance.

As Per Waldemarson became CEO in 2019, he emphasized internal talent development and saw expansion of Lifco's M&A capabilities as a necessity to maintain profitable growth. After hiring new M&A managers in key markets such as Italy, Germany, and the UK, the team today consists of around 20 people dedicated to M&A. Half of those are internally developed group managers. While the final capital allocation decisions are made by Lifco's board of directors, it is the group managers who actively drive the acquisition process. Per Waldemarson, essentially acting as Lifco's investment committee, oversees the process and ensures consistency and adherence to Lifco's stringent acquisition criteria.

Group managers, all deeply formed by Lifco's culture, are responsible for identifying acquisition candidates in addition to their internal board roles. When potential deals reach Waldemarson, they have already been thoroughly assessed as the best possible opportunities. This model ensures that Lifco's CEO is never a bottleneck in the decision-making process. By empowering group managers and placing trust in leaders trained within Lifco's system, the company maintains a highly efficient acquisition process, confident that its leaders will consistently make decisions aligned with Lifco's values and strategy.

The right (and shareholder-friendly) incentives matter

In many organizations, managers are incentivized to increase sales volumes, even if it comes at the expense of profit margins and returns on capital. Lifco's approach stands in stark contrast to this. Rather than prioritizing growth for its own sake, Lifco optimizes profitability and capital efficiency. Per Waldemarson, the CEO, often points out that "our best managers are the ones able to defend or increase margins." And to increase margins, Lifco encourages its managing directors to work to actively sell more of high-margin products and discontinue commoditized products with lower margins. This laser focus on specialization leads to higher pricing power, less competition, and thus higher margins and returns on capital.

Lifco's key governance principles are centered on minimizing bureaucracy and emphasizing performance measurement. In its decentralized structure, the company sets clear KPIs that all portfolio companies must follow, including earnings growth, organic growth, and working capital development. These KPIs are measured monthly, and there is no flexibility for group CEOs to modify or adjust them. Lifco aligns managers' incentives with these KPIs by linking their remuneration to EBITA growth, adjusted for a capital charge. Consequently, slow-moving inventory, or high receivables, will directly impact on a manager's compensation.

Fredrik Karlsson once shared Lifco's simple but effective tool on how to evaluate the performance of subsidiaries, which considers both profit growth and use of capital:

> "It would be based on a combination of profit and capital employed. For example, if the firm increased EBITA by \$100, the CEO might get 10%. But if his capital employed increases by \$100, he gets a penalty of \$2.5, so he or she ends up with a \$7.5 bonus. [Effectively a 25% ROCE hurdle (2.5%/10%).]"

In a conversation with a former CFO of a company Lifco acquired in 2015, we learned that one of their monthly KPIs was customer receivables. Lifco had a strict policy of writing down any receivables older than 30 days to zero. What do you do as a CFO of such a company?

You go the extra mile to reduce receivable days. This example perfectly embodies Lifco's almost frenetic focus on growth with strong cash flow. While each company alone may not significantly impact overall results, the cumulative effect of 250 companies applying this playbook becomes powerful. It is a system that has proven to attract high performers, who are well compensated for their results.

The most decentralized company

Over the years, we have analyzed numerous decentralized organizations, but rarely have we encountered a company as decentralized and averse to bureaucracy as Lifco. Despite being comprised of 250 portfolio companies and over 6,000 employees, Lifco operates with an incredibly lean structure, and its headquarters in Stockholm employs a mere handful of people. The head office is small, decorated with inexpensive furniture, and it is almost impossible to guess that a highly successful company hides within those walls. The decentralization runs so deep that the CEO doesn't have a secretary and is sometimes the only person in the office. During our visits to Lifco's headquarters, the CEO himself makes us coffee. Frugality is a core part of Lifco's culture, and the company's strong aversion to bureaucracy and complexity is deeply rooted in the management philosophy that can be traced back to Electrolux and Carl Bennet. This approach emphasizes full managerial responsibility at every level, ensuring that decision-making power stays close to the customers, where it has the most impact.

Or as Fredrik Karlsson, the former CEO, put it: "The complexity does not increase linearly. It increases exponentially relative to the number of employees. An employee is not a machine but a human being that needs to be kept satisfied and happy."

Maintaining a decentralized organization like Lifco eliminates the need for large corporate functions such as business development, strategy, HR, and finance. These are entirely managed at the individual company level. Lifco's guiding principle is to strip away unnecessary staffing, particularly middle management, which allows the organization to remain agile. A key factor in Lifco's ability to grow and scale has been its commitment to minimizing central staffing. For instance, only a handful of business controllers oversee the company's

250 portfolio businesses. This efficiency level is only achievable because Lifco refrains from intervening in daily operations as long as individual companies meet performance expectations. Lifco creates a structure that fosters profitable growth while keeping overhead low by empowering entrepreneurship and ownership at the subsidiary level.

An essential part of Lifco's decentralized culture is its strong focus on costs. Lifco minimizes costs "that do not directly contribute to the development of the businesses within manufacturing, sales or product development." In Lifco's experience, this results in lower costs and greater employee commitment.

A truly decentralized company like Lifco, where daily and operational responsibilities are delegated as close to the customer as possible, isn't just a nice-to-have—it's essential for the success of the acquisition-driven model. Without this level of independence at each business unit, the acquisition process at the holding company level can become sluggish and inefficient. Onboarding 20 to 25 or even 100 companies could easily overwhelm management.

Lifco's approach of delegating responsibility, empowering managers, and placing trust in them fosters leadership and builds an army of potential future leaders. Having the right leadership in each operating company is a top priority. Trusting capable, motivated individuals often yields returns far beyond any calculated projections. The COVID pandemic highlighted the importance of trust-based leadership and decentralization. When the pandemic hit, Lifco's companies didn't wait for directives from headquarters; instead, 97% of managers proactively adapted their businesses to the new reality—without any involvement from head office.

Allergic to bureaucracy—drawn to meritocracy

Like many other acquisition-driven compounders mentioned in this book, Lifco avoids micromanagement. It exercises its ownership primarily through the boards of its subsidiaries and has developed a more efficient way to scale its organization compared to many other companies. For instance, Lifco does not have business area presidents except for the System Solution business area. Instead, it operates with 15–20 group managers between top management and the operating companies without adding daily bureaucracy. Each group manager within Lifco is almost like a mini CEO. They serve as chairmen, governing 15–20 operating companies and scouting for acquisition opportunities. They are also Lifco's investment directors, who filter out the best possible acquisitions.

These operating groups hold two to three board meetings annually with their respective company; by comparison, Lifco's peers typically have chairmen responsible for 8–10 companies and hold 3–4 board meetings annually. This streamlined structure allows Lifco to scale more efficiently and quickly than its competitors.

Lifco excels at utilizing knowledge across the organization and between companies and business areas. It is common for group managers to take on the chairman role in companies outside their core expertise, which enhances knowledge-sharing and networking across the organization. What sets Lifco apart from its peers is its experience of having undergone a restructuring phase, scaled businesses like Brokk globally, operated distribution companies, and successfully managed niche, family-owned firms. Lifco effectively transfers this collective knowledge and experience to its subsidiaries through its boards, strengthening them in the process. A subsidiary in Lifco does not need to reinvent the wheel as it can just tap into the knowledge library of its other successful companies. If a group company needs help with expanding geographically or work with R&D, Lifco is there to help facilitate dialogue with managers of companies that have already succeeded in this. This is reflected in Lifco's impressive average organic profit growth of 7% since it went public in 2014—and the even more impressive 12% for its sector-agnostic division, System Solutions.

While Lifco doesn't micromanage, it does expect all its companies to adhere to its code of conduct and a few key principles. One of the most important is its clear pricing strategy: Lifco applies a standardized approach across all acquisitions, raising prices wherever possible and discontinuing products with low pricing power. In Lifco's way of looking at it, the best way to know if a product or service brings truly differentiated value is if you hike prices, and the customers still buy it.

The group management only intervenes when a company deviates from Lifco's internal performance metrics, which are margins, profit growth (EBITA) and cash flow generation. Even in such cases, Lifco offers the management team tools and resources to address the issues rather than imposing solutions. This hands-off management style fosters a sense of responsibility and accountability among employees for their company's performance.

A subsidiary under Lifco must comply with monthly financial reporting and monitoring. Lifco representatives, often group managers, take a board seat, monitor operations, and provide a discussion partner for subsidiary CEOs regarding strategy. Lifco invites subsidiary CEOs to annual gatherings to exchange ideas and discuss opportunities and challenges with group management. When Lifco notices results in their subsidiaries beginning to show deviations or negative trends, group managers promptly step in to analyze and assess the situation. They quickly identify underlying issues, ensuring any potential problems are addressed before escalating. This proactive approach allows Lifco to maintain performance across its diverse portfolio of companies. As a result, many business owners choose to continue running their companies well beyond the lock-up periods and initial put/call agreements after selling to Lifco.

Lifco's culture is built on accountability, responsibility, and performance. As a decentralized organization, it relies heavily on its managers to drive results. With a lean structure and minimal bureaucracy, there is no room for underperformance. What matters is delivering good numbers, and those who don't meet expectations are replaced. The same philosophy applies to acquisitions; if there is no consistency in financial performance, Lifco will not acquire the company. This straightforward approach has shaped the company over the years, attracting and retaining a team of high-performing individuals. Lifco has nurtured and developed its talent without needing a single HR person. Emphasizing Lifco's lean structure, the CEO Per Waldemarson once explained to us that: "hiring a HR person looks good for two years, but five years down the road we risk having five employees."

Lifco is all about meritocracy, and the only way to climb the ladder in Lifco is to perform. All group managers have been internally developed and trained into highly skilled leaders, mastering both small private acquisitions and operational excellence. Fredrik Karlsson placed significant emphasis on cultivating the next generation of culture carriers within Lifco—a tradition that Per Waldemarson has continued to foster. This focus on internal development has been critical to Lifco's successful growth. Without nurturing talent from within, the company could not have scaled the organization as effectively as it has.

From an investor's perspective, culture can often feel intangible, and no single metric can alone measure its success. However, a distinct pattern emerges in our conversations with Lifco's people. Everyone we have spoken to shares the same core values and perspectives, and Lifco's managers communicate in a uniform way. While difficult to quantify, this speaks to the strength of Lifco's culture—one centered on aversion to bureaucracy, emphasizing continuous improvements, and a laser focus on cash flow generation through simple KPIs.

Lifco's culture emphasizes simplicity and avoiding unnecessary tasks that detract from what truly matters: creating shareholder value. Internal meetings are minimized as much as possible, with issues being resolved quickly through phone calls or emails, reinforcing a culture of efficiency and decisive action. Its quarterly conference calls are notably brief, significantly shorter than those of other companies of comparable size. The company has never hosted a capital markets day, adhering to the belief that financial performance reigns supreme. In Lifco's view, there is little merit in devoting time to activities that distract from value creation.

Lifco's unique eye for talent

Fredrik Karlsson introduced one straightforward but successful principle: if you haven't been CEO of an operating company within Lifco, you can't advance to becoming a group manager. This policy, combined with a smart, cash-based incentive structure and significant managerial responsibility, has fostered strong employee loyalty. It's rare for leaders to leave Lifco; to date, only one high-ranking leader, an external hire, has done so. Lifco is deeply committed to preserving its performance-driven culture. Like the prime years of Electrolux in the 1970s and 1980s, Lifco rewards its managers generously when they deliver results. In fact, many Lifco managers earn salaries comparable to public company CEOs in Sweden, reducing any incentive to leave the organization. This approach ensures that Lifco retains its top talent while continuing to drive performance across the group.

Just as Carl Bennet had the ability to identify high-performing future leaders, so did Fredrik Karlsson. Under Karlsson's leadership, Lifco developed a high-performance culture focused on profit generation and an unwavering commitment to maximizing returns on capital. His time as CEO is evident not only in Lifco's financial results but also in his talent for developing an organization of leaders who share the same mindset and business acumen. One of the clearest examples is the current CEO, Per Waldemarson. His rapid rise within the company is a testament to Karlsson's eye for talent and his ability to foster leadership from within.

Despite Karlsson's extraordinary capital allocation skills, Lifco's evolution into the company it is today would not have been possible without the steady support of Carl Bennet, Lifco's majority shareholder. Together, they shaped a culture that remains strong under Per Waldemarson's leadership.

A powerful testament to the culture Fredrik Karlsson had developed at Lifco was his reaction following his departure in 2019. Not many CEOs would buy shares in the company they just got fired from. He has held onto every share to this day, underscoring his unwavering belief in the strength and future of the company he helped build.

When analyzing the reasons for Lifco's success, it is impossible to ignore the contributions of both Fredrik Karlsson and Carl Bennet. Together, they have been essential in developing Lifco's business model and culture. Although Lifco no longer employs Karlsson, he developed a strong business culture that still permeates the company.

5

For Entrepreneurs, By Entrepreneurs

Indutrade

IN SOME WAYS, horses are a strange place to start a chapter on an industrial conglomerate. But they're a good place, too, when it comes to Swedish industrial group Indutrade. Former CEO, Johnny Alvarsson, once said "our products should not be bigger than a horse." This prioritizing of smaller components has proven its value many times over.

Indutrade's success over many decades relies on its unwavering commitment to a few key drivers of self-funded, profitable growth. An entrepreneurial and trust-based culture is central, made possible by a decentralized governance model that grants high operational autonomy. Remarkably, every group company manages its own finance department, which are merely required to report monthly on profit and loss, the balance sheet, and cash flows. The group has consistently adhered to this lean operational approach, keeping the head office small and laser-focused on allocating capital wisely, as well as the follow-up of internal financial performance. It has diligently balanced autonomy with control. Even today, the head office remains small and efficient, consisting of only 25 people, about 0.25% of all group employees.

With a playbook continuously refined and improved over five decades through trial and error, Indutrade has built a well-oiled acquisition engine. Its industrial expertise, and a focus on small, continuous improvements, has not only strengthened its businesses, but also attracted other high-quality family-owned enterprises to join its journey. Its promise of being a perpetual owner has translated into a low-risk strategy. It has a remarkable stability in leadership with only three CEOs in 47 years. Indutrade has adapted to changing situations and managed to continuously refine its strategy without compromising discipline or losing focus on fundamentals.

Time is a friend to a wonderful business, and Indutrade exemplifies this with its patience, discipline, and commitment to steadily increasing intrinsic value. As the CEO, Bo Annvik, puts it: "We don't optimize for individual quarters or individual years; we think about long-term best practice, long-term performance improvements when we make investments, when we look at acquisitions and when we work with our companies."

Indutrade operates across five business areas spanning a broad range of industries, all of which are supported by megatrends: Industrial & Engineering, Infrastructure & Construction, Life Science, Process, Energy & Water and Technology, and System Solutions. The company's sales are at SEK 32.8bn ($3.28bn), with an EBITA margin of 14.5%. Since it was floated in October 2005, the company has delivered astonishing numbers: free cash flow per share has increased 14% CAGR, with a total shareholder return of 5,000% (22% CAGR).

Figure 5.1: Indutrade share price performance since IPO (2005)

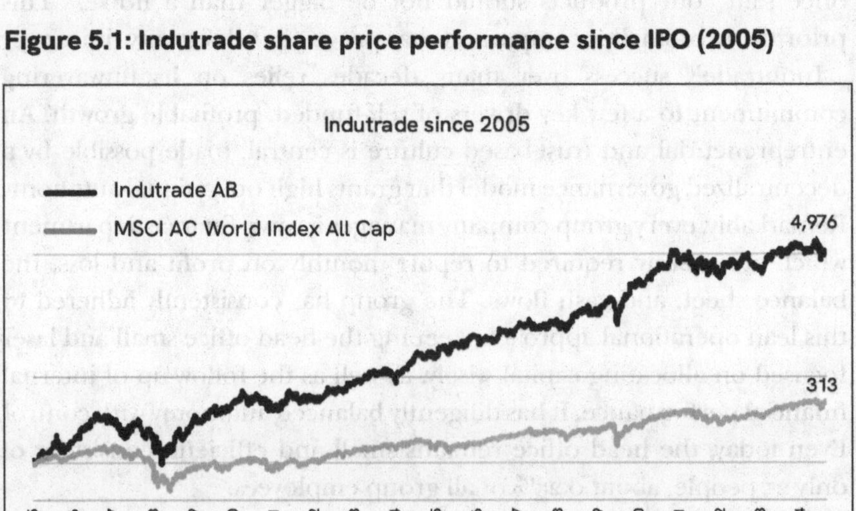

A diamond in the rough

Indutrade has a fascinating history that starts with the entrepreneurial spirit of a small Swedish company called Bengtssons Maskin. Founded in 1913, the company began as an importer and trader of products in various industries. As the firm expanded, it was acquired by the Tindberg family in 1953. During the Tindbergs' ownership, the company sharpened its focus into the value-added trading of components, mainly mechanical transmissions. It didn't just buy and sell gears, couplings, and drive systems—it improved, customized, or bundled those parts in ways that made them more useful to their customers. In 1978, the Tindberg family sold Bengtssons Maskin to the publicly listed company Wilhelm Sonesson, previously a wholesaler of pipes, pumps, and various other machinery and tools, that began operating more like an industrial holding company in the 60s and 70s.

Following the sale, one of the Tindberg sons—Gunnar, just 40 years old at the time—became the company's CEO, succeeding his brother. Gunnar Tindberg was resolute: under the new ownership, the company would continue to operate as an independent business, maintaining the same entrepreneurial spirit and autonomy.

Tindberg's mission was to grow by acquiring entrepreneurs with similar types of businesses. This resulted in the formation of the investment company AB Nils Dacke. The three companies that initially formed AB Nils Dacke (of which Bengtssons Maskin was one) established the foundation for what would evolve into Indutrade. A year after the formation of Nils Dacke, it was spun-out and listed on the Stockholm Stock Exchange with Wilhelms Sonesson as the largest shareholder. Gunnar Tindberg went on to conduct a series of acquisitions, including Colly Group in 1984, which was a cluster of companies that specialize in technical sales and solutions for manufacturing and engineering. Notably, Colly Group is still owned by Indutrade.

Gunnar Tindberg was an entrepreneur with a strong interest in technology, and a rare talent for identifying exceptional people. He loved to solve customers' problems, and he loved to buy and sell. "To close a deal gives me great satisfaction," he would say. [6] Tindberg was a master negotiator. A business owner who sold to Tindberg in 1995 remembers him fondly for his favorite phrase: "It's never too late to negotiate." He had personally experienced this when Tindberg, at the last minute, tried to further negotiate down the purchase price of his company. Tindberg always grasped that his growth plans would only be possible if he did not overpay for businesses. He would insist on paying a maximum of five times earnings. It is no coincidence that returns on capital during his leadership consistently surpassed 20%.

In our interactions with Tindberg, he always portrayed the people who worked with him as the heroes. In his view, they were the main reason for Indutrade's success. Although Tindberg retired over 20 years ago, we still meet people who worked with him. They describe him as one of the most outstanding leaders and mentors they have ever had.

At a time when acquisitions of trading companies were almost unheard of, Tindberg's approach was unconventional. He understood the importance of relationships: treating both suppliers and customers well, but also nurturing trust between subsidiaries and head office. He never bought a business before ensuring the company's suppliers would trust Indutrade as the new owner. And he always sought to treat potential acquisitions the way he would want Bengtssons Maskin to be treated. He prized businesses where know-how and customer confidence were central, and he gave them high autonomy, letting them retain their names, cultures and operations. He wasn't interested in fashioning a monolith.

Crucially, Gunnar also trusted the insights of Indutrade's best customers when it came to identifying potential acquisition targets. This is where Colly Group came in. During a meeting with the purchasing manager at Atlas Copco, a large industrial manufacturer specializing in compressors, tools, and vacuum solutions, Tindberg grasped the opportunity to ask about the company's most respected suppliers. The response from the purchasing manager: Colly Group. Gunnar took decisive action. He visited Colly Group's premises to conduct a firsthand assessment and introduce himself. What Gunnar Tindberg saw was a company capable of delivering products with exceptional mechanical strength. Colly Group had a formidable management team, and enjoyed predictable revenue streams, something Tindberg always saw as crucial. However, before acquiring Colly, he first had to convince its owner, who was living in Switzerland at the time. After several trips and persistent negotiations over a year, the seller finally agreed to sell.

By prioritizing relationships and leveraging customer insights,

Tindberg showed how partnership and mutual respect can drive successful acquisitions. When a promising opportunity arose, he moved swiftly to capitalize on it. His vision of making Indutrade a company built for entrepreneurs by entrepreneurs was being realized.

The northern star

A significant milestone in the history of Indutrade came with Industrivärden's acquisition of a substantial ownership stake in AB Nils Dacke in 1986. Industrivärden was, and still is, one of the largest listed investment companies in Sweden. It had noticed AB Nils Dacke, and it liked what it saw: strong leadership; a diverse range of customers, end-markets and geographies; a high return on capital, a solid balance sheet and strong profit growth.[7] Almost 40 years later, the same attributes could be used to describe Indutrade.

In 1989, Industrivärden made sure that any parts that were not focused on specialized industrial trading were sold off. It retained Dacke Component, a trading company of small and mission critical industrial components like valves, transmissions, filters and other similar products. Dacke was renamed Indutrade in 1990, with Gunnar at the helm.

Gunnar Tindberg's long tenure as CEO (1978–2004) was marked not only by nearly 50 acquisitions, but also by their extraordinary success. Ninety-five percent of those acquisitions were financially successful—a remarkable and almost unheard-of success rate.[8]

Acquisitions are essentially a "people game," and Tindberg's feel for personalities and relationships de-risked his acquisitions. He promised prospective sellers that he would help improve their businesses, and his background as an entrepreneur made him trustworthy. He stood apart from financially minded buyers in suits and ties. He was resolute in only buying businesses that met his stringent criteria: recurring-like revenue streams, high technical expertise, best-in-class products, and a potential of reaching a 10% margin. To him, these were signs of a high quality trading company. He explains to us that his belief was that "people and numbers are interconnected." Great people tend to drive great financial performance. Gunnar's "secret" was to find entrepreneurs sharing same core values, and to grant them freedom. This remains the north star of Indutrade's philosophy.

It is no coincidence that frugality marked Indutrade throughout

Gunnar Tindberg's leadership. Excess had no home there. During its first decade, cost consciousness was so strong that the head office was based out of a basement in a residential building in the mid-sized town of Malmö in southern Sweden. The office didn't even have a sign on the door, and only had room for one colleague in addition to Tindberg. Since then, Indutrade's head office has been based in the outskirts of Stockholm, far away from the fancy central business district and little upgraded.

Perhaps most impressively of all, Gunnar Tindberg's people-centric approach allowed Indutrade to grow both organically and through acquisitions without any addition of external capital. Sales and earnings grew by 100×, representing a 26-year CAGR of roughly 19.5%. In 2022, Tindberg was awarded a gold medal by His Majesty King Carl XVI Gustaf of Sweden, in honor of his contributions to Swedish industry and businesses.

Change in leadership and new growth opportunities

When Gunnar Tindberg decided to retire in 2004, Johnny Alvarsson succeeded him as CEO. At 54, the engineer—known for his expertise and passion for technology—was a perfect fit for Indutrade. In addition to his extensive experience as a public company CEO, he had relevant experience from different industries from Ericsson (1971–88), Zeteco (1988–2000) and Elektronikgruppen (2001–04). Elektronikgruppen was a listed acquisition-driven compounder focused on the electronics industry, and Zeteco was a supplier of niche products to the transport industry. Alvarsson had an impressive track record of profitable growth and was responsible for many successful acquisitions. Just as Gunnar Tindberg had grown Indutrade from a small company, Johnny Alvarsson had found similar success with Zeteco.

Alvarsson had grown that business from SEK 100m ($10m) in sales to SEK 2bn in sales ($200m)—an impressive 20× growth over the course of a decade. This was also notably profitable growth: returns on capital consistently surpassed 20%. His success didn't go unnoticed. In 1999, *Forbes* ranked Zeteco the 37th best small-cap company in the world out of 12,000 companies—an extraordinary achievement, especially in an era dominated by IT firms.[9]

For Indutrade's board, Alvarsson was more than just a proven leader—he was the ideal cultural fit. Shaped by early negative experiences in the more centralized and bureaucratic environment at Ericsson, Alvarsson strongly aligned with Indutrade's decentralized philosophy. His belief in autonomy was so deep that former colleagues recall that the word "synergy" wasn't even allowed to be mentioned.

As Johnny Alvarsson succeeded Gunnar Tindberg, Industrivärden—the owner of Indutrade—was in the midst of transforming into a pure-play investment company of public holdings. It contemplated selling or listing Indutrade. In October 2005, Indutrade was listed on the Stockholm Stock Exchange. Following the IPO, Fredrik Lundberg—through Lundbergsföretagen, a family-controlled listed Swedish investment company—became a major shareholder, and in 2012 the largest. Today it holds 26.6% of votes and capital. For Indutrade, Lundbergsföretagen was a perfect match with its philosophy of perpetual ownership of its companies. The Lundberg family is known for its long-term commitment and engagement; Fredrik is sometimes referred to as "the king of long-termism" in Sweden.

While Indutrade had successfully managed to grow through acquisitions of technical trading companies, Johnny Alvarsson favored growth through acquisitions of manufacturing (assembly) companies with proprietary products. It was something he had succeeded at in his previous roles. Alvarsson possessed a deep understanding of these companies, and had a great sense for technical details, impressing a number of entrepreneurs looking to sell their companies.[10]

Alvarsson saw that acquiring this type of company could not only increase their growth runway, but make the company more diversified and resilient in the process. Product companies offered greater scope for international expansion and organic growth compared to trading companies, which were usually local businesses. So redirecting acquisitions towards them would, with time, paradoxically make Indutrade's growth less dependent on acquisitions.

Alvarsson's strategy succeeded. He managed to increase the proportion of sales from companies with proprietary products from mid single-digits to almost 50%, and during his leadership the number of subsidiaries grew from 60 to 200.

Indutrade's international expansion also intensified under Alvarsson. He reduced overexposure to the Nordics by acquiring companies in geographies with similar cultures and values. He made a point of this by saying he would "never acquire companies in a country that has a beach facing the Mediterranean."

Alvarsson's expansion led Indutrade into the UK and the DACH (Germany, Austria, and Switzerland), where competition for deals was less fierce compared to Sweden. A third of the deals Alvarsson concluded were in these markets. He recognized that entrepreneurs, irrespective of country, faced the same challenges: particularly generational shifts, lack of resources, and the knowledge to grow their businesses. Selling their life's work to a decentralized company, where they could reap the benefits of collective wisdom while maintaining autonomy, would solve these issues. The success of its international expansion was pivotal for Indutrade.

When Johnny Alvarsson retired in 2017, he had grown Indutrade from SEK3.5bn ($350m) to SEK13.5bn ($1.35bn) in sales, representing a CAGR of 11%. EBITA expanded even more, from SEK 260m ($26m) to SEK1.5bn ($150m), a CAGR of 14%. Investors were rewarded with a total shareholder return of more than 1,000% (23.7% CAGR)—making the company one of the top performers on the Swedish stock market. This growth was achieved without diluting shareholders or stretching the balance sheet. The power of Indutrade's entrepreneurial and decentralized model was clear.

Evolution not revolution

In 2017, Alvarsson retired, and from one angle his successor seemed an unconventional choice. Bo Annvik had limited experience of decentralized organizations. Instead, he boasted a long and successful career within industrial companies such as Volvo Cars, SKF, Outokumpu, and Haldex, and extensive international experience from many different industries and application areas. The value of the latter, given Indutrade's geographical expansion, won out, and Annvik proved an excellent fit. While Tindberg understood technical trade and Alvarsson manufacturing (assembly) companies and international growth, Annvik blended the best of those two worlds.

Indeed, Indutrade's decentralized culture was so strong that Annvik quickly adopted its philosophy. "I didn't think the decentralized culture was so strong until I joined Indutrade," he told us. What also helped Annvik to settle in was continuity among Indutrade's leadership. Before assuming office, he personally called the senior leadership to assure them he did not aim to revolutionize Indutrade.[11] Continuity was king.

As new CEO, Bo Annvik grasped that to continue to grow Indutrade profitably without compromising returns on capital, even more capital needed to be deployed outside the Nordics. He needed places where the competition for deals was lower, but the quality of acquisition targets and price dynamics remained as attractive. It might have been easy to fall into deals for the sake of deals and scale for the sake of scale. But Annvik displayed his value investing skills: he sought the best deals at the highest returns, irrespective of business area or geography. He was always looking for the best long-term value for money. This was largely found outside the Nordics, with 60% of acquisitions completed in other countries.

Annvik is now eight years into his tenure, and he has succeeded at growing Indutrade while maintaining its family feeling and entrepreneurial spirit. One of his largest contributions is the increased collaboration and sharing of knowledge within the group. Annvik has also managed to improve processes and professionalize governance, developing people in-house to take on internal board positions—a vital necessity as new companies are added to the group. Centralized people development in a decentralized organization is, of course, a balancing act. To avoid unnecessary bureaucracy and over-centralization, Annvik entrusts decision-making authority to its experienced divisional managers and long-serving business segment leaders.

Rooted in industrial heritage, Indutrade always prioritized successful entrepreneurs that are great operators, the best at what they do. But as the portfolio shifted towards proprietary products, Annvik judged that there were even more possibilities to expand organically. He shifted to acquiring companies in industries with sustainable and structural growth tailwinds. He also pushed deal responsibilities for acquisitions out from headquarters. This increased the pool of people capable of making capital allocation decisions, and with that came a greater number of opportunities.

So far, under Bo Annvik's leadership, the company has grown sales from SEK 13.5bn ($1.35bn) to SEK 32.8bn ($3.28bn). During the same period, EBITA grew from SEK 1.5bn ($15m) to SEK 4.75bn ($475m). The share price has appreciated 300%, beating the overall Stockholm index by a factor of four which increased by 67% over the same period.

Buy great companies that generate money—and repeat

Indutrade's business philosophy for creating long-term shareholder value is simple. In the words of former CEO Johnny Alvarsson:

> "Indutrade has achieved steady growth since its start more than 35 years ago, and the key to our success is our focus on generating positive cash flow. With the money we earn we buy quality companies that generate more money, which enables us to buy more quality companies—it's that simple. This is how we grow and succeed at generating capital for new acquisitions as well as for a return for our shareholders."[12]

When Gunnar Tindberg was given the task of expanding Indutrade, it was natural for him to begin buying technical trading companies. Having grown up in his family's business, Bengtssons Maskin, he had deep insight into how these companies operated. But more than just understanding their mechanics, he recognized their strong commercial and financial appeal.

The companies Tindberg targeted were distributors of industrial essentials—valves, transmissions, fasteners, pipes, pumps, filters, and other consumables. These products were often critical to their customers' operations, yet typically constituted only a small portion of the total cost of a machine or system. This gave significant pricing power. Tindberg saw recurring patterns across these businesses: consistent sales; long-standing customer relationships; and dominant market positions within their niches. While their local nature limited organic growth, they generated substantial cash flow. To drive growth, Tindberg skillfully used that capital to acquire more similar businesses.

Tindberg also utilized Indutrade's passion and deep technical expertise to become their customers' problem solvers, effectively embedding themselves within customers' operations. And when these companies joined Indutrade, this only deepened. They went well beyond traditional supplier relationships.

One summer, one of Indutrade's customers—a car manufacturer—wanted to buy 50,000 units of a single product. The firm insisted on getting the price down as much as possible. Instead of agreeing to the deal, employees at an Indutrade company borrowed the technical specifications of the car, and spent an entire holiday cataloging potential improvements. They then returned the report to the customer. One of their suggestions was cutting the number of fasteners in half, saving time and money. Instead of selling 50,000 products at a low price, the company managed to sell half as many products at a higher price and thus higher margin. Tindberg had one key message to all his companies: don't sell single products—sell solutions that solve customers' problems. Thanks to this, Indutrade companies not only got better pricing power, but in many cases have been able to sell customers a wider range of products than initially sought.

Indutrade's reputation as a great home for technical trading companies was crowned with the award of the "Swedish Importer of the Year" in 1992 by the government-backed Swedish Commerce association (Svensk Handel). Many business owners chose to sell to Tindberg over the years not just because of the financial upside, but because he understood and respected what made them successful. He promised to preserve their names, cultures, employees, and management—recognizing their value as strong local champions.

Tindberg's ability to successfully acquire numerous small trading companies also came down to several other important factors. Sweden provided an ideal environment, as its small and fragmented market favored domestic importers with strong local presence and expertise: essential for adding value for customers. Due to limited market size, large suppliers often found it impractical to establish their own sales operations or logistics for low-cost components. Furthermore, as a pioneer in acquiring technical trading companies, Tindberg faced little competition. He recognized this opportunity and capitalized on it with remarkable success. The diamond in the rough started to shine.

Growth through acquisitions would not have been possible without the key ingredient: strong cash flow generation. Tindberg, Alvarsson and Annvik all made sure to keep bureaucracy at bay by not interfering in daily operations. Instead, they incentivized their companies to grow profits each year, but only if they generated attractive returns on capital. A company could not grow by decreasing its margins, by keeping too much inventory, or by agreeing too lofty payment terms with customers. Few other firms have consistently adhered to these simple principles over almost five decades, and under three CEOs.

This cash culture within Indutrade means that its subsidiaries understand the importance of generating strong cash flow independently, without involvement from the parent company. It clearly works: Indutrade has consistently converted its net income to free cash flow over several decades, resulting in a strong financial position. The company has never exceeded a net debt to EBITDA of 2.5×, despite paying dividends of 25% of operating cash flow since IPO.

We began this chapter with Johnny Alvarsson saying that the products Indutrade sold "should not be bigger than horses." Selling small and mission-critical products has always been its winning formula, and has created profound value for Indutrade's shareholders.

What all three CEOs share is a belief that sustainable growth has to generate strong returns on capital, widely exceeding the cost of capital. This has been built into Indutrade from the start. Shareholder value is only created by profitable growth that produces a sufficient amount of cash flow in relationship to the capital that goes into the business. As a result, Indutrade's only external financial target in the first years was that the return on capital employed should exceed 20%, a target still used today.

Tindberg's approach—which shaped Indutrade's acquisition strategy—was deeply people-centric. He personally negotiated and closed most deals in the sellers' family homes. For him, it was important to earn the trust and approval of founders' families. He had an ability to make people feel like true owners of their business—even after a sale. Such an approach allowed Indutrade to acquire companies at attractive prices, often at mid-single digit multiples, with little competition.

With no strict limitations to a single vertical, Indutrade enjoys the flexibility to be highly selective—acquiring only businesses that align with its criteria. It typically pays 5–8× EBITA multiples, thanks to its focus on smaller, less competitive targets with annual revenues between $5m–50m.

Growing big by staying small

As Indutrade has grown nearly 1,000 times larger in sales since its founding in 1978, the company now faces new challenges—one of the most significant being the need to deploy increasing amounts of capital while maintaining high returns. Bo Annvik has recognized this and has taken decisive steps to address it. To position Indutrade for sustained profitable growth, he announced a reorganization in 2023 of its eight business areas (including three country-based areas) into five international business areas focused on specific business segments. By focusing less on where companies are based and more on what kinds of products they make and who their customers are, group companies can share knowledge more effectively across similar businesses—making it easier for them all to grow.

Annvik's approach is also based on the belief that if companies in the same business area are better connected, it'll be easier to find good new companies to acquire. This shift has already accelerated the pace of acquisitions under his leadership. Annvik also recognizes that clustering similar businesses within adjacent industries reduces risks and minimizes potential surprises; these are areas where they already have a deep knowledge of challenges and opportunities.

To sustain its historical growth rates while maintaining high returns, Annvik has set a target for each business area to complete 3–4 acquisitions per year. This ensures a steady pipeline of potential deals. By granting each business area the autonomy and incentives to pursue its own growth, Indutrade functions as a collection of "mini-Indutrades," allowing it to scale efficiently while preserving its entrepreneurial spirit.

The more individuals and teams engaged in deal sourcing, the more time top management has to focus on capital allocation decisions. Over the past 20 years, the company's commitment to delegated responsibility for acquisitions has been instrumental in sustaining its steady pace of growth. Business area managers, segment leaders, and managing directors are the "local antennas" that nurture a broad and effective network for identifying acquisition candidates. This decentralized approach now accounts for half of Indutrade's acquisitions, demonstrating the strength of local decision-making.

Annvik has successfully decentralized M&A responsibilities, albeit the board takes final capital allocation decisions, in line with Swedish governance practices. With years of experience, Indutrade's teams and experienced leaders have developed a keen ability to identify companies that fit the company's DNA. A key example of its trust-based, decentralized culture is that no add-on acquisition takes place without the approval of local management, reinforcing a strong sense of trust, ownership and accountability among leaders.

To fully capitalize on future growth opportunities as Indutrade continues to expand, Bo Annvik is determined to scale the organization without introducing unnecessary bureaucracy. His strategy hinges on two key principles: professional ownership and scalability. As previously mentioned, involving more people in identifying M&A opportunities has been crucial to Indutrade's success. To prepare for the next phase of growth, Indutrade has promoted its most senior managing directors to business segment leaders. Business segment leaders are the key link between business area managers and subsidiaries, responsible for driving growth through acquisitions. This initiative not only gives experienced leaders from within Indutrade greater responsibility for driving growth beyond their own businesses, but also creates opportunities for younger talent to step into managing director roles.

These structural changes address two common challenges faced by acquisition-driven compounders as they scale: expanding the pool of leaders capable of executing acquisitions and managing generational transitions within Indutrade's more than 200 companies. Additionally, business segment leaders—leveraging their deep experience within the group—take on internal board roles, implement Indutrade's operating model, and provide governance and support for subsidiaries. This frees up subsidiaries to focus on their core operations and customer relationships. Business segment leaders are key to facilitate knowledge sharing, strengthen professional governance, and drive collaboration across different areas of expertise.

Saying no to mediocrity

True mastery in multi-decade acquisition-driven growth lies in the discipline to reject mediocrity, prioritize quality, and remain steadfast even when tempting opportunities arise. For 47 years, Indutrade has exemplified this discipline, supported by its long-term owners who have provided stability through both economic booms and periods of uncertainty. At one point, Indutrade's acquisition pipeline was thinner than usual, prompting the CEO to inform the company's main owner, Fredrik Lundberg. To the CEO's relief, Lundberg simply replied, "There's no need to worry—we're in this for the long haul, not to maximize the next quarter." That moment perfectly captured the essence of Indutrade's long-term mindset.

While the company's annual growth may seem unremarkable from the outside, Indutrade recognizes that the true power of compounding lies in sustainability. Growth is not about speed alone but about endurance—ensuring that each acquisition strengthens the foundation for long-term success. This commitment has allowed Indutrade to uphold its strict cultural criteria while confidently entering new geographies, industries, and product areas. A prime example of this strategic expansion is its life science division, which now accounts for a quarter of total sales—up from just a tenth two decades ago.

For Indutrade, success is not just about securing deals at low multiples—it is about acquiring the right companies without compromising on quality or cultural fit. By prioritizing long-term profitable growth, Indutrade has fostered continuous, incremental improvements in its subsidiaries post-acquisition—whether by raising prices or jettisoning unprofitable customers.

Many family-owned businesses are often hesitant to raise prices, fearing they might lose valuable customers. Indutrade's experience has shown that the actual risk of losing customers this way is relatively low. The pricing power enjoyed by Indutrade's companies was well shown when a managing director reviewed the profitability of various products and identified one with an unusually low margin. When he informed the customer that a price increase was necessary, the response was, "This is crazy." Despite the initial pushback, the customer eventually agreed. A few months later, the managing director realized he had mistakenly raised the price of the *wrong* product—resulting in that item now having an exceptionally high profit margin.[13]

If you sell, we will help you grow

From the very beginning, Indutrade has been built on a foundation of autonomy and entrepreneurship. When Gunnar Tindberg embarked on Indutrade's expansion journey, he drew upon his industrial expertise, business acumen, and experience from his own family-owned business. He knew that success would come from one simple promise: if they sold their companies to Indutrade, he would help them grow and develop.[14]

By keeping his promises, Tindberg gained the trust of business owners, making Indutrade an attractive acquirer. One of Indutrade's managing directors once explained the fast decision-making that characterizes its companies. A good idea could come up in the morning around coffee time—after lunch "it is already decided and executed."[15] This entrepreneurial ethos continues to thrive. As a result, many entrepreneurs have chosen to stay with Indutrade well beyond their earn-out periods—and often go on to recommend the company to other potential sellers.

Indutrade's dedication goes beyond acquisitions—it also nurtures growth from within its own ecosystem. Take Colly Flowtech, for instance. Founded as an internal start-up in 2007, the company has grown into a leading distributor of valves, hoses, and pumps, now generating close to SEK 300m ($30m) in annual revenue. It stands today as one of Indutrade's most successful and profitable ventures, and an example to inspire the rest of the group.

Another key factor in sustaining entrepreneurial drive is the benchmarking system introduced by Johnny Alvarsson 20 years ago. In our conversations with managing directors, we have heard them describe how the benchmarking system fosters healthy competition among companies. Despite being successful before joining Indutrade, positive incentives rather than pressure have been proven to inspire them, with internal competition driving improved performance post-acquisition.

Alvarsson once illustrated this with the story of a 65-year-old manager who had consistently achieved a 10% profit margin. Four years after the benchmarking system was introduced, he increased his profit margin to 18%. The manager's explanation: "You challenged me!" In Indutrade, business leaders are motivated to push their limits. Many aspire to rank at the top of the benchmarking system, fueled by the company's prestigious five-year performance award and quarterly rewards for exceptional results.

Visiting Indutrade's subsidiaries provides firsthand evidence of this culture—performance awards are proudly displayed on office walls and in windows.

A unique culture of trust and continuous learning

The trust-based, transparent, and open culture that Gunnar Tindberg established remains at the heart of Indutrade today. Driven by a vision to create a home for entrepreneurs, Tindberg understood that honesty, openness, and an entrepreneurial spirit would naturally attract like-minded sellers. In our conversations with employees—both past and present—they often describe Indutrade as a close-knit family.

Tindberg had a remarkable ability to build trust with entrepreneurs. Confident in Indutrade's reputation, he would encourage potential sellers to "call anyone and ask how we are as an owner." His hands-on entrepreneurial background, far removed from big and bureaucratic corporations, made him relatable. His successors have been exceptional in living up to this.

Alvarsson and Annvik have also added to it by introducing an internal directory listing all group companies, along with the names of managing directors, business segment leaders, and business area managers. This list is accessible to all employees. Networking and collaboration is encouraged across the organization. Beyond strengthening internal connections, the directory has also played a strategic role in acquisitions—potential sellers can contact anyone within Indutrade for a reference. Sharing this list externally is akin to offering a long-term quality guarantee; it signals confidence in Indutrade's business model, its people, and its decentralized philosophy—helping it win deals.

Warren Buffett once famously said that "the more you learn, the more you earn." Continuous learning has been essential to Indutrade's success. One example of this played out back in 2006. Alvarsson invited top leaders from ITW, Illinois Tool Works, an American industrial conglomerate with $15.9bn in sales, to share their experience of expanding through acquisitions. ITW had managed to grow to 800 subsidiaries and he wanted Indutrade to learn from their journey.

This learning culture empowers employees at all levels, sharpens decision-making, and strengthens the company's ability to navigate complexity. Continuous development is actively embraced by every level in the organization. Board meetings include presentations from internal leaders and external experts.

Annvik reinforces this philosophy through comprehensive three-year post-acquisition reviews, which help refine Indutrade's approach, optimize decision-making, and share valuable insights across the group. Case studies documenting acquisition outcomes are regularly shared with the board, ensuring that strategic decisions are based on real-world experiences. This practice not only strengthens Indutrade's governance but also cultivates a deeply embedded culture of informed decision-making and ongoing improvement across the company.

We had the privilege of experiencing this firsthand. When we were invited to share our insights on how larger acquisition-driven compounders had scaled their organizations to drive growth through acquisitions, we encountered an atmosphere that felt more like a meeting of minds than a boardroom: open, welcoming, and filled with genuine curiosity. The board listened intently, asked thoughtful questions, challenged ideas, and exchanged perspectives that enriched the conversation.

People build success, long-term owners sustain it

When Bo Annvik took the helm in 2017, he made leadership development a key priority. Recognizing the need for competent and forward-thinking leaders in an ever-evolving world, Annvik set out to equip Indutrade for the decades ahead. He introduced voluntary knowledge hubs focused on critical areas such as digitalization, value-based pricing, sustainability, and international expansion. Additionally, he placed strong emphasis on capital allocation, ensuring that decision-makers across the organization are well-informed, strategic and rational in their approach.

If there was competition on how instrumental the right people, management teams, and owners can be in a company's stability and success—Indutrade would be a winning contender. For nearly half a century, engaged and competent leaders have upheld a long-term vision, a disciplined approach, and an unwavering commitment to increasing intrinsic value. This enduring dedication is reflected in Indutrade's financial strength over five decades, demonstrating the stability and foresight of both its management and ownership.

All three of Indutrade's CEOs have played a pivotal role in shaping the company's success. Their leadership has been strengthened by engaged and committed owners who have provided unwavering support and upheld long-term principles for shareholder value creation. Few companies are fortunate to have owners who measure success in generations rather than quarterly results.

This long-term perspective has also attracted highly competent and deeply committed board members, many of whom have dedicated significant time to Indutrade. Some directors have served for as long as 18 years. The commitment of Indutrade's largest owner, Lundbergsföretagen, is particularly notable. Chairman of the board, Katarina Martinsson, is actively involved in acquisition decisions and regularly visits companies across the group, engaging directly with employees and reinforcing the ownership commitment.

Just like Berkshire Hathaway, Indutrade is built on the strength and vision of countless entrepreneurs and dedicated individuals. In the early years of Indutrade, Hans-Erik Ovin, then CEO of Wilhelm Soneson, saw something extraordinary in Gunnar Tindberg. Instead of hesitating due to Tindberg's unconventional family-entrepreneurial background, Ovin encouraged him to embark on an ambitious acquisition journey, one that would lay the foundation for Indutrade's long-term success.

The journey was shaped by other outstanding people as well. Claes Hjalmarsson, who joined Indutrade in 1984 through the acquisition of the Colly companies, played a pivotal role in more than 100 acquisitions as Alvarsson's right hand. Similarly, Peter Eriksson, the former MD of Alnab AB (acquired in 1995), became a cornerstone of Indutrade's growth journey. Not only did he lead his company to continued profitability after the sale, he also helped build the Flow Technology division (valves, pipes, and pipe systems) and initiated Indutrade's internal training programs. His journey became a blueprint for what long-term success within the Indutrade ecosystem could look like. By the time he decided to retire, he had grown Flow Technology into 20% of Indutrade's group sales. Even today, his dedication to Indutrade remains strong, as he continues to serve as a senior advisor to the management team.

These leaders weren't exceptions—they were part of a culture that nurtured talent from within. The results speak for themselves: high employee retention, seamless leadership transitions, and a company that continues to grow without losing its entrepreneurial DNA. At

Indutrade, leadership isn't just appointed—it has to be earned through performance. In a business world often defined by turnover and short-term thinking, Indutrade's approach stands out—proving that investing in people is the most sustainable growth strategy of all.

To grasp Indutrade's philosophy of patient, long-term value creation, it's essential to understand its primary owner, Lundbergsföretagen, one of Sweden's largest investment companies. Fredrik Lundberg, Chairman of Lundbergsföretagen, shares his views on long-term value creation, offering insight into the thinking that also drives Indutrade's approach:

> "Our commitment to the portfolio companies is long-term. It is simply not possible to pursue active ownership successfully without taking a long-term view. Time is an important factor for an investor. This is when the compound interest effect really has an impact. It is therefore important to persevere and work hard."[16]

Conclusion

Indutrade is a compelling example of a successful acquisition-driven compounder with many of the ingredients for long-term success. Since its IPO in 2005, Indutrade has delivered an impressive total shareholder return of 5,000% (CAGR 22%).

Built upon the religion of decentralization and a deep belief in entrepreneurship and autonomy, with the support of owners with a multi-decade view, Indutrade has stayed disciplined regardless of macroeconomic conditions. Nurtured by a strong cash culture, the company has developed many great private market investors that have continued to programmatically make small acquisitions year after year with one focus: to increase intrinsic value.

In essence, Indutrade displays several characteristics that represent a successful acquisition-driven compounder: sensible leverage and risk profile, sustained high reinvestment rates, superior returns on capital, disciplined M&A practices, emphasis on organic growth within acquired entities, an unwavering focus on capital efficiency, and scaling of M&A capabilities. With steadfast ownership committed to long-term stewardship and minimal CEO turnover, Indutrade has adhered to its core strategy while continuously evolving and delivering exceptional shareholder returns.

6

A School of Value

Bergman & Beving

IN THE FALL of 1984, Warren Buffett published an article called "The Superinvestors of Graham-and-Doddsville" in the Columbia Business School magazine.[17] In this piece, Buffett highlighted a group of investors whose guiding principles were deeply embedded in the traditions of the value investors Benjamin Graham and David Dodd. Despite pursuing diverse paths and selecting different stocks, all these investors adhered to the fundamental principles of value investing. The outcome was a series of impressive investing track records that defied randomness.

Sweden's Bergman & Beving, with its five spun-out companies, provides a similar example. It forms a kind of ecosystem: the Superinvestors of Bergman & Bevingsville, if you will. All constituent parts adhere to a common set of principles crucial for their success as independent entities. Much like the investors in Buffett's article, these companies operate with a shared ethos, marked by two notable characteristics: a dedication to decentralization and a commitment to self-financed growth through simple profit goals, allowing each individual within the system to make a meaningful impact.

The first profit goal is simple, yet not easy: to double earnings every five years. This ambitious target pushes the companies to stay innovative and search for new profitable growth opportunities. But growth alone isn't enough. It must be sustainable. The second goal, crafted by the engineering background of the company and the financial brilliance of its former CEO Anders Börjesson, focuses on maintaining a strong cash culture.

Subsidiaries must adhere to a simplified return-on-capital metric that translates into a profit-to-working capital ratio of over 45% (P/WC >45%). In other words, for every dollar tied up in working capital, companies must consistently generate more than 45 cents of profit. The simplified ratio reflects Bergman & Beving of the 1980s and 90s. At the time it mainly owned distribution companies, which typically did not have any tangible assets except working capital. The beauty of the ratio was that everyone in the organization could understand and impact it. Numerous successful acquisition-driven compounders find inspiration in the notable influence of the Superinvestors of Bergman & Bevingsville, which have demonstrated how powerful the combination of time and great capital allocation can be.

Rooted in a common philosophy, this ecosystem nurtures talents from within. It turns operators into disciplined capital allocators, and instills a mindset of frugality at every level. The result has been the creation of exceptional shareholder value. Its leaders are more than just skilled operators; they possess a deep understanding of what it takes to build enduring value over time. In many ways, the Bergman & Bevingsville ecosystem is simply a collection of powerful cash-generating companies.

Bergman & Beving and its spin-offs have compounded earnings before tax 690 times since listing, concluding an impressive CAGR of 14% over 48 years. A sum of $1,000 (invested in Bergman & Beving at its IPO in September 1976, is today worth almost $7.5m, excluding dividends received, if all the shares in the various spin-offs have been held. That marks an astonishing CAGR of 20% over 49 years.

Until the IPO in 1976, Bergman & Beving was run like a family company, its acquisition growth strategy first evolving after 1967. Its growth has, with only minor share dilution, been achieved completely with self-generated cash flow.

In 2021, Sweden's largest economic newspaper, *Dagens Industri*, described the company as "The Ancestor of Stock Market Rockets." It is hard to disagree.

Figure 6.1: Bergman & Beving by the numbers

SEK million	**Earnings Before Tax**	**Market Capitalization**	**Date**
Bergman & Beving 1976	7.5	24	September 1976
Bergman & Beving	297	8,242	May 2025
Addtech	2515	85,933	May 2025
Lagercrantz	1298	43,000	May 2025
Momentum Group	241	8,785	May 2025
Alligo	349	5,528	May 2025
Addlife	477	21,548	May 2025
Total	**5,177**	**173,035**	
CAGR since 1976	14%	20%	

$ million	**Earnings Before Tax**	**Market Capitalization**	**Date**
Bergman & Beving 1976	0.75	2.4	September 1976
Bergman & Beving	30	824	
Addtech	252	8,593	
Lagercrantz	130	4,300	
Momentum Group	24	879	
Alligo	35	553	
Addlife	48	2,155	
Total	**518**	**17,304**	**May-25**
CAGR since 1976	14%	20%	

A passion rooted in technology

The Bergman & Beving story starts with Arvid Bergman, a Swedish student from the mid-sized town of Norrköping, who studied electrical engineering in Germany. In the 1890s, his path crossed with that of Fritz Beving, a German student with a similar passion for technology. After his studies, Bergman took a job as engineer at the Wuppertal-Elberfeld power station. Beving worked at The Tudor Accumulator Co. in England. A few years later, he returned to Germany and joined the Wuppertal-Elberfeld power station, where he reunited with Arvid Bergman. Together, they moved on to Brown Boveri (now ABB), and an idea they once dreamed of in school—to start a company together—began to take shape. In October of 1906, they moved back to Sweden and founded Bergman & Beving, a trading company focusing on importing technological products to the industrial sector in Sweden. The start of the business was marked by the signing of the first agency agreement with the German company, Carl Schenk. The business thrived despite the challenges of war and the founders' deaths in the 1950s.

From day one, Fritz and Arvid built a culture rooted in frugality, simplicity, and accountability. In fact, their cost-consciousness was so strong that they famously persuaded their first customers to cover their initial salaries and furnish their office. This mindset rippled throughout the company, and would leave its mark on firms later spun out from it. (One former subsidiary CEO recalls winning an internal performance contest in the 1980s; the grand prize was not a lavish trip or bonus, but two pens. Performance was valued—frugality was sacred.)

This entrepreneurial mindset was paired with a clear mission: to deliver best-in-class technical solutions to clients. Fritz and Arvid's leadership was agile and forward-looking, always seeking new avenues for growth, and quick to adapt to changing conditions—like when they switched strategy in the 1920s to focus on more advanced products with higher margins. This spirit continues to shape the Bergman & Beving ecosystem to this day.

Venture into acquisitions

In the early 1940s, Bergman & Beving demonstrated its agility by making a bold move into the life sciences sector through a partnership with Radiometer. This ultimately laid the foundation for its many holdings in the lab and diagnostics markets—with its Meditech division finally formed in 1997.

In the 1960s, when many small and medium-sized businesses were up for sale at attractive prices amid widespread family business pessimism, Bergman & Beving once again made a bold and unconventional move. It ventured into acquisitions, a field in which it had little experience. At this time in Sweden, serial acquisitions without synergies or integration were unheard of. Despite being pioneers and modest in size, Bergman & Beving thrived thanks to its entrepreneurial spirit. Leadership had a deep belief in the firm's philosophy and business acumen, trusting that their prioritization of simplicity, passion for entrepreneurship, and history of deep technical expertise would resonate with the businesses they sought to acquire.

The first acquisition—Johan Lagercrantz AB, in 1967—marked an initial foothold in the electronics technology field. The firm, established in 1938, had dealt with components and equipment from its inception, trading with notable brands like General Radio and Du Mont. This was to be the first of many purchases. By the time Bergman & Beving came to spin off Lagercrantz and Addtech in 2001, it had made close to 200 acquisitions.

During the 1980s, the group enjoyed a strong market position, with distribution rights for over 300 companies and a 15% market share in the electronics distribution business in Sweden. In 1987, it was awarded "Importer of the Year" by the Swedish Commerce association (Svensk Handel). A year before, the prize had been awarded to Hennes & Mauritz, one of the most promising Swedish companies in decades. This solidified the group's reputation as a great trading business, which in turn helped to position it as a preferred buyer of similar businesses. Bergman & Beving's winning approach to acquisitions was to let companies continue to operate autonomously under their existing names while adhering to its fundamental principles.

Intensified competition emerged with the expansion of the European Union, which allowed for parallel imports. This, coupled with the growing commoditization of some products, significantly impacted trading companies like Bergman & Beving. But the company never let a good crisis go to waste. These challenges prompted it to shift towards niche-oriented companies, and to emphasize adding value beyond mere distribution. Just as it had navigated two world wars and other crises, Bergman & Beving once again proved its ability to adapt. This has been critical to its survival and development.

Two defining decades

Significant changes in the 1980s and 1990s would define the company's future. When Tom Hedelius, the CEO of Svenska Handelsbanken, became chairman in 1982, one of his most significant decisions was to make

Anders Börjesson the first external CEO. This marked a shift in Bergman & Beving's management strategy; the company had only had four CEOs over the past 84 years, all of whom had been significant shareholders. Nevertheless, Börjesson had been part of the management team since 1979 and had a deep understanding and affinity for the cultural ethos of the organization. Börjesson launched the profit over working capital metric (P/WC): essentially, how much profit the company generates for every dollar tied up in inventory, receivables and payables, i.e., the day-to-day running of the business. The metric has stood the test of time for over 40 years and continues to serve as a vital guiding tool, influencing all aspects of business operations and acquisitions.

The P/WC metric was not the only impactful change: a greater use of internal academies or courses to boost abilities in key areas, played a significant role in "transforming engineers and individuals from non-sales backgrounds into proficient business professionals."[18] Already established in the 1960s, these academies increased collaboration and networking among employees within the group. They also created an internal feedback loop for improvements in sales, exports, customer service and capital and resource allocation. And they stressed the importance of closer customer relationships: companies within Bergman & Beving became partners and problem solvers for their customers rather than mere suppliers. Employees shaped by these internal academies have made important contributions to the group's success over the decades. Bergman & Beving deemed the internal academies and the investments in its people so crucial to the future success of the company that in the 1980s it spent close to 10% of its cost base on them.[19] The enduring value these investments had generated has far outweighed the costs.

Pioneering serial acquisitions

The Superinvestors of Bergman and Bevingsville's superior shareholder value creation over multiple decades is thanks to their disciplined value investing philosophy, strong cash culture marked by frugality, and intelligent capital allocation supported by self-funded growth. For decades, they've stayed true to a simple yet powerful decentralized operating model that permeates the entire organization. The only time they have failed to create shareholder value was when they briefly departed from its principles, as we will return to later.

By 2000, primarily under the leaderships of CEOs Anders Börjesson and Pär Stenberg, the company had completed almost 200 acquisitions, with a staggering 85% of them being accretive to earnings-per-share growth. This success wasn't due to luck. Through a disciplined and methodical approach, Bergman & Beving identified entrepreneurs who shared the same core values. Free from bureaucracy, they ensured a smooth deal-making process, and there was no burden of lengthy agreements typical of M&A transactions. It was about simplicity, as well as the discipline not to overpay for acquisitions: the essence of value investing. The brilliant, down-to-earth strategy significantly de-risked acquisitions, leading to a track record that few can rival.

What sets Bergman & Beving's Superinvestors apart is not just their great confidence and ability to venture into unfamiliar territory through acquisitions. It's their ability to pass on hard-earned wisdom—teaching the value of strong customer and supplier relationships, allocating capital rationally, and striving for operational excellence. That mindset lives on today, embedded in every company that carries the Bergman & Beving legacy featured in this book.

Figure 6.2: The Bergman & Beving ecosystem

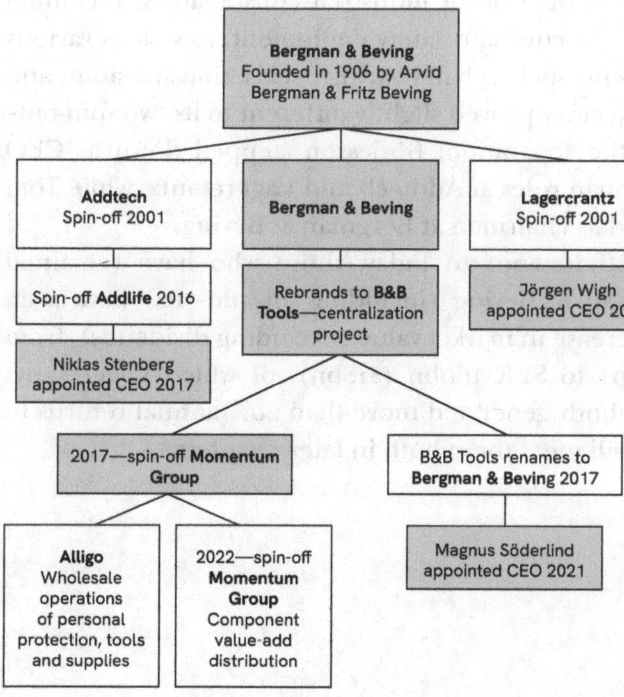

New century—three companies

Bergman & Beving's market value had increased from SEK 24m in 1976 to SEK 3.5bn in 2001—an astonishing increase of 140× since its IPO. However, Anders Börjesson, then CEO, had begun to feel that the company (at the time boasting sales of SEK 9bn) had become too large and dispersed. When he no longer recognized all the managers at the annual conference, he decided that something had to change for the company to maximize shareholder value.

Börjesson wanted Bergman & Beving to be the best company—not the largest. He and Tom Hedelius (chairman) concluded that the best way to increase Bergman & Beving's shareholder value was to separate the businesses into three smaller entities, each from a lower base that could grow profitably in its respective niche. Bergman & Beving was therefore split into: Addtech (industry), Lagercrantz (electronics), and Bergman & Beving (product companies and wholesale operations mainly to construction and industry-related businesses). The aim was to highlight the company's underlying value and enable each entity to focus on growth as individual units. Subsequently, Bergman & Beving focused on the sale of industrial consumables, including tools, machinery, protective and safety equipment, as well as various industrial components such as ball bearings, seals, transmissions, and automation. Its trajectory proved slightly different to its two spin-outs.

After finalizing the separation, Börjesson stepped down as CEO and took the chairman roles at Addtech and Lagercrantz, while Tom Hedelius continued as chairman at Bergman & Beving.

From the spin-off in 2001 to today, those who have remained invested in Bergman & Beving (including all-spin-offs) have seen another 50-fold increase in market value (excluding dividends), from SEK 3.5bn ($350m) to SEK 180bn ($18bn), of which Lagercrantz and Addtech have both generated more than 20% annual returns to shareholders. We will meet them both in later chapters.

Figure 6.3: The Bergman & Beving family over the years

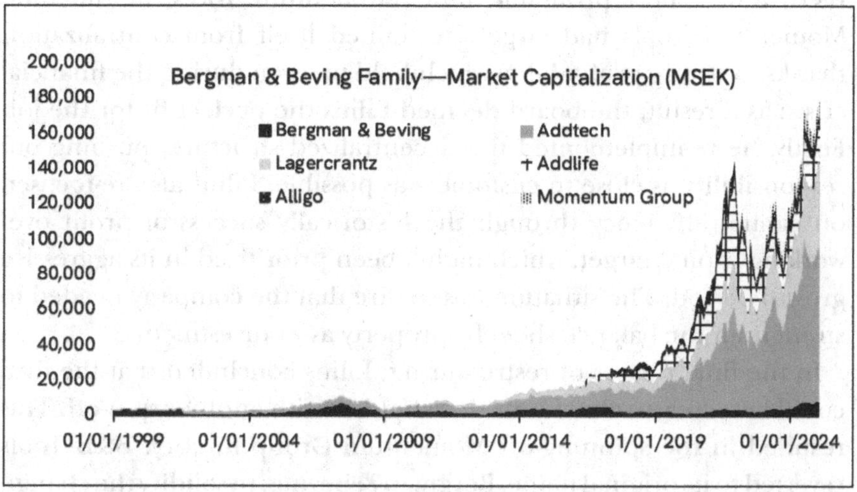

The centralization experiment

After spinning off Lagercrantz and Addtech in 2001, Bergman & Beving took a decision that would leave a mark for more than a decade—they deviated from its established DNA of decentralization. In pursuit of efficiency gains and economies of scale, the company aimed to transition to a one-company approach despite a century-long track record of successful decentralization. It marked the beginning of a decade-long experiment. The hope was to extract synergies by integrating product companies with wholesale and the many reseller entities they bought.[20] In the midst of this, the company changed its name to B&B Tools in 2007.

While the anticipated efficiency gains appeared promising in PowerPoint presentations, in practice they failed to materialize. In the pursuit of an integrated company, between 2002 and 2009 the company acquired and integrated over 100 resellers. This led to an almost five-fold increase in operating profits over the course of only six years. And the soaring share price contributed to increased investor confidence in the centralization strategy. But when profits fell dramatically by more than 50% in 2009, the company's leverage grew too high. Its balance sheet had swelled too fast in the wake of the aggressive acquisition pace.

To lead the restructuring of B&B Tools, the board appointed

Ulf Lilius, now CEO of Momentum Group. Lilius was the head of B&B Tools' most profitable unit, Momentum Tools, at the time. Momentum Tools had largely restrained itself from centralization, thanks to strong profitability which held up even during the financial crisis; as a result, the board deemed Lilius the perfect fit for the job. Firstly, he re-implemented the decentralized structure, pushing out responsibility as close to customers as possible. Lilius also re-focused on capital efficiency through the historically successful profit over working capital target, which hadn't been prioritized in its aggressive growth period. The situation was so dire that the company needed to strengthen the balance sheet by property asset divestments.

In the final phases of restructuring, Lilius concluded that the firm could best create value for its shareholders with another spin-off. This resulted in the spinning-off Momentum Group in 2017. B&B Tools reverted to its original name, Bergman & Beving, to solidify the change. The restructuring and subsequent spin-off involved separating the value chain, with Bergman & Beving retaining wholesale operations and product companies, while Momentum Group took charge of the technical reseller businesses and component value-added distribution.

Bergman & Beving's bold centralization and vertical integration project, aggressively acquiring over 100 companies, in the short term led to the stock outperforming both Addtech and Lagercrantz. However, the cracks in their aggressive centralization strategy were revealed when the financial crisis hit. It proved a painful lesson. There are no shortcuts to creating long-lasting shareholder value, and too fast growth seldom leads to value creation.

Profit over working capital

Fritz and Arvid, the eponymous founders of Bergman & Beving, always had a distinct focus on profitability. This focus remained when the company later pursued ambitious growth through acquisitions while adopting a profitability benchmark, which involved maintaining profits divided by working capital (P/WC) at levels exceeding 45%. Put simply, every dollar allocated to net working capital had to produce a return surpassing 45%, akin to the mindset behind Buffett's $1 Test:

"We test the wisdom of retaining earnings by assessing whether retention, over time, delivers shareholders at least $1 of market value for each $1 retained."[21]

This target not only generated a self-sustaining business model that enhanced per-share value creation, but also provided resilience in navigating the ups and downs of the business landscape ever since it was introduced.

The P/WC metric was introduced in 1981 when Anders Börjesson joined the management team of Bergman & Beving. During his studies at the business school in Lund, Sweden, during the late 1960s and early 1970s, Börjesson had discovered the benefits of an asset-light approach commonly used by successful entrepreneurs. In particular, he drew inspiration from entrepreneurs like Ingvar Kamprad (founder of IKEA) and Erling Persson (founder of Hennes & Mauritz), who had successfully adopted this strategy.[22]

As Addtech and Lagercrantz were spun off from Bergman & Beving in 2001, they created an internal book called *The Idea and the Soul* (*Tanken och själen* in Swedish), which outlined their fundamental business principles. This book originated from a series of seminars held in 1995 by Bergman & Beving. It is relatively short, consisting of approximately 80 pages, and is distributed to all employees to convey the company's culture, strategy, and value creation. The book is written in a way that every employee can understand, and provides practical examples. One key focus is naturally the P/WC metric, demonstrating how every employee can contribute to returns.

According to the Superinvestors of Bergman & Bevingsville, a business is considered self-financed when the return on working capital (P/WC) is higher than 45%. By achieving P/WC > 45%, the business can generate the necessary cash to cover taxes, interest, and dividends, and make required investments in existing businesses through capital expenditures, working capital, and financing acquisitions. The goal of being self-financed means that growth, whether organic or through acquisitions, will not dilute current shareholders through equity raises or rely heavily on debt financing. It highlights the importance of capital efficiency in generating cash.

The logic behind the original goal of exceeding a 45% return was straightforward: 15% of returns would cover taxes, another 15% would go toward dividend payments, and the remaining 15% would fund future growth.

Why use working capital instead of invested capital in the denominator? A trading or value-added distribution company, like those under Bergman & Beving, primarily relies on working capital rather than fixed assets, which are often outsourced. Hence profit over working capital is a suitable proxy for asset-light companies and an adequate measure of overall capital return.

The formula is simple and consists of two elements: the impact from the profit and loss statement, and the impact from the balance sheet. If a distribution company earns $9 on each $100 it sells (a 9% margin is typical for a trading business), and wants to achieve a P/WC ratio of 45%, it can hold a maximum net working capital of $20 ($9 divided by $20 equals P/WC 45%).

To boost the ratio, there are six levers the company can pull. To improve profit, a company can increase sales volumes, raise prices, or reduce costs. The same applies to the working capital. The easiest way to decrease working capital is by reducing inventory, speeding up customer payments, and extending supplier payment terms. All of these efforts positively affect the profit over working capital ratio.

Employees in group companies are encouraged to foster strong relationships with the right customers and suppliers and to have a solid grasp of inventory levels. Essentially, this framework both educates and heightens awareness about excelling in sales. It imparts valuable lessons on prioritizing the most profitable customers, nurturing relationships, adopting value-based pricing, and comprehending the consequences of providing discounts. These last two choices can result in significantly divergent cash flow outcomes.

Minor adjustments, continuously improved upon, create a positive feedback loop that enhances cash conversion, strengthens resilience, and increases the company's self-sufficiency for growth, ultimately leading to long-term value creation for shareholders. The best-in-class companies excel in sharing best practices across multiple levers simultaneously. They successfully boost cash flow and achieve substantial organic growth without resorting to coercive measures that could stifle the entrepreneurial spirit within their operating companies. This balance is a delicate equilibrium, refined only through experience and iteration.

The focus model

Aiming for a P/WC ratio of 45% or higher is important, but Bergman & Beving also adheres to an internal benchmark known as the "Focus Model." This model essentially serves as a capital-allocation prioritization tool applied to all operating companies within the group. Their performance is evaluated accordingly.

This framework inspires companies that do not find themselves in the top rankings to improve. The repeated message among its companies—"we strive to be at the top of these rankings"—underscores the influence of this approach. This benchmarking system provides more than just paper gratification. It represents success, and with success comes operating freedom.

The "Focus Model" for different P/WC levels is as follows:[23]

- Above 45%: Increase profits mainly by increasing revenue (organic and acquisitions).
- 25–45%: Increase P/WC by improving working capital turnover and profit margins for "proof of concept." Only make revenue growth investments within areas with a P/WC ratio well above 45%
- Below 25%: Increase P/WC before increasing revenues, as the business is too working-capital intensive. Focusing on improving working capital turnover and profit margins.

The P/WC ratio serves various purposes, such as assessing operating units, evaluating product performance, analyzing markets and customers, and as a tool for assessing acquisitions, irrespective of substantial or minor bolt-on additions. Companies reaching P/WC of 45% or more are encouraged to make acquisitions and grow organically. If P/WC is between 25–45%, add-on acquisitions could be allowed on clear grounds, and below P/WC of 25%, no add-on acquisitions can be considered.

Furthermore, this metric is consolidated at the group level, with all employees' incentives tied to it—creating full alignment between employee efforts and shareholder interests. The overarching goal is for all employees to quickly see measurable impacts on financial performance. Aggregated accounting metrics just aren't as relatable.

This theme is prevalent among best-in-class compounders. They emphasize straightforward profit objectives that genuinely make a difference, often smartly tying them to incentives. The recurring lesson is to avoid unnecessary complexity. It's about establishing an internal language that resonates, especially with small business owners who may have engineering backgrounds and not be well-versed in financial terminology.

In Bergman & Beving and its spin-offs, this is all made as relatable as possible to employees, and backed up with practical examples so that everyone grasps how they can make a positive impact. Warehouses are seen as piles of money, not products. Salespeople are encouraged to raise prices, avoid discounts, and ask customers for quicker payments, while negotiating longer terms with suppliers. Clear, actionable habits like this create a strong, systematized cash flow culture.

A new reality for Bergman & Beving

Following the spin-off of Momentum Group in June 2017, Bergman & Beving had to focus on its current operations. The wholesale business of B&B Tools wanted to become less dependent on Bergman & Beving's product companies in order to be more competitive and independent post-spin off. Unfortunately, this had a negative impact on Bergman & Beving: it lost almost 10% of its revenue. The company had to replace the lost profits.

To steer Bergman & Beving after the spin-off, the board appointed Pontus Boman, the former deputy CEO of B&B Tools and one-time CEO of Essve, the maker of screws and fasteners, and one of Bergman & Beving's largest companies. He was not dealt an easy hand. Despite this, during his four-year tenure, Boman managed to increase sales from SEK 3.8bn ($380m) to SEK 4.3bn ($430m). During the same period, EBITA increased from SEK 220m ($22m) to SEK 270m ($27m).

Despite the increase in both profit and EBITA, margins remained subdued. The return on capital employed was stuck at levels barely covering the cost of capital. The board decided they needed a change, and sought a leader with a growth mindset and familiarity with acquisitions. They looked for such an individual within the Bergman & Beving group of companies. Magnus Söderlind was soon appointed.

Introducing the Lagercrantz playbook

In May 2021, Magnus Söderlind stepped into the office as the CEO of Bergman & Beving with a clear mandate from the board: accelerate growth, improve returns on capital, and enhance cash flow generation to increase shareholder value. Bergman & Beving was eager to return to the same profitable growth as the 1980s and 1990s, and Söderlind was the right leader to take it there.

His track record was impeccable. He had spent 14 years at Lagercrantz as both deputy CEO and head of M&A, and played a pivotal role in transforming the company into a highly successful business. During his tenure at Lagercrantz, the company's market capitalization grew from SEK 850m ($85m) to SEK 18bn ($1.8bn). At Lagercrantz, Söderlind specialized in acquiring high-margin companies with proprietary products that delivered strong returns. Over the course of his tenure, he demonstrated significant talent for making deals in the private market, leading more than 50 successful acquisitions.

However, Söderlind's qualifications also extended to a deep passion for decentralization. The combination proved ideal and the transition was seamless, not least because Magnus had been the deputy CEO of Jörgen Wigh (Lagercrantz's CEO), who also serves as the board chairman at Bergman & Beving. To underscore his confidence in Bergman & Beving's future, Söderlind made a significant personal investment in the company, purchasing over 300,000 shares with his own money, a stake worth SEK 80m ($8m) today.

Söderlind embarked on a strategic transformation to drive its next growth phase. Central to this effort was reinforcing the company's "Focus Model," with greater empowerment of operating units. Söderlind's approach was clear: to grant managing directors more autonomy in their decision-making while holding them accountable for meeting clearly defined financial targets within a three-to-five-year time frame. It was no small feat. Transitioning from centralization to autonomy takes time, especially after operating in muddied waters. But Söderlind didn't shy away from the challenge. He made it clear that things had to change, and took action. One of his first steps was to change the leadership across Bergman & Beving's legacy portfolio, appointing new managing directors in several businesses.

Söderlind's priorities centered on profitability. Drawing on an approach similar to the one used at Lagercrantz, he started by phasing out low-margin, high-volume products. The result was a gross margin increase from 41% to 47%, contributing to a substantial rise in operating profit. The strategy was clear: increase returns and make the company more resilient by diversifying into new niches. Acquisitions became a primary driver of growth, setting an ambitious target of adding SEK 50m–80m in EBITA annually. However, Söderlind deliberately targeted only financially strong companies with EBITA margins above 15% and solid growth potential. Since he took office, Söderlind has acquired more than 20 companies, all meeting these criteria.

Beyond financial criteria, Söderlind's plan was to focus on B2B companies with long histories, strong financial track records, and dominant positions in expanding niches. These companies are often asset-light, and when they grow, they produce a lot of cash flow. Companies have been acquired at multiples averaging 6–7× EBITA, demonstrating Söderlind's discipline. But beyond numbers, the key is finding companies and leaders that align culturally with Bergman & Beving's values, and want to stay committed post-acquisition.

The winning game plan

Söderlind's game plan wasn't just about numbers. It was about reshaping the culture—moving back to what Bergman & Beving was originally built on. Internally, he ensured the entire organization understood the seriousness of the new strategy, introducing the ambitious "500/ten/45" financial targets (SEK 500m in operating profit, 10% EBIT-margin and P/WC of at least 45%). The goal was clear: to reach these targets by the fiscal year ending in March 2026 and the P/WC target by the following year. At the time of writing, improvement is already evident: Söderlind has improved the P/WC ratio from 22% to 31%.

Söderlind's commitment to increased profitability is unambiguous: all companies within the group must achieve a P/WC of 45% within 3–5 years. What you measure is what you get. To drive his point home, Söderlind revamped the incentive structure for managing directors. In a company with P/WC <25%, the bonuses are 80% tied to P/WC and 20% tied to Earnings Before Tax growth. The bonuses of the companies with a P/WC >45% are instead weighted 80% to profit growth and 20% to improving P/WC. This way, the bonus system is aligned with group capital allocation priorities.

Söderlind has also redefined how profit growth is measured. Subsidiaries and divisional managers are now evaluated on Earnings Before Tax (EBT), including internal interest on all capital used. This shift from the previous EBITA-based metric emphasizes the cost of capital and acquisition-related assets—no interest may be deducted from profit calculations—pushing managers to pursue capital-efficient growth and apply a value-investor mindset.

These aren't just lofty goals to impress investors; they are critical performance markers for every division and manager within the company. Results matter more than ever in the renewed meritocratic culture. Managers have the freedom to lead, but with that freedom comes accountability. If they don't deliver, they won't stay. It represents a new era defined by empowerment, responsibility, and the pursuit of profitable growth. Söderlind has turned vision into execution, and consistently improved profitability and margins.

Though selling is not part of the core strategy for Bergman & Beving, Söderlind has already set the stage by divesting the underperforming company, Skydda (offers protective safety gear for the construction industry), that had been owned by Bergman & Beving since 1994. The move sent a powerful message—there are no sacred cows. If a business doesn't deliver on cash flow and profitability, it doesn't belong. Performance is the only north star.

In its renewed strategy, all divisions are responsible for driving both organic and inorganic growth. When considering where to allocate capital between divisions, the division with the deal that generates the highest return on capital wins.

Treating people like true owners

Bergman & Beving's philosophy is simple. If you have companies that are led by capable management and you give them autonomy to run their operations, they will also act like true owners of the businesses. The job of Bergman & Beving is not to run its companies, it is to obtain and retain people who continue to be passionate and excited even after selling their life's work, and to empower and incentivize them to become even better. This is very different to the general perception of how companies should be governed, a world away from centralization and "management knows best." Out of 1,400 employees, only a handful are employed at HQ.

In Bergman & Beving today, every company is responsible for its operations, including profit and loss, balance sheet, and cash flow. The function of the small HQ is to trust but verify by following up on subsidiary performance and wisely allocating the capital generated.

Bergman & Beving even takes decentralization a step further. In addition to autonomy for daily decision-making, they trust their entrepreneurs with acquisition responsibilities. Though the board of directors makes the final capital allocation decision, Bergman & Beving puts faith in its people to generate ideas that align with their acquisition criteria. This empowers local leaders, enhances their sense of ownership, and incentivizes accountability. Interestingly, the company operates with only one central M&A resource, primarily assisting with brokered deals and internal due diligence. This minimalistic approach ensures that the focus remains on empowering individual businesses.

Within Bergman & Beving's decentralized framework, the three distinct business areas (Safety Solutions, Industrial Equipment and Core Solutions) and their group companies operate independently, without enforced synergies or collaboration. Networking and cooperation occur only voluntarily, further reinforcing the trust culture. The role of the headquarters is not to micromanage but to facilitate—to provide opportunities for managing directors, strengthening them with the tools and autonomy they need to thrive. Even though Bergman & Beving does not micromanage its companies, it practices active ownership through the boards of the individual companies. These boards, which are composed primarily of individuals with current or former experience at Bergman & Beving, ensure that the culture and governance principles of the parent company are applied consistently across the entire group.

A suite of capabilities for growth

At Bergman & Beving, the commitment to continuous evolution and adaptability is deeply ingrained. The eagerness to earn more money runs through the very fabric of the company—an ethos that underpins the ability to fully seize opportunities for growth. This is a simple concept, yet far from easy to execute.

The company equips its businesses with the tools necessary for capital-efficient, profitable growth—whether organic or through acquisition. Central to this are the divisional managers, who play a vital role in driving this agenda. They inspire, challenge, and empower their companies to grow profitably, while also shouldering the crucial responsibility of lowering barriers for new entrants to the group—adroit onboarding is key. Together, these elements keep the flywheel in motion—ensuring long-term value creation.

At the core of Bergman & Beving's strategy for continuous improvement is the "B&B Toolbox"—a suite of capabilities designed to help each group company reach its full potential. This toolbox offers targeted support across several critical areas, including acquisition execution, international expansion, access to functional expertise, and the development of professional governance structures. Used extensively throughout the organization, the B&B Toolbox facilitates the exchange of knowledge and encourages collaboration, both within the company and with external partners. Moreover, it focuses on crucial elements such as people development and motivation, ensuring businesses under Bergman & Beving's umbrella are equipped to achieve sustainable, long-term success.

An ecosystem of culture carriers and informed investors

The importance of the people behind the success of Bergman & Beving and its spin-offs cannot be overstated. They are powerful examples of "culture carriers." In the 1980s, when Bergman & Beving introduced new simple profit targets and guiding principles to set the stage for a new era of self-funded profitable growth, its people adapted. When Ulf Lilius restructured the company after the failed centralization project, its people adapted. When Magnus Söderlind put the company back on track for profitable growth, its people once again proved the ability to adapt.

None of this would have been possible without owners with a long-term mindset, and great leadership. Bergman & Beving's nine CEOs since its foundation in 1906 have fostered a family-like spirit built upon trust. This ethos weaves throughout the entire organization, creating a culture that serves as a guiding principle for every decision and interaction. This shared sense of purpose offers a competitive advantage when attracting new entrepreneurs.

A clear reflection of this culture can be seen in the interactions between the board of directors, senior management, and employees. Meetings often begin with hugs. Trust and a family-oriented culture is a way of life at Bergman & Beving.

All companies stemming from Bergman & Beving have a long-standing tradition of developing leaders and capital allocators from within. Most leadership appointments have been internal, and all Bergman & Beving CEOs have been internal recruitments, except Magnus Söderlind. Yet Söderlind is as close as possible to an internal recruit, having spent over 14 years in the decentralized culture of the Bergman & Beving spin-off Lagercrantz.

One of the most influential figures in shaping Bergman & Beving was its former CEO, Anders Börjesson. Under his leadership, the company delivered shareholder returns that few others could match. Colleagues remember him as a master of decentralization—granting operating companies full autonomy and accountability—while he himself focused relentlessly on capital allocation. What set him apart was his investor's mindset, still uncommon in Swedish industry at the time. Börjesson approached capital as a scarce resource, allocating it rationally to its highest and best use. If a subsidiary lacked sufficient profitable reinvestment opportunities, he had no hesitation in reallocating its cash elsewhere in the group, where returns were stronger. One former manager recalls how Börjesson reallocated surplus capital from his company—an unwelcome surprise at the time—only to realize later that it was a brilliant move, freeing funds to be invested where they created the most value. He mastered small private acquisitions and created an ecosystem of similarly capable leaders. Börjesson was also a pioneer in recognizing the value of smart, simple and profitable cash-based targets. Along with Torsten Fardell and Pär Stenberg, he was instrumental in driving the company's highly successful acquisition strategy throughout the 1980s and 90s. During their leadership, the company achieved an impressive 18% annual compound growth in earnings per share through both acquisitions and organic growth. A clear testament to their investor capabilities, Bergman & Beving delivered a remarkable 25% annual total shareholder return in this period, including reinvested dividends.

Although Anders Börjesson is no longer actively involved in the company or on the board of directors—aside from his role as Chairman of the election committee—his legacy still epitomizes the company. His two children, Fredrik Börjesson and Malin Nordesjö, now serve as board directors, representing the second generation of family leadership. The Börjesson family's commitment to Bergman & Beving remains strong, with the family holding the company's largest voting power.

Table 6.1: The CEOs of Bergman & Beving

Company name	Founded	Name	Joined	CEO since	CEO end
Bergman & Beving	1906	Arvid Bergman / Fritz Beving	1906	Shared roles	
		Knut Stenberg	1924	1947	1964
		Carl T. Säve	1957	1964	1980
		Pär Stenberg	1960	1980	1990
		Anders Börjesson	1979	1990	2001
		Stefan Wigren	2001	2001	2012
		Ulf Lilius	2004	2012	2017
		Pontus Boman	2007	2017	2021
		Magnus Söderlind	2021	2021	

Conclusion

Despite a misstep into centralization, a failure that took some years to correct, Bergman & Beving has proven that it can rise from the dust. Sooner or later, every company will face challenges. Setbacks do not determine a company's future; the important thing is how quickly it can adapt and learn from previous mistakes. Bergman & Beving had deep roots in decentralization, and a long-standing entrepreneurial spirit, and was able to return to both. The company has thrived and learned valuable lessons that will make it even stronger in the future.

What has truly set Bergman & Beving apart has been its ability to execute a proven acquisition strategy while maintaining cultural alignment. It has focused on acquiring high-quality companies with strong financial performance, and demonstrated extraordinary capital discipline, ensuring that every acquisition enhances shareholder value creation. Furthermore, its long-standing commitment to self-funded growth and a cash-driven culture exemplifies its financial prudence and resilience. Leadership has played a crucial role in the company's enduring success. Its family-oriented culture, which fosters trust, loyalty, and long-term commitment, has become a competitive advantage, attracting like-minded entrepreneurs who want to be part of the Bergman & Beving legacy. With the support of the Börjesson family as committed shareholders, the company has stood the test of time, and ownership remains in the hands of people who understand its greatness and want to grow it for the coming decades.

When Söderlind took the helm, Bergman & Beving's share price was far from its 2007 all-time high. Following the financial crisis, Bergman & Beving's aggressive growth strategy had led to a loss of trust from investors, and the share price had struggled to recover. Initially, the market was skeptical about the new direction. However, Söderlind stayed focused and committed, delivering consistent earnings growth quarter after quarter. The company's financial results changed the narrative two years into his leadership. As Bergman & Beving posted consecutive quarters of profitability, the share price started to perform. The shares are trading near its all-time high again today, marking a remarkable turnaround.

7

Escaping Commoditization

Lagercrantz

IMAGINE THIS: A company suddenly burdened with warehouses full of unsold electronics—custom, high-value components, all designed for a once-promising client that collapsed without warning. This was Lagercrantz in the early 2000s. As a value-added distributor, it had provided specialized components to a Norwegian mobile phone venture. The goal? To challenge industry giants like Nokia and Ericsson. But when the venture went bankrupt, Lagercrantz was left holding the pieces figuratively and literally.

The warehouses were full, the clients were gone, and the financial hit was immediate. Market capitalization hit rock bottom at SEK 360m ($36m). It was a harsh wake-up call—a reminder of the fragility of relying too heavily on one client, especially in an industry as fiercely competitive as electronics. Faced with shelves of unsold stock and no buyers, Lagercrantz was at a crossroad.

It was clear: something had to change.

This pivotal moment pushed the company to rethink its entire strategy. No longer willing to be at the mercy of others, the firm decided to take control of its future. The answer? A gradual shift from distribution to ownership. Lagercrantz began acquiring and developing niche product companies. This wasn't just a new direction—it was a transformation that brought higher margins, greater flexibility, and, ultimately, resilience.

A fresh start: embracing new horizons

Lagercrantz is today a $4.3bn market cap Stockholm-listed acquisition-driven compounder offering world-leading, value-creating technology through proprietary products and those of leading suppliers. The group has been under the leadership of CEO Jörgen Wigh since 2006. Lagercrantz was one of three companies that emerged when Bergman & Beving was split into three separately listed companies in 2001. Its prior connection with Bergman & Beving—which was listed in 1976—means that Lagercrantz had an extended presence on the stock exchange. The roots of Lagercrantz lie in its initial configuration under Bergman & Beving, consisting of the electronics and Lagercrantz divisions. In fact, Bergman & Beving's journey in the electronics sector began with its very first acquisition: Johan Lagercrantz's company, in 1967, a components distributor that had been established in 1938.[24]

Before Jörgen Wigh took the helm at Lagercrantz, he joined Bergman & Beving in August 1998 as head of business development, later leaving the group in June 2001. When Lagercrantz needed restructuring, Jörgen Wigh returned to the company at the beginning of 2006. Under his leadership, Lagercrantz has achieved a 28% annual total shareholder return (as of May 2025), making Lagercrantz more than a 100-bagger. During the same period, free cash flow per share has grown at an annual rate of 16%, with an average return on invested capital of 19%.[25]

Figure 7.1: The emergence and evolution of Lagercrantz[26]

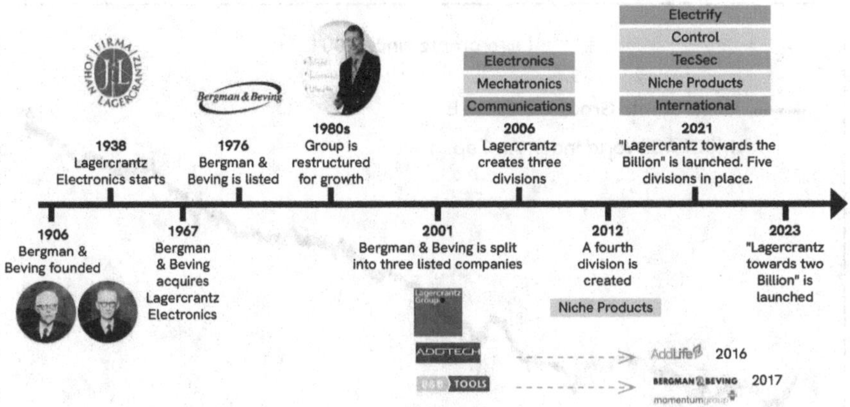

Today, the group is one of six businesses stemming from Bergman & Beving. The 2001 decision to split the group was based on product categories, with Lagercrantz initially leaning more towards electronics and telecom. However, its portfolio has significantly diversified over time. Lagercrantz now spans various sectors across five key divisions, primarily in the Nordics and Northern Europe. The company is not content with restricting its expansion to these regions and is establishing and intensifying its presence in the UK. Lagercrantz also has its sights set on markets such as Germany, Netherlands, and Belgium.

With a workforce of approximately 2,800 employees spread across over 80 business units in Northern Europe, Lagercrantz boasts sales of SEK 9.4bn ($940m) and earnings before tax of SEK 1.3bn ($130m), a testament to its consistent growth trajectory over the years. Lagercrantz operates through five distinct divisions—Electrify, Control, TecSec, Niche Products, and International—each specializing in unique technologies. Each company occupies a leading position within its specific niche market. As a generalist acquirer, Lagercrantz benefits from considerable flexibility, facing no sector-specific constraints that could hinder its adaptability. The group enhances the performance of its profit centers by holding regular board meetings, which foster both decentralization and collaborative interactions among the companies.

Figure 7.2: Lagercrantz share price performance since 2001

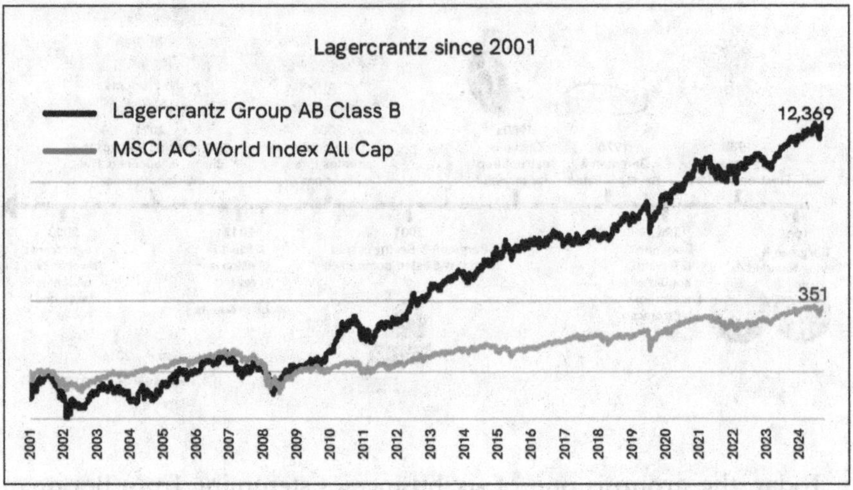

Flirting with centralization: an early lesson

After the 2001 spin-off from Bergman & Beving, Lagercrantz faced a tumultuous start. The semiconductor wholesale segment encountered substantial challenges, particularly after the dotcom crash. Sales plummeted—almost halving from post-spin-off levels—and profits turned into losses, primarily due to ongoing profitability issues in the electronics division.

In response, Lagercrantz took decisive action. It swiftly relocated production to streamline operations. However, major international players posed significant hurdles. The company embraced centralization and embarked on an international expansion strategy, aiming for economies of scale to regain stability and drive growth.

So, as with B&B Tools, Lagercrantz's early years as a spun-out group were marked by an inclination towards centralization. The prevailing industry landscape largely influenced this decision. Like B&B Tools, the temptation of achieving significant synergies and leveraging economies of scale was too great. Lagercrantz's motivation was particularly strong given its role as a value-added distributor of electronic components. In this industry, scale often translates into a considerable competitive advantage.

The drive towards centralization manifested in various ways, with the company even experimenting with a central warehouse for all its operations. The idea was to streamline logistics and reduce costs. However, this move quickly proved more problematic than beneficial. The centralized warehouse model created confusion and ambiguity regarding ownership and responsibility. As the company grappled with these challenges, it became increasingly clear that the centralized structure wasn't aligning with Lagercrantz's operational reality.

Changing mindsets

However, the shift back to decentralization around the time Jörgen Wigh joined as CEO was not a simple one. It was a multi-year process that necessitated a fundamental change in mindset, impacting the organizational chart and the company's culture. Wigh had to confront deeply ingrained habits and practices that had taken root during the period of centralization. Managers who found it challenging to adapt to the new decentralized way of operating had to be replaced.

Value-added distributors like Lagercrantz serve as vital links between suppliers and customers; their business model thrives in markets with numerous small players on both sides. Yet, during this period, dominant customers like Ericsson wielded substantial negotiating power, placing pressure on smaller distributors like Lagercrantz. Meanwhile, larger competitors—Arrow, Avnet, Eurodis, and Future Electronics—leveraged their advantages of scale, securing better terms from suppliers and intensifying the competitive landscape.

Unlike pure "box movers"—companies that merely transport products with gross margins of around 10%—Lagercrantz and its competitors adopted a value-added approach. These box movers focused solely on logistics, engaging in transactional relationships. By contrast, Lagercrantz went beyond simple distribution. The company provided additional services, such as technical support, product customization, and system integration. This commitment to delivering added value allowed Lagercrantz to generate higher gross margins.

Yet this distribution model had its limitations. Contracts often included geographic restrictions and other constraints, curtailing growth and flexibility. The company's smaller scale further hampered its market position within this fiercely competitive industry.

The pivot: taking control of your destiny

In the 2004–05 annual report, then-group CEO Per Ikov (still at the group today) acknowledged the challenges, outlining a new acquisition direction:

> "Key acquisitions will be made within the framework of selected technology areas to strengthen our market position and add development competence. Acquisitions may also be made to enter new, expansive niches. An element of proprietary products is an important factor when acquiring companies."

To drive change and inject fresh perspectives, Jörgen Wigh joined Lagercrantz as a consultant upon the request of the Börjesson family, playing a pivotal role in infusing new ideas and accelerating the strategic shift initiated by Per Ikov. By February 2006, Wigh officially assumed the CEO role, leading the company towards a decentralized mindset and paving the way for a new path forward.

Wigh led a strategic shift to ensure the company's future success, focusing on acquiring product companies with intellectual property rights and extended product life cycles. This strategy not only afforded greater sales flexibility and higher margins but also retained outsourced production, optimizing returns on capital. Concurrently, the management team steered Lagercrantz back to its Bergman & Beving heritage, promoting decentralized decision-making to cultivate a more adaptive and responsive organizational structure. This holistic approach positioned the company for resilience and growth in a dynamic business landscape.

Jörgen Wigh shifted Lagercrantz's focus. He moved the company away from pure value-added distribution and set sights on acquiring product companies, particularly those in niche markets. Several objectives guided this pivotal change:

- Greater control over market position: Owning product companies reduced reliance on external suppliers and provided more negotiating power.
- Higher profit margins: Product companies typically yield better margins than distributors.

- Longer product lifecycles: Focusing on products with extended lifecycles offered stability, unlike the rapid obsolescence common in electronics distribution.
- Geographic flexibility: Owning proprietary products facilitated easier expansion into new markets.

Cable shoes

This decision marked a turning point for Lagercrantz. The first step came with the acquisition of Nordic Alarm in early 2006, a leading Swedish provider of integrated security systems for high-security environments. It was a slightly different model—a system integrator—but aligned well with Jörgen Wigh's goal of building market-leading positions in specialized technical niches such as security. The acquisition of Elpress, just a few months later, solidified this transformation.

Elpress, recognized for its proprietary products like cable shoes, crimping tools, and pre-insulated connectors, became "a real cornerstone" of Lagercrantz's transition and future success.[27] Unlike the short product lifecycles typical in the electronics industry, Elpress built its reputation on durability. The company specialized in electrical connection systems—particularly cable shoes or lugs—designed with lifecycles of up to 30 years. These metal connectors, used to safely attach the end of an electrical cable to another cable, a terminal block, or an electrical device, ensure safe, durable, and efficient power connections in industries ranging from energy and telecommunications to industrial machinery and transportation. Aimed primarily at market segments with high requirements for performance and service levels, Elpress's focus on long-lasting, critical products made it a perfect fit for Lagercrantz's new direction. Lagercrantz acquired the company for just six times its pre-tax profit, and since then Elpress has increased earnings four times.

Although Elpress wasn't a high-growth business, it demonstrated steady, sustainable growth—around 9% in the years preceding the acquisition, driven by increasing demand for electrification. This reliability resonated with Jörgen Wigh's strategy of acquiring businesses with durable, profitable product lines. Consistent cash flow generation was crucial for maintaining a self-funded growth model. This success further fueled Lagercrantz's appetite for companies with proprietary products and higher margins, and these endeavors reinforced the company's shift from a distributor to a developer of niche businesses.

The new division: Niche Products

In 2012, Jörgen Wigh made an important move that redefined Lagercrantz's future. He established Lagercrantz's fourth division, Niche Products. For the key role of leading the division, Wigh handpicked Jonas Ahlberg, a former management consultant and two-time entrepreneur. Until then, Lagercrantz had operated with just three divisions: Electronics, Mechatronics, and Communications. However, as the company expanded, not every acquisition fit neatly into these categories.

Niche Products changed everything. It allowed the company to house a wide range of acquisitions under one roof. Instead of trying to squeeze companies into rigid divisions, Lagercrantz began grouping them into clusters based on their unique areas of expertise. This shift, driven by Ahlberg's vision, allowed the company to acquire businesses like Asept International—known for its ketchup dispensers—Tormek, and Wapro. Tormek, acquired in 2018, developed a unique sharpening system that has set the standard in modern edge tool sharpening. Wapro, acquired in 2017, is a market leader in high-quality check valves and flow control systems. Both companies would have been difficult to place within the previous structure.

The impact was immediate. Niche Products took off, growing quickly by snapping up businesses that didn't conform to traditional industry labels. Its success lay in focusing on "product companies"—those with distinctive products and strong brand identities.

This shift wasn't a minor adjustment; it changed Lagercrantz at its core. Back in 2006, when Wigh became CEO, around 62% of the company's sales came from value-added distribution. Today, that's down to just 12%. Meanwhile, the share of proprietary products, which comprised only 13% of sales under Wigh's early leadership, has skyrocketed to 78%. This dramatic transformation has opened new avenues for higher profit margins and stronger organic growth, especially in exports.

The focus on proprietary products has become a cornerstone of Jörgen Wigh's strategy, enabling the company to tap into higher-margin opportunities. It's a far cry from the days of value-added distribution, where growth was more limited, and margins were thinner, largely due to the geographical boundaries of that business model.

Driving growth with precision: how Lagercrantz balances ambition and returns

Lagercrantz has well-defined growth objectives that encompass return metrics. The company aims to achieve 15% annual earnings growth over a business cycle, with a minimum of one-third attributed to organic growth and the remaining portion driven by 8–12 acquisitions per year. Importantly, Lagercrantz aims to maintain a return on equity exceeding 25%, converted internally to a return on working capital of no less than 45% per business concept and profit center. Return on working capital is measured as operating profit (EBITA) as a percentage of average working capital. The emphasis on P/WC follows a similar focus as the other independently operated companies from Bergman & Beving. This metric informs their acquisitions, product development efforts, variable compensation, CEO compensation, and quarterly benchmarking across the group.

Focusing on return on working capital as a measure of return on capital is well-suited for a company like Lagercrantz. There are two critical reasons for this. Firstly, it helps maintain the entrepreneurial spirit by emphasizing factors that employees can directly control, such as pricing, costs, and terms of trade (e.g. payment terms with customers and suppliers). Secondly, Lagercrantz owns product companies with intellectual property rights, outsources production, and operates value-added distribution companies. Consequently, the denominator of the return metric predominantly comprises accounts receivable and inventory minus accounts payable, reflecting the company's asset base. Historically, the company has successfully met these targets. The self-funded approach, balancing both organic and acquisitive growth, highlights the significance of strongly emphasizing return metrics. This emphasis is essential for Lagercrantz to sustain its growth trajectory.

Moreover, the emphasis on return metrics is anything but arbitrary. It is driven by the need to sustain a consistent pace of acquisitions, which, in turn, demands predictability and robust cash flow conversion.

Steady revenue streams and robust cash conversion rates are crucial for implementing a self-financing acquisition strategy, enabling the organization to preserve financial stability without dependence on external funding sources.

Furthermore, upon completing the onboarding process, cash flow and return on working capital become the common financial language within these companies. Essentially, these firms operate as highly efficient cash flow generators, a necessity dictated by their business models.

Since 2006, Jörgen Wigh has successfully acquired over 80 niche businesses. He has demonstrated a return-focused approach in every facet of the company, particularly in working capital management, margin tracking, and the profit-to-working capital ratio (P/WC). Moreover, as production is typically outsourced, capital intensity is low, and organic growth is always evaluated against the required incremental capital compared to alternatives.

This growth has not only occurred without dilution for shareholders but with a decreasing share count of 17% over this period. Lagercrantz has proven that a growth pathway based on self-financed growth without straining the capital structure is more prudent in the long term.

In addition to financial considerations, Lagercrantz places significant value on responsible stewardship of the companies it acquires, which involves not merely buying businesses indiscriminately but carefully selecting those that align with the company's goals and can be effectively integrated into its existing structure, often with a technically focused overlap. Lagercrantz is acquiring not just businesses but talent, technologies, and market positions. Each acquisition brings new employees, unique skills, and fresh perspectives into the company.

We once reached out to an entrepreneur who had sold his company to Lagercrantz. During our first call, he was clearly on the move and told us to ring back at 7 o'clock the following Wednesday. Naturally, we assumed he meant 7 p.m.—but he actually meant 7 a.m. When we called back, we began the conversation in the typical Swedish fashion, with a bit of small talk. We asked if he was on his way to work and suggested he could take the call from the car. His response caught us off guard: "I've been at work since 5:30 a.m." What stood out wasn't just his continued dedication post-sale, but the story behind why he sold to Lagercrantz. Despite receiving "much higher offers" from both an industrial player and a private equity firm—both of which he had negative past experiences with—he and the other five owners chose Lagercrantz. They were nearing retirement, he explained, and appreciated that "they understood our business, and CEO Jörgen Wigh made a strong impression—he was clear and direct about how he intended to develop it."

Jörgen Wigh not only recognized Lagercrantz's potential to pivot into acquiring highly specialized businesses with proprietary products almost 20 years ago. He also set the company on a path for geographic expansion. With a strong cultural foundation and a decentralized approach, he successfully led Lagercrantz into new markets in recent years. A prime example is the UK, where the company has established a local presence to scale its operations effectively.

Furthermore, acquisitions often provide Lagercrantz with access to new markets or strengthen its position in existing ones. Acquired companies may have established customer bases, brand recognition, or distribution networks that Lagercrantz can leverage to expand its reach. This is a highly effective way to accelerate the company's growth and increase its market share. Acquisitions can also provide Lagercrantz with access to new technologies or capabilities. By acquiring companies with unique technological assets, Lagercrantz can enhance its product offerings, improve its operational efficiency, or gain a competitive edge.[28]

As observed with many acquisition-driven compounders in this book, the divisions and segments appear distinct and well-organized from the outside. However, internally, these labels hold little significance. Fundamentally, Lagercrantz operates as an investor without being tied to particular labels. Each segment shares a common purpose: to seek out highly specialized businesses promising robust returns while maintaining certain consistent themes.

Notably, the "niche" segment, with its diverse clusters beneath, houses many of the generalist product niche businesses. These businesses are the driving force behind the escalating share of proprietary products. Conversely, the "international" segment typically includes numerous legacy businesses that operate with a value-added distribution model.

Back to basics: reviving decentralization and entrepreneurial spirit

Lagercrantz's journey towards its current decentralized structure has been marked by experimentation and adaptation. While the concept of decentralization was already present within the Bergman & Beving culture before the spin-off, its application varied across different divisions. Some embraced decentralization wholeheartedly, like Bergman & Beving Industries (which evolved into Addtech) and Bergman & Beving Meditech (today Addlife). By contrast, others, such as the Tools division and Lagercrantz itself, favored a more centralized approach, particularly when managing logistics for their larger business units.

Lagercrantz's initial years as a separate entity saw an expansion of this centralized mindset, especially within the electronics division. This approach was partly influenced by the leadership's comparisons with industry giants like Ravnet, known for its extensive, centralized logistics networks. The prevailing belief was that a centralized structure would lead to greater efficiency and cost savings, especially in a division dealing with complex supply chains.

However, Lagercrantz's leadership, particularly Jörgen Wigh, recognized that a decentralized model, where individual companies had more autonomy and accountability, aligned more effectively with its long-term growth strategy. The vision was to create an environment where entrepreneurial spirit could flourish, and subsidiaries could adapt quickly to the unique challenges and opportunities within their respective markets.

However, the transition to a decentralized model was not without its challenges. The company's leadership had to overcome resistance from managers accustomed to a traditional, top-down hierarchy. These managers, comfortable with receiving directives from above, needed to be convinced of the value of a more autonomous and decentralized approach. This cultural shift required patience, persistence, and a willingness to make difficult decisions.

Theory vs. practice: when reality challenges the plan

One of the most telling anecdotes that illustrates Lagercrantz's challenges in its transition to a decentralized model is the story of the central warehouse. With the goal of streamlining logistics and optimizing costs, Lagercrantz embarked on an experiment to establish a central warehouse for all of Northern Europe. The initiative, driven by the promise of increased efficiency, aimed to create a central hub for managing inventory and distribution.

However, the centralized warehouse soon revealed unforeseen complexities. While efficient in theory, the very nature of a central warehouse created issues when it came to managing sales and inventory across a diverse range of markets. Clear lines of accountability became blurred, and the question of ownership, particularly concerning inventory management and responsibility for meeting local market demands, remained ambiguous. As Jörgen Wigh pointed out, the central warehouse model presented a fundamental question: "Who owns the warehouse? Who is responsible for the warehouse?"

The challenges posed by the central warehouse model underscored a critical realization for Lagercrantz's leadership: centralization, while seemingly straightforward in its implementation, can create unforeseen complexities and stifle the entrepreneurial spirit they sought to cultivate. This realization led to a pivotal decision to dismantle the central warehouse and return to a decentralized approach where each country would manage its own warehouse operations. This decision marked an important step towards the decentralized structure that defines Lagercrantz today.

The shift from the central warehouse model represented more than just a logistical change; it symbolized Lagercrantz's commitment to empowering its subsidiaries. By relinquishing a degree of control and entrusting individual units with greater responsibility, Lagercrantz laid the foundation for the decentralized structure that would become a hallmark of its corporate identity. This commitment to empowering subsidiaries through decentralization would ultimately enable Jörgen Wigh to foster an environment of entrepreneurial thinking, agility, and responsiveness to market dynamics, setting the stage for its sustained growth and success.

Cost synergies and hard integration? Think again!

Rather than imposing a hard integration, Lagercrantz carefully integrates newly acquired companies, preserving their unique identities and operational frameworks. This includes retaining the original company name, profile, and locations, ensuring the business continues as-is. By leveraging the capabilities of each company's existing employees, customers, suppliers, and partners, Lagercrantz fosters continuous growth within established relationships and practices.

When possible, the company prefers that the managing directors of acquired companies stay on post-acquisition. Leaders are granted a high degree of autonomy and given full responsibility for the company's success, merely being required to report financial figures to the senior management monthly. With incentives that reward profit growth and ensure strong cash returns, this attracts high-performing companies and leadership teams to join Lagercrantz. The group follows a management-by-objectives approach, where every subsidiary develops comprehensive business plans that define clear targets for growth, earnings, and return on working capital. While goal formulation is prioritized, subsidiaries have considerable freedom in determining the most effective means to achieve their objectives.[29]

As a perpetual owner, Lagercrantz expresses its ownership through the board of each subsidiary. The activities of the subsidiary boards are diligently monitored by division heads, ensuring oversight and alignment with the overall group's goals. Quarterly meetings of subsidiary boards are typically convened to assess operational activities and ensure the successful implementation of the approved business plans. These gatherings provide a platform for evaluating progress, identifying areas for improvement, and taking necessary measures when required.

A winning long-term strategy for Lagercrantz's decentralized operations has been to refrain from focusing on cost synergies. Instead, it infuses its acquisitions with energy, structure, and professionalism. The group brings a fresh perspective and professional approach that helps reinvigorate companies that may have become complacent, smoothing generational transitions and enhancing professionalism. Rather than dictating synergies, Lagercrantz allows collaborative and operational enhancements to emerge organically from within the companies, driven by their initiatives and discoveries. Already high-performing companies within the group help to set role models for how success can be achieved. After all, the group doesn't buy turnaround businesses. It acquires good businesses that don't require any huge fixes. These businesses possess vital local knowledge, and are best equipped to make decisions regarding marketing, products, customers, suppliers, and more. For such companies, decentralization is crucial to continue thriving after acquisition.

Toolboxes and support: the choice is yours

A central part of Lagercrantz's strategy is the creation of global hubs to support exports. The core idea is to take the specialized products developed by its portfolio companies—many of which originate in the Nordic region—and introduce them to international markets.

As a larger corporate group, Lagercrantz is well-positioned to pursue these export opportunities. Unlike smaller, independent firms that may be hesitant to take on the risks of international expansion, Lagercrantz is more willing to establish subsidiaries in foreign markets such as the United States.

This strategy has already produced tangible results. For example, Tormek—a leader in sharpening systems for edge tools like knives, chisels, and woodcarving tools—has seen substantial growth thanks to improved access to the U.S. market. Similarly, Wapro, which designs innovative solutions to manage and prevent flooding, has achieved strong market penetration in the U.S., resulting in impressive organic growth.

Lagercrantz's International division plays a key role in executing this export-focused approach. It extends the group's successful "niche products" strategy to global markets by building product-specific companies within the division itself. This model, already proven within the group, has led to the formation of successful clusters—such as the marina cluster—and has fueled the growth of companies like Schmitztechnik in Germany and DPC Ilse in the UK.

Overall, the aim is to drive organic growth by leveraging the strengths of individual product companies and supporting their global expansion through these hubs. This not only facilitates knowledge sharing but also strengthens their positions in specific niche markets worldwide.

In addition to the hubs, Lagercrantz supports growth and development through a range of practical resources. The Lagercrantz Growth Fund offers financial backing for strategic initiatives. Business Improvement Modules (BIMs) and access to functional experts help strengthen internal capabilities across key business areas.

Furthermore, the Lagercrantz Academy delivers specialized training led by internal experts, promoting continuous learning throughout the group. Stable and financially strong ownership builds long-term trust, while a wide network of group companies encourages the exchange of best practices and innovative ideas. This knowledge-sharing culture is reinforced through annual gatherings and academies focused on best practices in areas such as pricing, working capital management, and entrepreneurial principles.

The company cherishes its entrepreneurial spirit, prioritizing cash flow and self-funded growth—a balance distinguishing it from its peers.

An example of how it maintains a competitive spirit and creates a cash culture among operating companies is its internal "Champions League," where all companies are benchmarked against each other based on the "Focus Model" to determine how each subsidiary performs compared to the rest of the group.[30]

The "Focus Model," far from being mere bullet points in an investor presentation, is a core element deeply embedded throughout Lagercrantz, embodying a commitment to entrepreneurship and excellence shared by every employee.

A prime example is its subsidiary, Radonova. During our visit to Radonova's headquarters, the first thing that caught our attention was a wall adorned with diplomas. These were not just any awards; they represented pride in victories in their internal "Champions League," where subsidiaries vie against each other to achieve cash flow-related objectives. Ingrained through an internal entrepreneurship handbook, this unique competition illustrates a deep-seated culture of excellence and achievement. The ethos of prioritizing cash-return goals is integral. They are a commitment shared by every employee across Lagercrantz, and ultimately they produce above-average entrepreneurs.

This distinctive competition, reinforced through their internal entrepreneurship handbook, demonstrates a profound culture of excellence and achievement. This ethos highlights what sets the companies in this book apart: a robust cash culture, meticulously honed and perfected through persistent trial and error. While acquisitions are within reach for many, the true challenge emerges in the careful nurturing of acquired companies and the cultivation of a high-performing culture.

The 100-bagger architect

Jörgen Wigh has not just been any CEO. With a strong devotion to Lagercrantz's enduring success, he has also rewarded shareholders with more than a 100-fold increase in total shareholder value. Before joining Lagercrantz, he had proven himself as vice president at Bergman & Beving, founded PriceGain, worked as a management consultant at McKinsey & Co., and served as an investment manager at Spira Invest. He brought valuable experience that has become a key foundation for Lagercrantz. Before stepping into his leadership role, he worked as a pricing consultant, gaining deep insights into the critical role of pricing. This expertise has proven invaluable, benefiting many of Lagercrantz's highly specialized companies.

The Börjesson family demonstrated faith in Wigh's potential when they recruited him in 1998 to Bergman & Beving. Despite his relatively young age, they recognized his skills. For them, it was not surprising that Wigh performed well, and when they sought new leadership for Lagercrantz in 2006, he was the perfect match.

Jörgen Wigh has significant insider ownership, ensuring strong alignment with shareholders in Lagercrantz's success. He holds 1.2% of the capital and 2.9% of the voting rights in the company. Additionally, the company's incentive plans are directly tied to return on capital and organic growth, focusing on key drivers of shareholder value.

Other important people who contributed to Lagercrantz's continuous success are Peter Thyssel, the CFO; Jonas Ahlberg, head of M&A; and Andreas Heder, head of the control division.

Peter Thyssel has been with the company since December 2021. He is involved with all acquisitions and responsible for group sustainability and IT. Before joining Lagercrantz, he was the CFO and IR director of RaySearch Laboratories for close to seven years.

Jonas Ahlberg, senior executive vice president, took on the role of head of M&A in April 2024. Since joining the group in 2012, he has played a key role in developing the Niche Products division at Lagercrantz.

Andreas Heder led the M&A and business development department at Lagercrantz before Ahlberg took over. He has 25 years of international experience in telecommunications, specializing in corporate development and M&A. Heder joined Lagercrantz in June 2021. He transitioned to his new role as head of the control division in April 2024.

Niching down

Looking back at Lagercrantz's journey, a clear picture emerges of a company that not only survived a significant crisis but managed to transform the very core of its existence. From being in a vulnerable position as a distributor of electronic components, Jörgen Wigh took an important step toward ownership and the development of the company's own niche products. This ability to iterate and course-correct along the way is a key trait common among all nine companies featured in this book.

Under Jörgen Wigh's leadership, decentralization became not just an organizational structure but a guiding philosophy that unleashed entrepreneurship and local adaptability. By focusing on acquiring niche companies with their own, often long-lived products, Lagercrantz created a more stable and high-margin-oriented business. The establishment of the Niche Products division symbolized this new direction.

The consistent emphasis on self-financed growth and return on working capital has supported this transformation, enabling an impressive series of small private acquisitions while the share count remained stable. At the same time, a strong cash culture—reinforced by rigorous benchmarking and knowledge-sharing platforms—has further strengthened financial resilience and operational efficiency. Jörgen Wigh's ability to build a culture characterized by entrepreneurship and results orientation within decentralized units—illustrated by the "Focus Model" and internal competition—demonstrates a deep understanding of how to create long-term growth and shareholder value.

In the broader perspective, Lagercrantz stands as a valuable example of how strategic insight and the ability to course-correct can turn a challenging situation into a lasting success story. The company's journey from a peripheral player in a demanding market to a robust group of market-leading niche businesses reflects a remarkable ability to adapt, learn, and create a distinct identity based on decentralization, a focus on proprietary products, and strong financial discipline.

8

Riches in Well-Defined Niches

Addtech

THEY SAY A company's true strength is revealed in tough times, not easy ones. Just a year into his role, Addtech's current CEO, Niklas Stenberg, faced one of the company's greatest challenges. Addtech had been hit by a major ransomware attack. IT systems in 80 of its 130 subsidiaries—responsible for half of the group's sales—were shut down. In most large corporations, operations might have stalled while employees waited for direction. But not at Addtech. The company's decentralized, entrepreneurial culture kicked in. Instead of waiting, employees picked up pens and phones, contacting customers and suppliers to serve them manually in order to keep business moving. Despite many subsidiaries being offline for over a month, the company impressively increased sales by 12% that quarter—a testament to its resilience and responsiveness. Addtech isn't just any company; it's a story of adaptability, fast decision-making, and turning crisis into opportunity.

Investors who have remained invested in Addtech since its spin-off from Bergman & Beving have witnessed the company achieve an impressive 19% CAGR in free cash flow per share. A $10,000 investment in Addtech in 2001 would have increased to $1.2m by 2025, or $2.2m if all dividends were reinvested—a staggering 26% CAGR.

(A $10,000 investment in the former parent company Bergman & Beving, including its later spin-offs, during the same period would have increased to $63,000.)

But first, let's take it from the start. The 2001 spin-off of Addtech from Bergman & Beving was more than a corporate restructuring. It unleashed entrepreneurial energy across a network of companies, all driven by a shared passion for industrial technology. The results exceeded all expectations, delivering performance and returns at an entirely new level.

Addtech's success stems from two simple yet not easy goals: increase profits annually by 15%, and generate a return on working capital (P/WC) of more than 45%. It has achieved this through disciplined capital allocation, acquiring family-owned businesses run by exceptional people with proven success at serving customers in small industrial niches. Its people diligently identify and cultivate acquisition candidates that share the same entrepreneurial mindset and core values. Even more impressive is that Addtech also found the keys to unlocking these companies' full potential with its small-scale autonomy approach.

At the core is an unwavering belief in autonomy and managerial responsibility. Through benchmarking, networking, and sharing best practices, Addtech helps its companies improve. It utilizes smart cash-based incentives to turn its companies into cash-generating machines. It uses this cash flow to acquire new businesses. And then it does this repeatedly, year in and year out.

Recognizing the value generated by its own spin-off, Addtech has successfully applied a similar internal strategy. One notable example is the 2018 Automation unit spin-off from the Components division, establishing an independent business area. It allowed Addtech to replicate its success on a smaller scale, effectively creating mini-Addtechs that leverage emerging structural growth opportunities.

Addtech is an industrial group with revenues of SEK 21.8bn ($2.18bn) and an operating profit (EBITA) of SEK 3.2bn ($320m). It operates across five business areas, each well-positioned to leverage megatrends: Automation, Electrification, Energy, Industrial Solutions, and Process Technology.

Figure 8.1: Addtech share price performance since 2001

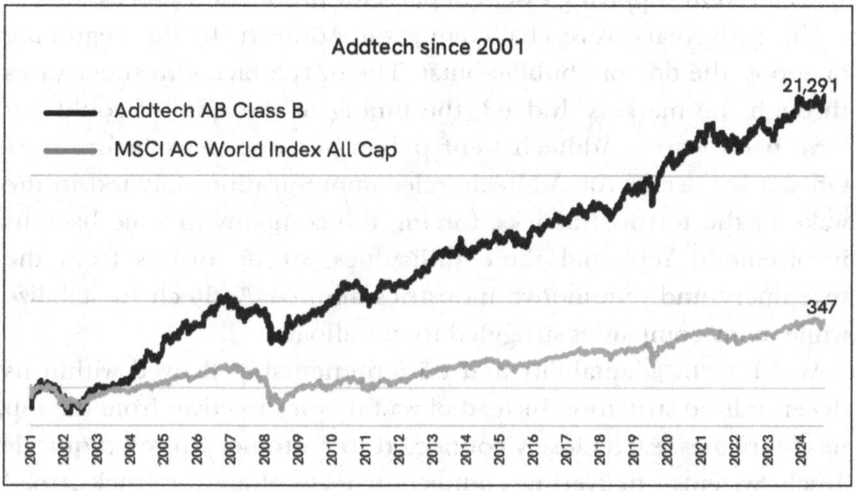

First footprints in fresh snow

Addtech represented the original core industry business area of Bergman & Beving, and the name reflects the company's original mission: to add value to its customers through expertise in technology. True to its philosophy of nurturing leaders from within, Addtech's first CEO, Roger Bergqvist, was no stranger to the business.

Having spent 28 years at Bergman & Beving, Bergqvist was well-equipped to steer Addtech as a stand-alone company. Bergqvist joined Bergman & Beving in 1973 as a managing director, and later advanced to the role of CEO of Lagercrantz before it was spun off. He had also headed Bergman & Beving's Industry division before he became the CEO of Addtech. During his time at Bergman & Beving, Bergqvist had helped shape a decentralized organization. He was laser-focused on consistent profit growth, prioritizing high returns on capital and strong cash generation. He strongly believed that Addtech's success was not only about achieving strong operating earnings; the goal was also to "generate an excellent return on invested capital."

At the time of its listing, Addtech comprised 50 companies and was organized into three business areas. The Production division focused on electronics, engineering, and the automotive sector. Transmission catered to the broader manufacturing industry. Components specialized in supplying essential parts for production processes.

The early years were challenging for Addtech. In the beginning of 2000s, the dotcom bubble burst. The 9/11 attack sent shockwaves through the markets. Indeed, the timing of the spin-off could not have been worse: Addtech went public just one week before 9/11. Once a key sector for Addtech, telecommunications faltered in the wake of the terrorist attacks, forcing the company to scale back its involvement. Yet amid these difficulties, strong orders from the machinery and automotive industries allowed Addtech to stabilize while many companies struggled to stay afloat.

At Addtech, adaptability and entrepreneurship thrived within its decentralized structure. Instead of waiting for directives from the top, its companies, each closely connected to customers, pivoted quickly. Tesch Systems—delivering connection technology for trucks, road machines and antennas—strongly exemplified this, rapidly pivoting and growing an automation business to 15–20% of its sales and helping it navigate a tough market.

Instead of rushing into acquisitions, Roger Bergqvist focused on improving operations. Margins increased from 3.6% at IPO to 6.7% in 2004/05. Even when he began acquiring in pursuit of more diverse income streams, he did so cautiously. With high acquisition prices and market uncertainty, Bergqvist remained rational and selective, refusing to overpay for the sake of expansion—an approach deeply embedded in Addtech's DNA. Rather than chasing deals, the company prioritized supporting relationships with existing customers. This strategy strengthened Addtech's balance sheet, allowing it to pursue acquisitive growth from a position of strength a few years later.

The year 2003 marked a notable shift that ensured continuity of previous successes. Tom Hedelius and Anders Börjesson, already major shareholders and key figures in its leadership, formalized their control over the company. They became the largest shareholders in Addtech, today holding 15.2% and 16.5% of the votes, respectively. Having Börjesson as a committed long-term owner—the key person behind Bergman & Beving's successful acquisition strategy—ensured that there would not be any change of strategy, culture, or philosophy. The architect of decentralization would never centralize.

Having learned valuable lessons from the dotcom era, and recognizing the company had significant exposure to cyclical industries like telecommunications and automotive (which made up 34% of sales in 2001), Roger Bergqvist wanted to make Addtech more diversified and less vulnerable to market swings. These sectors had historically been attractive, but Bergqvist was open-minded, always seeking opportunities for more stable profits. It led to the acquisition of Bergman & Beving's MediTech business, a Nordic distributor of instruments and consumables in the life science sector.

MediTech, with roots in Bergman & Beving going back to 1941, provided Addtech with steady, non-cyclical cash flows, and it operated with a decentralized structure. It was a relatively low-risk addition to the portfolio, despite accounting for around 25% of revenue. Roger Bergqvist was very disciplined on price and only paid a 6.5× earnings multiple. When the life science division was later spun off as AddLife in March 2016, it was listed at a market capitalization of nearly SEK 2.1bn ($210m). For Addtech shareholders, this translated into an 11× return over only 11 years—an impressive 28% CAGR.

Same but different

When the financial crisis struck in 2008, sales plummeted and profitability took a hit. In some segments, orders dropped by as much as 30%. However, Roger Bergqvist's wise but somewhat unconventional decision to buy the life science business in 2005 proved to be a saving grace, just as it had been for Bergman & Beving in the 1970s when its industrial businesses struggled following the aftermath of the oil crisis. While industrial sectors struggled, the life science and energy divisions remained relatively stable. This crisis, even more than the 2001 dotcom bust, highlighted the importance of resilience. Advanced, technologically sophisticated products, performed more steadily than standard offerings.

Simultaneously, Addtech was in the midst of a leadership change. Johan Sjö, a 41-year-old rising leader with deep roots in Bergman & Beving, was appointed CEO. With a background in equity research and corporate finance, he brought a sharp understanding of disciplined capital allocation. He took decentralization to the next level, shifting more autonomy and responsibility to divisional leaders. He even closed the central M&A function and transferred acquisition responsibilities to the divisions. He also divided the company into four distinct divisions, and within each division the companies addressing a certain market segment were gathered in groups, called "business units." The change was not just a corporate reshuffling—it was a strategic realignment to better reflect Addtech's business model and encourage collaboration among subsidiaries.

To ensure a smooth transition, Sjö appointed experienced managing directors to lead the business units while in some cases maintaining their MD roles, reinforcing an internally driven rather than top-down approach. The reorganization allowed Addtech to even more effectively pinpoint structural growth areas by prioritizing acquisitions within adjacent industries. In search of new opportunities, group companies utilized relationships with both suppliers and customers to identify growth opportunities.

Despite the challenges of the financial crisis, Addtech's decentralized philosophy and formidable cash culture kept its subsidiaries focused on protecting cash flows. Although profits plummeted 42% in 2009, operating cash flow declined by only 5%—a testament to the agility of Addtech's small companies, which quickly adapted their inventory levels to match shifting market conditions. Even in its toughest year, the company maintained a high double-digit return on capital employed (ROCE)—a benchmark many companies struggle to achieve even in favorable conditions. Its conservative risk profile and solid balance sheet allowed Johan Sjö to quickly resume acquisitions, and by 2012 the company had expanded to over 120 subsidiaries, up from 50 at the time of the IPO in 2001.

Internal promotion and same philosophy

When Johan Sjö retired as CEO of Addtech in 2018 to focus on external board roles, the company had a clear successor: Niklas Stenberg. A rising star from within Addtech's own ranks, Stenberg began his career as a lawyer before joining Bergman & Beving in 2005, specializing in M&A. He held several leadership roles in Addtech between 2010 and 2015, eventually joining the management team as Head of Power Solutions, before being appointed CEO.

Niklas Stenberg stayed true to Addtech's decentralized culture, adding a stronger emphasis on internal knowledge-sharing to continue to grow profitably. "The key is to offer opportunities, not impose them," he noted, highlighting the need to preserve a sense of ownership among its business leaders while encouraging collaboration between the companies.[31]

Seven years into his role, Stenberg has delivered on his vision. He further increased Addtech's divisions' focus within certain verticals, and encouraged acquisitions in adjacent niches, accelerating deal-making from within the business areas. Under his leadership, half of the company's acquisitions have come from outside the Nordics, proving that Addtech's decentralized philosophy and "house of brands" appeal, as one entrepreneur described its collection of great businesses, can resonate with entrepreneurs across borders.

What started on a small scale has, during Niklas Stenberg's leadership, developed into an internal network of around 15 managers, all trained internally in fostering organic growth and executing small private transactions with a high degree of success. This approach addresses a common challenge faced by acquisition-driven compounders as they scale. Rather than increasing the size of each deal, Stenberg distributes responsibility among more people to handle a higher volume of transactions.

Cooking in customers' kitchens

At Addtech, change is the only constant. It has not only managed to adapt but has also emerged stronger from each challenge it has encountered. "There are opportunities in every market condition," its former CEO Johan Sjö once said; "you just need to seize them." While many companies maximize short-term profits, Addtech embodies the Bergman & Beving philosophy of focusing on activities with a long shelf-life. This was stressed by the former CEO of Bergman & Beving, Anders Börjesson: "Recession or boom. What is the difference from a management perspective? In my opinion, there are no decisive differences. I believe that philosophy and overall goals are long-term approaches and should not be adapted too much to economic trends." This ethos, and its unique ability to prioritize long-term decision-making, even during economic downturns or cyber-attacks, makes Addtech unique. Its approach to risk and return focuses on identifying scalable growth opportunities that deliver strong returns on capital, regardless of economic cycles.

Addtech's approach is underpinned by a learning culture that enables the organization to avoid past pitfalls. Such an open-minded approach has permitted Addtech to identify and capitalize on new opportunities. The commitment to staying ahead in an ever-changing market has been made possible by "cooking in the customers' kitchens."[32] By staying closely attuned to the market and customers' operations, Addtech has identified trends and used those insights to develop new growth areas that thrive independently within its decentralized structure.

Following the dotcom era, Addtech's management displayed a dynamic and responsive leadership when they searched for new income streams that were less tied to macroeconomic cycles. With the help of internal networks, they identified the energy sector as a promising opportunity and took a decisive step in 2006 by acquiring Gevea, a company specializing in high-voltage transmission equipment. Despite energy only being a minor part of Addtech (7% of sales), the selling founders were so confident in Addtech's vision that they didn't even consider other buyers. Since then, through acquisitions and organic growth, the energy division has grown to become the company's largest division, accounting for nearly a third of total revenue.

In the post-crisis years, Addtech's management once again showed responsive leadership. Its industrial businesses had grown faster than its life sciences division, which had shrunk to 15% of total sales. Seeing greater potential for profitable growth and better returns on capital due to lower acquisition costs in industrial niches, Sjö made a strategic decision to allocate capital toward these areas. In early 2016, he spun off the life sciences division, rebranding it to AddLife. For Addtech, this proved a good decision. Since the spin-off, Addtech has outperformed AddLife shares, appreciating almost 1,250% compared to 690% for AddLife—both beating the broader Swedish index by a factor of 12 and seven, respectively.

This prioritization of companies with high technical expertise in structurally growing niches, in combination with dynamic leadership, has enabled Addtech to focus on high-return opportunities, while systematically stepping away from business at the maturity curve. The spin-off of AddLife was a testament to this disciplined approach to capital allocation—constantly evaluating and comparing investment opportunities to maximize returns.

Idea and soul

Addtech wouldn't have been able to grow as much without its strong cash culture, cultivated over decades. It is deeply embedded in Addtech's operations, shaping the way employees think and work. Instilled across all levels, it ensures that every employee understands how their daily actions contribute to the bigger picture. For a salesperson it is to set the priority of selling high-margin products with favorable payment terms. For a warehouse employee, it's all about keeping stock levels lean without risking shortages. Addtech recognizes that true success isn't built on a single grand initiative but on countless small, incremental improvements—whether in pricing, working capital management, or sales—that collectively drive significant impact.

A key element in fostering this culture is its internal book, *Idea and Soul*, a legacy from Bergman & Beving. Given to employees who complete its internal business school, the book lays out the company's core business principles in about 80 pages. The true emphasis of the book is on fundamental business principles and practical applications that drive business performance. A central theme is the importance of the P/WC metric, demonstrating how every employee plays a role in maximizing returns. The *Idea and Soul* promotes entrepreneurship, simplicity, and a long-term perspective; the key foundations of Addtech's self-financed growth model. This philosophy not only sustains its business over time but also sets Addtech apart from the private equity model, which often prioritizes short-term cost synergies and exit strategies.

A compelling illustration of the impact of these principles is found in the story of a former CEO of Addtech's Life Science business unit, spun out to form AddLife in 2016. His decision to join Addtech had been significantly influenced by *Idea and Soul*. "The reason I accepted the job at Addtech was actually the book," he recounts. Following an interview in Stockholm, as he was about to return to Lyon in France, the CEO of Addtech presented him with the book, asking him to share his thoughts. Captivated by the content, he found himself unable to put it down until the last page was turned. Intrigued by its pragmatic approach to business, he called the CEO to ask if the company genuinely lived by those principles. Assured by the CEO's response, he eagerly accepted the position. The former CEO recalled that Addtech's approach to business analysis and improvement was so straightforward and effective that even consultants from prestigious firms like Boston Consulting Group have been taken aback.

Self-funded ethos

When Anders Börjesson introduced the P/WC metric over 40 years ago, he probably didn't imagine the long-lasting impact it would have. His self-financing approach has ensured that growth does not dilute existing shareholders through equity raises or over-dependence on debt financing. It is no coincidence that Addtech, since it was spun-off in 2001, has converted more than 100% of its net income to free cash flow, and compounded its free cash flow per share by 19% annually. This has been achieved by continuously high returns on capital, 25% on average since IPO and 20% on average for the last ten years. The reinvestment rate of 80% of their cash flow since IPO has been invested into acquisitions and supported organic growth. Remarkably, this disciplined approach has remained consistent under three different CEOs.

This unwavering financial prudence exemplifies Addtech's risk-averse philosophy. As for acquisitive growth, price discipline is paramount. The higher the price paid, the greater cash conversion needed to enable self-financing growth. It's like buying a rental house. If you buy it cheaply, the rent easily covers repairs and lets you save up for a second property. But if you pay too much, the rent barely covers costs—and now you need the house to generate a lot more cash just to break even, let alone grow. By maintaining this balance, Addtech ensures that growth remains sustainable without compromising financial stability.

Furthermore, the deeply seated cultural ethos of a self-funding business model also translates into an ultimately low-risk business model, as it naturally limits the pace of growth. Only so much cash flow is available to finance growth in a self-funding manner, ensuring that the development is sustainable and benefits all stakeholders over the long term. In effect, the common denominators that usually lead to failures among acquisition-driven companies—too rapid pacing of acquisitions and overstretched balance sheets—have effectively been avoided in Addtech as a side benefit of operating a self-funding business model.

Recognizing that cost-cutting and margin expansion have natural limits, Niklas Stenberg emphasizes revenue growth as the primary driver of long-term profitability. He keeps things simple: employees are encouraged to focus on achievable improvements, such as price optimization, geographic expansion, and market share gains, rather than goals like simultaneously launching new products to entirely new customers. Every subsidiary and department is evaluated based on its impact on profitability, reinforcing a company-wide understanding of the return contribution.

The same disciplined mindset applies to working capital management, which is the denominator in the P/WC KPI. The easiest way to lower working capital is to reduce inventory, improve the time of client payments, and increase supplier payment terms. All of this is something that every senior management team in every large corporation focuses on. However, in Addtech, it is relatively easy to implement as each employee in the smaller group companies is measured on it. By continuously emphasizing that each underlying company must generate a profit on its working capital above 45%, leadership in Addtech has created a high-performing culture in which each individual understands his or her role in how value is created. Though some might view this rigorous financial monitoring as micromanagement, Addtech achieves the opposite.

Drink coffee like a Swede—and do a lot of deals

How has Addtech mastered the deal making of small acquisitions of niched industrial companies? By leveraging the collective insights of its approximately 4,000 employees across 150 companies, viewing each individual as a crucial "antenna" attuned to market dynamics and customer needs. Patience and persistence—including drinking lots of coffee with entrepreneurs—lies at the heart of this.

Addtech employees are encouraged to stay in touch with acquisition candidates as much as possible. This process enriches the company's acquisition pipeline with interesting leads, and cultivates an organizational culture that values and encourages contributions from all levels within the company. Subsidiaries are motivated to recommend potential acquisition targets to business area managers, and they sometimes engage in smaller bolt-on acquisitions on their own, transforming the acquisition process into a collaborative effort that transcends a traditional centralized approach. Many of these informal conversations span years, allowing the company to help sellers navigate the emotional process of selling their life's work. This approach not only builds trust but significantly de-risks acquisitions. By the time a deal is on the table, Addtech has gained a deep understanding of the people behind the business, ensuring a smoother transaction. Interestingly, our conversations with management and employees note that failed acquisitions are rarely due to financial misjudgments, but stem from cultural mismatches. As a result, more than 80% of Addtech's acquisitions come from within its internal networks.

A strong contributor to success has been to explicitly target stable, profitable, cash-generating businesses within industrial niches the company fully understands, and where there is also a strong alignment in culture and core values. Addtech's bread and butter are small family-owned businesses around $10m–$20m in deal size. By strictly adhering to both quality and price, Addtech has consistently paid very attractive earnings multiples below 7-8× for its acquisitions. These deals are typically too small to attract significant attention from bigger industrial players or private equity, which puts Addtech in a favorable position.

This proactive approach not only positions Addtech favorably when a sale becomes a possibility, but also provides Addtech more time to demonstrate how its offering differs from other buyers. One compelling example of this came with an acquisition Addtech undertook 12 years ago. One of the two founders was hesitant to sell the business, and opted to talk to one of Addtech's suppliers, hoping to hear that Addtech was not a good owner so that he could walk away without regrets. In fact, the supplier told him the opposite. So, after taking time to get to know the company and employees further, a deal was made. The initially reluctant entrepreneur remained CEO of his firm, and later climbed the ladder to become a business unit manager within Addtech.

Leadership in Addtech has a strong aversion to acquisitions where the seller's top priority is the sale price. Rather than relying on synergies or operational improvements in its valuations, it consistently enhances the earnings of acquired companies by applying its business expertise, further boosting overall returns. Almost ten years ago, Addtech acquired a family-owned business where the retiring father left behind two sons—only one of whom wanted to continue running it. Lacking the capital to buy out his brother and invest in growth, he turned to Addtech. They promised him support if he sold. After the acquisition, Addtech's leadership provided funding for key hires and guided him through the transition, helping him grow the business beyond his father's legacy. Within just a few years, the son who became CEO had doubled the business—a great deal for Addtech. Grateful for the support, he remembers one of his proudest moments: he could share the success with his father over Christmas.[33]

Although historically committed to acquiring 100% of its targets, Niklas Stenberg prefers a more flexible strategy to letting entrepreneurs keep an ownership stake if it helps seal a deal. This adaptability highlights Addtech's responsiveness, particularly in cases where entrepreneurs are willing to sell their business but prefer not to fully exit. From Stenberg's perspective, a deal that ensures long-term commitment, even if not structured according to traditional principles, is better than no deal at all.

As a perpetual owner in no rush to grow, leadership knows that the best deals are not the fastest ones—but the ones worth waiting for. "In order for us to succeed with acquisitions, the moment must be right for all parties," said former CEO, Roger Bergqvist. "Only then can a take-over and implementation in our group be successful. We must maintain our momentum without getting carried away." And the company is highly selective and stringent on its criteria, with only one out of 100 potential acquisition candidates making the cut.

Interestingly, a notable pattern emerges in our discussions with other acquisition-driven compounders: Addtech is the company they encounter the least in brokered transactions. Ultimately, becoming a preferred buyer and buying the best companies at the most attractive prices requires a trustworthy long-term commitment and a shared industrial mindset with sellers.

Unlike some of its Bergman & Beving peers, Addtech has taken decentralization even further, adopting a fully distributed M&A strategy. When Johan Sjö took over as CEO in 2008, he inherited a well-run organization. However, he recognized that to position Addtech for continuous growth, he needed to increase acquisition activity. To achieve this, he delegated all acquisition responsibilities across the organization, believing that training and empowering those closest to operations in deal-making would increase Addtech's appeal as a buyer and help the company make more and better-quality informed decisions. Niklas Stenberg has continued on the same path.

Stenberg remains the overarching capital allocator, overseeing all possible investment opportunities. Albeit, in accordance with Swedish governance practices, final approval comes from the board. Addtech's culture is so deeply embedded among employees that by the time investments reach Stenberg, they are invariably deeply anchored in Addtech's values and criteria. As such, the board has not yet rejected any acquisition proposals.

A warm welcome to the Addtech family

Behind every Addtech acquisition is a dedicated entrepreneur and his or her employees, whose hard work has built the company's success. Addtech views each acquisition as a lifelong commitment—much like marriage—where trust, transparency, and honest communication are essentials for a lasting partnership. To ensure a seamless transition for family-owned businesses, the team takes a hands-on approach. After the paperwork is signed, they visit each acquired company, hosting morning meetings and breakfasts to personally meet employees, answer questions, and ease concerns. Remember the entrepreneur reluctant to sell his business? Addtech proved that it was the right buyer when it helped him to bridge the selling process by showing up to his company's offices the day after closing to answer all questions from employees: "and there were a lot of questions," the entrepreneur recalls. Addtech's open and approachable style resonates deeply with family-run businesses, where strong relationships and shared values are key to long-term success.

When acquisitions are embedded in the business model, success improves with each repetition. To foster this expertise, Addtech trains its business unit leaders to conduct internal commercial due diligence and valuations, reducing reliance on costly external consultants. Formalities like suits and ties are set aside in favor of a hands-on, trust-based approach, ensuring that those leading the deals also receive the support they need. This method cultivates an internal network of informed investors, aligning acquisition decisions with the company's culture and long-term goals.

Beyond acquiring companies, business unit leaders are responsible for driving post-acquisition organic growth, ensuring a strong cultural and financial fit. Much of Addtech's high returns stem from its ability to create value from helping its acquired companies grow organically, while allowing them to remain operationally independent. CellTech, one of Addtech's companies in its battery division, serves as a neat example of this. While historically profitable, after it was acquired, Addtech armed it with better customer segmentation and profitability analysis. By actively de-selecting unprofitable customers and focusing on profitable ones, the company not only increased profits, but increased growth by a double-digit percentage.[34]

Cultivating simplicity

Addtech's deeply rooted philosophy of local managerial responsibility and accountability is simple. When it acquires a company, it provides it with tools and capital to grow. Since its spin-off in 2001, Addtech has remained steadfast in this decentralized approach, even as its former parent company, Bergman & Beving, shifted toward centralization—a path Lagercrantz followed in its early post-spin-off years. Management's refraining from centralization was enabled by the company being much more diversified by comparison, and less affected by the late waves of the dot-com era. There was no need to stray from a proven decentralized strategy, no reason to "fix" what wasn't broken.

Management grants full autonomy to group companies. Each subsidiary may develop its operations and growth strategy as it sees fit, as long as this aligns with Addtech's overarching business model and meets its group-wide targets. Nevertheless, there remains a strong focus on collaboration between business units, who often share common R&D, suppliers and production needs. This is particularly evident among segments that share similar markets or challenges, such as the battery or automation division.

Grouping its business units based on similar end-markets is important for several reasons. Firstly, when entrepreneurs with businesses within the same industries are able to interact, healthy internal competition starts. The internal benchmarking systems that spur competition release energy and incentivize companies to improve. Secondly, as all of Addtech's business units are incentivized to grow profits each year, it encourages them to find similar businesses to acquire. Thirdly, the more managers who have trained their acquisition skills through internal business schools, the more efficiently Addtech can utilize those skills to scale the organization efficiently as it grows.

In conversations with entrepreneurs from Addtech, we often hear how these benchmarking systems motivate them to improve. This healthy competition has not only contributed to performance but also made it more attractive for other sellers to become part of the Addtech family. When companies are empowered to thrive and grow, they become the best ambassadors.

In addition to granting autonomy to operations, Addtech encourages its companies to make organic investments however they deem will create the most value. One of these organic investments that has turned into a huge success is the company Caldaro, providing joysticks, pedals, sensors and marine controls for industrial use. The company was started in 1993 as a greenfield project within the industry business area in Bergman & Beving. Impressively, it grew into a business of SEK 100m ($10m), with 20% operating margins, in less than a decade. Caldaro is still so successful that Addtech employees refer to it as the "Rolls-Royce" within its industry.[35]

Even though companies share overarching group targets, every individual company has sub-goals, tailored to the company's profile. For instance, trading companies do not share the same goals as companies with proprietary products. Adjusting goals and incentives to the nature of each company's business, while maintaining shared overarching goals, ensures that each company stays motivated. The goals reflect real possibilities.

Granting subsidiaries full autonomy over operations does not mean Addtech is a hands-off owner. On the contrary, it is active in empowering the companies to become better. Overall, Addtech deploys a "pull" rather than a "push" strategy. A company within Addtech has all the freedom to choose which parts of the toolbox it wants to utilize—and no obligation to select any. Addtech's active ownership is also expressed through the governance of its subsidiaries, managing each company through its board. Addtech puts in place a chairman, often a business area or unit manager, who helps each company set its strategic direction. These chairmen also help to drive its businesses forward and fill an important role as carriers of the Addtech culture.

Reaping the benefits of a learning organization

Imagine working for a company that fosters a culture where autonomy and encouragement are more than ideals. Since the 1960s, Addtech has invested in its people by sending a significant portion of employees to its internal business school. Employees are taught business acumen, negotiation techniques, value-based selling, among other subjects aiming at driving profitable growth. These courses are both general and tailored to specific company needs. The school is a key part of building Addtech culture, and is also important for internal networking. The idea running through this is that a successful business is a co-creation. While some companies treat business school as a short-term cost, Addtech sees it as a long-term investment. With over 500 participants each year, the courses are kept short to minimize disruptions to daily operations. It is particularly important for Addtech's leadership development.

One of the most notable events in Addtech's calendar is the annual gathering of its managing directors. These meetings often carry an informal vibe, and the goal is for mutual support and open dialogue to flourish among its leaders. Addtech's culture is on full display. Conversations flow freely over a relaxed drink. Discussions revolve around business opportunities, strategies, and experiences. It's a striking example of how Addtech finds the balance between autonomy and collective effort. It illustrates a culture where every member is a key driver of their success and, by extension, that of the entire organization.

This balance is hard to achieve, and seems to be a success factor distinguishing the best companies from the rest. It involves finding the right mix of entrepreneurial drive and a sense of ownership. It means synergies are enabled—but voluntary. And it relies on the balance being tailored to the unique circumstances of each business; some need to be much more autonomous than others. Ideally, company culture should be so compelling that founders of acquired companies are motivated to stay beyond their earn-out period.

An ecosystem of talented leaders and private market investors

The Superinvestors of Bergman & Beving—including Addtech—have a remarkable track record of developing talent and cultivating strong leaders. Within Addtech's entrepreneurial and decentralized ecosystem, ambitious individuals have thrived, rising through the ranks, creating shareholder value along the way. But the real magic isn't just in identifying great leaders—it's in keeping them.

A testament to this is Addtech's exceptional leadership stability: in 24 years as an independent company, it has had just three CEOs. Many of its business area managers and leaders—most of whom were promoted internally—have been with the company for over a decade. The strong emphasis on both internal promotions and proprietary deal-making makes Addtech stand out from its peers.

One compelling example is Malin Enarsson, Addtech's CFO. She started as a business controller in one of the group's companies in 2004, steadily climbing through various roles before earning a place on the senior management team. Her journey reflects a broader insight: at Addtech, leadership is cultivated, not imported.

This stability in leadership has been key to the company's consistent execution over the years. As many within Addtech put it: why change a winning strategy that's worked for over a century? And unlike many companies where executives rise through sales, marketing, or technical expertise, Addtech leaders are taught to think like investors from day one. No matter if they pursue organic investments or propose acquisitions, they opt for the options with most attractive long-term returns on invested capital. Furthermore, given the high focus on profitability and stringent reporting requirements in running an organization like Addtech, one might expect a high turnover rate among senior management teams of acquired companies. However, CEOs of acquired companies often remain well beyond their lock-up or earn-out periods—the company clearly creates an environment where great leaders want to stay.

Troika of value creators

There is a famous saying that culture eats strategy for breakfast. If there is one company where this is evident, it is Addtech. Its strength is its ability to nurture and develop leaders with a striking combination of operational knowledge and investor skills. This reduces the risk of deviating from its long-term vision. Among the top of these investors are Addtech's three CEOs. All three of them have generated immense value for shareholders, significantly outperforming the broader market.

Roger Bergqvist's tenure (2001–08) was characterized by adapting the business to become less dependent on telecommunications in the post-dotcom era. He initiated a move into energy, today Addtech's largest business area. Under Bergqvist's leadership, sales grew from SEK 2.4bn ($240m) to SEK 4.2bn ($420m), and the share price appreciated 237%, outperforming the broader Stockholm Stock Exchange by a factor of four.

Johan Sjö (2008–18) continued to build on this foundation by further strengthening Addtech's resilience, diversifying beyond the Nordics. He decentralized M&A responsibilities and introduced the business structure that laid the foundation for growth in niches with structural growth. After ten successful years at the helm, he had delivered almost 600% in total shareholder returns. Under his leadership, Addtech grew from SEK 4.4bn ($440m) to SEK 8.4bn ($840m) in sales.

Niklas Stenberg (2018–present) has directed more capital towards expanding Addtech's geographic footprint outside the Nordics. He has also put a focus on internal collaboration and knowledge sharing, highlighting the potential for relationships to drive growth. During his tenure, Addtech has continued to foster leaders from within, turning local managers into even greater leaders and private market investors. So far, under Stenberg's leadership, Addtech's share price has delivered a remarkable 590% return, ten times the broader Swedish market's performance.

Another of the most important assets enabling Addtech's sustained value creation has been its stable shareholder base. The company has benefited from long-term majority shareholders with a generational perspective that recognize that value creation is a marathon, not a sprint. Although Anders Börjesson and Tom Hedelius are now well beyond retirement age, they have maintained a long-term view of their ownership in Addtech. Malin Nordesjö, Börjesson's daughter, currently serves as chairman of the board, representing Tisenhultgruppen (the Börjesson family office), while Fredrik Börjesson, his son, is a newly elected board member. Henrik Hedelius, Tom Hedelius's son, also represents the Hedelius family on the board.

Conclusion

Reflecting on Addtech's success, much of the shareholder value comes from the company's ability to acquire great companies with leaders who share the same core values. Addtech ensures these companies thrive and grow within the organization. When people are treated with respect, given autonomy and a sense of ownership, they take responsibility—and remarkable things happen.

The cumulative effect of fostering a cash culture at Addtech—characterized by highly decentralized decision-making and autonomy through a feeling of ownership—creates the right entrepreneurial spirit. This culture is supported by an ecosystem that includes career opportunities, a toolbox for operational efficiency, academies for learning, and a collaborative environment for sharing knowledge. In this environment, synergy gains are welcomed—but not forced.

With a multigenerational focus, Addtech has always adapted to changing market conditions and come out stronger. The company has time and time again stood firm by acquiring great family-run businesses at attractive prices that share the same values—and views on future opportunities. When others have been greedy, Addtech's leadership has adhered to its guiding principles.

9

The Software Laboratory

Constellation Software

MARK LEONARD HAD grown tired of the venture capital game. At Ventures West, the endless cycle of building companies only to sell them off felt uninspiring. He wanted something different—something that could last. Instead of chasing the next big thing, Leonard saw an opportunity in the world of vertical market software (VMS), a space few were focused on. Unlike large, general-purpose ("horizontal") software used across many industries, VMS companies build tailored software for a single, specific job—software that's often essential to keeping the customer's business running smoothly.

Have you ever considered the program that controls a chicken coop, helps police reconstruct a crime scene, or manages cemeteries and traffic lights? These are just a few of the countless niche verticals powered by software that may seem tedious at first glance, but which are mission-critical, deeply integrated into operations, and make switching to something else painful. From a financial perspective, this translates to steady, recurring revenue streams with high margins. Not so boring after all.

However, owning just a few such small companies could be risky—they often rely on a single offering and a tiny team of employees.

Moreover, they typically lack opportunities for organic reinvestment: what to do with the cash they generate? Leonard had an idea: What if he could own a collection of them under one roof? He could acquire and nurture dozens, even hundreds, of these stable, cash-generating companies by creating a holding company—or, better yet, a permanent home for these businesses. This structure would allow him to reinvest the cash flows from one business into acquiring more, creating a self-sustaining growth cycle. In effect, a reinvestment engine. With each new acquisition, he compounds growth as the underlying businesses continue to generate returns.

This breakthrough moment would establish Mark Leonard and Constellation Software as a patient architect of a permanent capital vehicle in the vertical market software space—the creator of a model designed to endure and grow, much like Warren Buffett's Berkshire Hathaway. As we'll see, this approach evolved into a data-driven experiment grounded in first principles and the scientific method. It was built to foster an ideal corporate structure and learning culture, deeply rooted in autonomy and Mark's favorite childhood mantra, "Live free or die," which he embraced while building flamethrowers in his bedroom. With plenty of iterative improvements along the way, the goal, directly and indirectly, was to delay the onset of mean reversion—and, in some ways, to defy the laws of financial gravity as the company grew larger.

Since the company went public in 2006, it has compounded its operating profit by almost 33% annually or 150 times. This has been achieved without a dilution of shares, and without leveraging the balance sheet to the teeth. With Leonard's commitment to generating high returns on the company's investments, Constellation has averaged a ROCE just above 30%. What is the secret sauce? Reinvesting all of the free cash flow into small acquisitions of VMS companies—and repeating the process over and over again. Constellation Software has typically maintained a net cash position, relying on internally generated free cash flow as the primary source of capital. In exceptional cases Mark Leonard has stated that he is open to using both debt and equity to fund growth.

The beginning of a multi-bagger journey

In 1995, aged 39 and raising four children, Mark Leonard established Constellation Software—and, remarkably, still serves as its CEO 30 years on. With only a $25m investment from his previous venture, Ventures West Capital, he has compounded Constellation's value to over $100bn over 30 years—without issuing a single additional share since.

Leonard is one of the most rational people we have ever met, and in 1995 he saw the world of venture capital with a clarity that few possess. Creating and selling companies for quick returns began to feel misaligned with his growing vision. He was looking for something different—something that would outlast him, an investment vehicle with a permanent capital base that could continue to generate returns indefinitely.

Leonard's path to VMS was influenced by a mentor who understood high-quality business models: Steve Scotchmer. An engineer, operator, and long-term investor, Scotchmer built his fortune with Bay Mills Ltd, a manufacturer of engineered materials.[36] For 35 years, he guided Leonard, introducing him to enduring business models, the discipline of permanent ownership, and the insights of investors like Warren Buffett and Charlie Munger. His influence extended beyond mentorship—Scotchmer served on Constellation's board of directors from 2000 to 2021, a role through which he helped embed his operating and investing philosophies in the company's culture and long-term approach. According to Leonard, those philosophies remain foundational to Constellation Software.[37]

Backing masters of capital allocation

The story of Constellation Software offers fascinating insights into what can happen when intelligent capital allocation meets a decentralized business model, all driven by the quiet genius of Mark Leonard. Leonard's expertise in capital allocation and commitment to decentralization is exceptional, positioning him as an exemplary CEO and a subject ripe for in-depth study akin to those made of Warren Buffett. We have yet to meet a CEO who has instilled a learning culture as deep as his. Leonard approaches Constellation

Software like a physics lab, conducting controlled experiments to collect precise data over time.

Experiments are the Constellation Software way of life. Suppose Leonard wants to test how new hurdle rates—the minimum return expected—affect the performance of individual subsidiaries. He will apply changes to one set of companies, keeping another as the control group, then compare the results over time. This approach allows Constellation Software to refine its processes continuously, always striving for incremental improvements. It is a mindset shared throughout the company, from the board of directors down to individual subsidiaries.

The company constantly evaluates itself, questioning traditional ways of approaching things. It also studies the history of other successful companies. All the key lessons are folded into Constellation over time. What better way to know if spin-offs work than trying it yourself, while also studying others' efforts? And not just by studying books: Leonard travels across oceans to collect first-hand knowledge. We had the opportunity to meet Leonard on his recent trip to Stockholm, where he visited Bergman & Beving and its spin-offs Lagercrantz and Addtech to learn from their successes.

The playbook

While VMS businesses are not always providing substantial reinvestment opportunities on their own—their focus is so narrow, there are few opportunities to profitably make use of all the cash they generate. VMS businesses are a perfect fit for Constellation Software. Combine the attractive cash flow of a VMS business with an organization built upon an investor mindset, efficiently reallocating capital into other high-return acquisitions, and you end up with a company that generates a ton of free cash flow—then uses it to generate yet more. This is what Constellation has done for the last three decades.

The companies Constellation typically seeks to acquire are small and specialized software firms spanning a range of niches: software for traffic control and waste management, booking systems for golf clubs, church-related administration, mortgage and real estate lending, dental, library management, and bowling centers. The company operates in over 100 specialized verticals, the most prominent being transit and healthcare. Approximately 50% of the company's revenue derives from government software, a dependable and consistent source of recurring income.

There is a misconception about Constellation Software. Many believe that it only buys companies of high quality. That's true of many of the compounders in this book, and perfectly praiseworthy. But Constellation will buy companies that *aren't* profitable. That's where its playbook comes in handy. Given its repeated experience in the software space, the company knows exactly which strings to pull to improve a seemingly low-quality business. Incremental improvements and high returns on investment prevail.

Because of the specialization of the software, and the limited market size, larger companies often deem it impractical to enter the space of each VMS. Consequently, Constellation Software is frequently dominant, ranking as the top or second player in these niches.

The highly customized nature of VMS, serving mission-critical functions, also entails significant economic risks and business disruptions for customers contemplating a switch. This situation, in turn, grants Constellation pricing power and results in sticky revenue streams with high margins. This is proven by Constellation's low churn rate of around 4%, meaning that the average customer will stay with them for 25 years.[38] Moreover, the underlying business model often relies on recurring revenue, yielding substantial free cash flow that fuels the company's acquisition agenda.

Figure 9.1: Constellation Software's share price performance since IPO

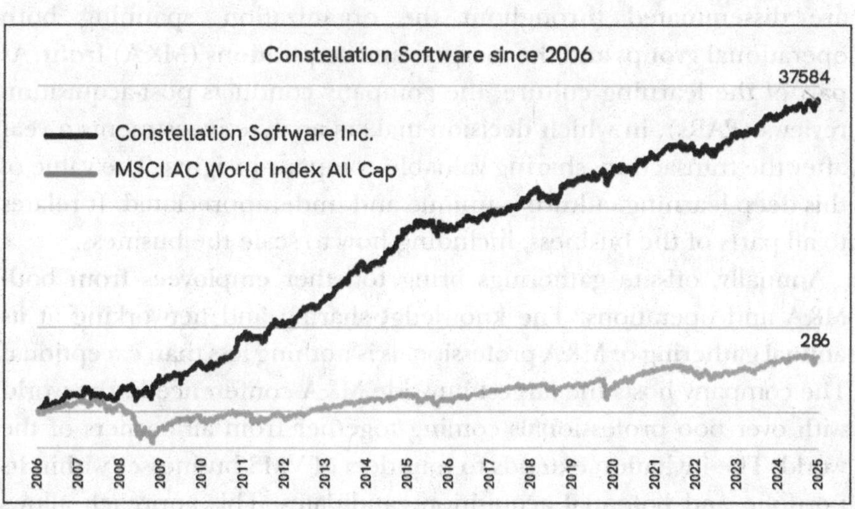

Creating a learning culture

Leonard has always been a profound learner. In the world of VMS, he drew inspiration from Jack Henry, another company known for growing through acquisitions. However, Leonard took a different approach. Jack Henry sought to extract synergies and paid a premium for growth in one vertical. Instead, Leonard focused on acquiring lower-priced companies, not chasing quick synergies, and invested in various verticals to avoid concentration risk. In his mind, this would ultimately generate higher returns on capital and, hence, stronger cash flow generation. He was correct in his thesis and executed it in a way that created generational wealth for him and his employees.

While many CEOs with the kind of success Constellation has had would love to be in the pages of Wall Street newspapers, Leonard has maintained a low profile. The CEO of one of the world's largest and most acquisitive software companies is a little-known figure. The company avoids Wall Street as much as possible and, like others in this book, favors frugality. Which other $100bn company does not even have quarterly conference calls?

This level of anonymity is quite unusual. However, Leonard's annual letters have provided valuable insights into his business and investment philosophies. Under Leonard's guidance, Constellation Software has ingrained a culture of continuous learning, sharing best practices, and offering coaching and mentoring. These principles are disseminated throughout the organization, spanning both operational groups and the mergers and acquisitions (M&A) front. As part of the learning culture, the company conducts post-acquisition reviews (PARs), in which decision-makers analyze investments a year after the transaction, sharing valuable company insights. The value of this deep learning culture is unique and underappreciated. It relates to all parts of the business, including how to scale the business.

Annually, off-site gatherings bring together employees from both M&A and operations. The knowledge-sharing and networking at its annual gathering of M&A professionals is nothing less than exceptional. The company hosts the largest buy-side M&A conference in the world, with over 600 professionals coming together from all corners of the world. The invitation extends to founders of VMS businesses within its portfolio and potential acquisition candidates. This approach allows them to immerse themselves in the company's culture of continuous learning, with case studies covering a range of topics, like how to enter a new geography. Constellation shares updates on recent acquisitions and the financial performance of acquired businesses. Senior executives, including Mark Leonard, typically present the company's M&A strategy and lessons from previous acquisitions. The event also serves as an opportunity to network with colleagues. The company wants people to feel they are part of something bigger. CEOs of other acquisitive companies are also invited to share their knowledge and expertise.

Where other companies may seek to polish numbers to meet quarterly expectations of earnings per share growth, Constellation has chosen another path. The primary performance indicator utilized over many years is "ROIC + organic growth." In Mark Leonard's annual letters, he shows how those two metrics work in parallel to create shareholder value. ROIC represents the cash return generated from acquisitions, ensuring that the company does not overpay, while ROIC + organic growth signifies the overall increase in the company's total value. In other words, Constellation is guided by long-term capital discipline (which leads to real positive outcomes), not short-term market optics.

Scaling the acquisition team

Unlike many other businesses, where capital allocation is the responsibility of top management, Constellation Software has a decentralized policy. Portfolio managers make most acquisitions, a highly scalable model. In recent years, Constellation Software has increased the number of employees involved in acquisitions. To accelerate its pace of acquisitions, Constellation Software has implemented a uniquely decentralized capital allocation model—unlike anything seen before in corporate M&A. The company has granted its most tenured portfolio managers full autonomy to make capital allocation decisions for smaller deals. Armed with so-called "hunting licenses," these managers independently pursue acquisitions that meet Constellation's stringent hurdle rates. Mark Leonard has reinforced this structure with incentive plans that reward effective capital deployment at the operating group level—while penalizing the bonuses of those who fail to deliver results.

Having conducted over 1,000 acquisitions over the last 20 years,

Constellation Software has a unique repeatable model for buying smaller companies at scale. It has developed a data set, knowledge base, and relationships few can rival. Historically, most acquisitions have been small software companies with sales of $1.5m–$2m, acquired for low prices due to their size and dependency on single verticals or customers. Many acquisitions have been acquired for less than $5m, a size impossible for private equity or industrial players to replicate.

Constellation leans heavily on data, and benefits from its exposure to numerous similar companies within its niches. This exposure allows it to draw upon insights from various software companies when assessing pricing, cost structures, and other vital aspects. One of the most important inputs into the model for acquisitions is the retention rate. This metric tells how much potential price increases Constellation can drive without sacrificing customer loyalty or product stickiness. This data advantage forms a crucial competitive edge when bidding for companies.

Constellation Software of the future

John Maynard Keynes once said "When the facts change, I change my mind. What do you do, sir?" Mark Leonard has a similar mindset. While VMS has proved a rich hunting ground, Constellation Software is open to changing course if it sees a change in long-term market dynamics.

Leonard's key takeaway from studying business history is the belief that businesses constantly need to adapt and change in order to stay in the game. We met Leonard while writing this book, and he put it in terms of evolution rather than revolution: gradual changes to strategy that over years transform a company. Examples could be finding new growth areas or spinning out subsidiaries.

Topicus and Lumine Group are two recent examples of the latter. Lately, the company has also been engaging in carve-outs of software companies from large corporations. These are more complex than small acquisitions but provide opportunities to deploy large amounts of capital. These more significant acquisitions, coupled with the possibility of acquisitions outside its conventional VMS domain, could potentially lead to significantly higher capital deployment and sustained robust earnings growth—if Constellation gets it right. The "experiments" above are part of the laboratory framework mentioned at the beginning of the chapter.

In his 2018 shareholder letter,[39] Leonard discussed growth areas outside VMS to address the question of "where does it end?" His answer was that all profitable industries and companies attract competition, and the companies that can adapt to change are the most successful. On several occasions, Leonard has cited the rise and fall of the newspaper industry as a useful analogy for the future of software. Today, VMS enjoys high returns on capital. The industry therefore attracts a lot of competition: that will eventually lead to falling returns on capital. The few newspaper businesses that have survived are those that gradually diversified out of traditional newspapers into other media. "One day Constellation may find that VMS businesses are too expensive to rationally acquire," said Leonard. "If that happens, I hope we'll have had the foresight and luck to find some other high ROE [return on equity] non-VMS businesses in which to invest at attractive prices." As of the time of writing, the company has not entered into any other major business segment, but it would not be a surprise if the company were to announce such an acquisition.

Finding attractive acquisition targets is not always easy, and larger targets come with their own challenges. In particular, they tend to draw considerable interest from private equity firms and publicly listed companies, driving prices up. This, in turn, results in reduced returns on capital for whoever acquires them: put simply, you have to tie up more capital for less bang per buck. Leonard has shared his views on making more significant acquisitions at higher multiples. The best use of capital is, of course, to buy many small software companies at low multiples, since these small acquisitions generate a substantial return on capital. But Constellation's internal study showed that deploying capital to make occasional significant acquisitions makes sense—if not to the same degree. They work financially, so long as return on incremental capital exceeds the cost of capital. Significant shareholder value can also be created if the company is able to deploy a *lot* of capital at these lower returns. The path of Warren Buffett is an apt comparison here: he has deployed large amounts of capital at relatively low returns (still above the cost of capital) in substantial deals (e.g. railroad company BNSF, or Kraft Heinz). A recent major acquisition by Constellation Software was Altera in May 2022. Constellation acquired the company for $400m, and the firm generated $88m in free cash flow in 2024—generating a much higher return on capital than most deals of this size.

In recent years, Constellation Software has increasingly delegated responsibility for acquisitions to lower ranks within the company. This has helped to scale its M&A opportunities. In terms of capital allocation, the company has announced two initiatives: increasing its number of substantial VMS businesses, while developing investing competence beyond the VMS sphere. Resources are being expanded; hurdle rates are being lowered. As long as these acquisitions generate a return on capital above the company's cost of capital, this can work.

There will probably be more significant acquisitions from Constellation Software in the years ahead, even venturing beyond the traditional VMS sector into niches within horizontal software (already explored somewhat) or other non-software domains. From talking to Mark Leonard, we understand that a group of people in Constellation Software today are working solely on identifying non-software acquisition opportunities.

The man, the myth, the legend

After meeting Mark Leonard in person in 2024, it became clear that Constellation Software plans to become a different company, renewing itself gradually through controlled experiments. Could this be the future of sustainable corporate growth? After meeting Leonard, it seemed clear to us that any opportunities outside of vertical market software will need to have similar economic characteristics, such as long contracts and/or sticky customer relationships. That could lead the company into niche industrials, where some of the other companies in this book are already thriving.

If Constellation Software's skillset encompasses capital allocation more broadly, a gradual move out of software could be an intriguing prospect. It may well enter new markets with financial characteristics similar to vertical software—and it may well find similar success. What's noteworthy about Leonard's letters is how far in advance they telegraph moves. As early as 2015, Leonard was discussing plans to increase the number of acquisitions. These plans materialized a few years later, resulting in a much higher volume of acquisitions (and, in turn, strong and profitable earnings growth).[40]

In terms of sheer numbers, "owner-operator" acquisitions will continue to dominate in the years ahead. Carve-outs make for larger deals, though fewer in number.

Constellation Software accounts for just 3% of total software acquisitions worldwide. The company is well aware of the opportunities. Navi Hehar, a previous VP at Constellation Software, spoke on this subject in 2022:[41]

> "One of the deals I closed, I obviously can't talk about the specifics of it, but you wouldn't believe the returns on this thing. It was shocking. You'd be surprised, man, there's still a lot of low-hanging fruit out there, just like free money out there, that Constellation is uniquely positioned to exploit that other people just can't seem to figure out how to do. It's unbelievable, it's really hard to fathom."

"Live free or die"

Mark Leonard's passion for decentralization and autonomy runs deep. His independent spirit was evident from a young age—a time marked by defiance of authority and a relentless drive to chart his own course. He recalls his school days, where challenging his teachers earned him more than one trip to the principal's office. For Leonard, this wasn't just youthful rebellion but the beginning of a lifelong commitment to independence and self-determination. His favorite motto, "live free or die," is one he truly lives by.[42]

Leonard's commitment to a decentralized, autonomous structure is rooted in his lifelong belief in independence. His rebellious spirit, evident even in his youth when he built flamethrowers, shapes Constellation's structure. "Live free or die" translates into a management philosophy where autonomy isn't just valued—it's essential. It has to be earned through delivering on key ratios that drive shareholder value: like organic growth, profitability, and client attrition. The company has a decentralized set-up—but with strict financial criteria governing this. As long as underlying companies deliver on key ratios, they are free. According to a former employee of Constellation Software we spoke to, the company "runs as a machine where rules and mathematics replace feelings." At the front-end of the company, client satisfaction has a high priority—but if you run a subsidiary with low profitability, you have to prioritize profitability ahead of client satisfaction.

Over time, Leonard's disciplined, data-driven approach to capital allocation and experimentation has turned Constellation into a compounding machine. With a rational framework that treats each acquisition as a long-term investment rooted in return on capital, he has created a cycle of reinvestment that continuously amplifies growth. Constellation now stands as a powerful testament to the strength of a decentralized approach, essential for scaling and building enduring value that grows with each cycle.

This independence shapes how he leads Constellation Software. Leonard dislikes being told what to do; he finds persuasion through rational arguments more rewarding than mandates. In running Constellation, he has attracted a team of like-minded individuals who share this need for autonomy. He empowers his operating group managers to make their own capital allocation and strategic decisions, entrusting them—and the portfolio managers and business unit leaders they oversee—with a rare degree of autonomy to succeed or fail, so long as they maintain strong financial discipline and uphold CSI's core principles. Subsidiaries have to report on a rolling four-quarter and four-year basis. Leonard has built a culture where mistakes are data points, essential inputs that drive constant evolution and adaptation.

Leonard acknowledges that a hands-off approach can produce different interpretations of autonomy across Constellation's various units. But rather than seeing this as a weakness, he embraces it as a source of strength. Each variation is an experiment, a chance to uncover new ways of solving problems and growing the business. This decentralized structure enables Constellation to harness a diversity of approaches, fostering an environment where leaders aren't just following a manual—they're writing it as they go.

Vertical market software—the beauty of pattern recognition

Vertical market software, despite its customization, possesses homogeneous characteristics that make it highly suitable for an acquisition-driven growth strategy when combined with capital allocation and decentralization. This is because specialization in software, as opposed to being a generalist acquirer across different niches, leads to a wealth of repetitive processes and best practices focused on a single area of expertise. Simultaneously, the extensive dataset resulting from owning similar companies within each niche allows for the standardization and subsequent decentralization of acquisition responsibilities to individual operating groups. In turn, it serves as the foundation for the significant volume of annual acquisitions at Constellation Software. Essentially, VMS's homogeneous nature and the many opportunities it provides facilitate Constellation's unique acquisition pace. Meanwhile, the customization of software necessitates decentralized operations.

Decentralization is a hallmark of Constellation Software, and for this structure to work effectively, a significant amount of trust is necessary. Establishing trust requires a long-term investment horizon. As with most decentralized business models discussed in the book, the underlying companies can learn how to run a successful company from best practices over many years. Constellation Software can constantly evaluate each underlying company's strategies due to its own insights into various VMS companies. Best practice can be applied to other subsidiaries in the system but is not forced upon them from headquarters. This unique insight is also a competitive advantage in the acquisition process since Constellation Software knows what measures the target company needs to implement to increase profitability and cash flow. One example is pricing. A secret sauce in Constellation Software is pricing increases based on insights on client attrition. There are instances where Constellation Software has increased prices several hundred percent based on very low client attrition numbers.

"Tit-for-tat" theory—in practice

Authority in Constellation Software is delegated to individuals. The company does not take over the day-to-day management of its vertical market software subsidiaries. In his writeup "Constellation Software: A capital allocator's culture":[43] Roi Lipovetzky (research analyst at Oakmount Capital) describes a mindblowing statistic regarding decentralization in Constellation Software.

> "If someone is looking for evidence for decentralized culture, he should probably look for the number of employees in the headquarters compared to the total company. In Constellation Software, a company with approximately 25,000 employees, only ten people sit in the headquarters at Toronto (a ratio of 1:2,500)."

Leonard shares some thoughts about the cooperation theory in his 2014 shareholder letter, where he draws on the conclusions from a book called *The Evolution of Cooperation* by Robert Axelrod:[44]

> "When Constellation Software was much smaller, we used to run annual offsite meetings. Working on the curriculum for one of the offsites, I asked our academic advisor about game theory. He said 'tit-for-tat, that's pretty much all you need to know.' That clever but unsatisfying explanation eventually led me to the book and article that I'm recommending this year—*The Evolution of Cooperation* by Robert Axelrod, and a related journal article (jointly, "EoC"). EoC is a short and accessible introduction to the prisoner's dilemma game. EoC has provided me with models for thinking about a number of business problems. In Chart 1 [left out], you'll see that our head office expense as a percent of Net Revenues has halved from 1.9% in 2005 to 0.9% in 2014 while ROIC has increased from 17% to 37%. Trust trumped central bureaucracy in our case."

The book's main conclusion is that a so-called tit-for-tat strategy is very beneficial in all kinds of relationships, as well as in an organizational context. You always start with a friendly invitation and hope that the other party will respond similarly. The book gives a somewhat optimistic view of cooperation and has clearly influenced Leonard and the way he has structured Constellation Software.

In a business context, tit-for-tat means that the head office provides a lot of autonomy and trust from the beginning and helps the subsidiary companies develop. In turn, the subsidiary companies sense this freedom from above and respond by cooperating and ultimately making business decisions that benefit headquarters, themselves, and shareholders. When this long-term, two-way cooperation develops in these decentralized business models, all parties benefit—not least shareholders.

Visualization of Constellation Software

The visualization in Figure 9.2 shows the structure of Constellation Software, a collection of hundreds of niche software companies spread across six operating groups and dozens of different verticals. Each vertical might be dedicated to software for specific areas such as "library management" or "people transportation."

Figure 9.2: A visualization of Constellation[45]

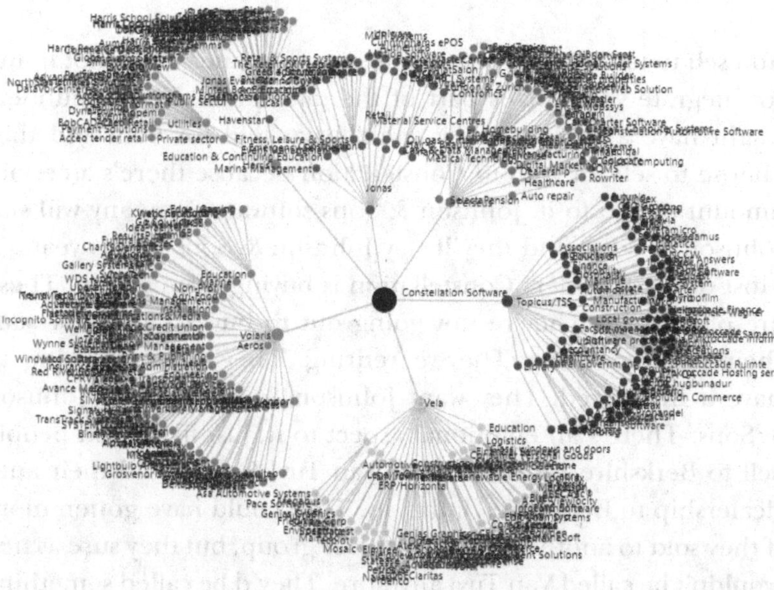

The structure of Constellation Software is highly decentralized, with six operating groups that, by themselves, could function as independent, publicly traded companies. Each operating group is granted responsibility for conducting its acquisitions, and deeply involved in capital allocation decisions beyond this, as well as strategic decisions. Each operating group has its own DNA and culture and operates as a mini-CSI. In 2021, Topicus was spun off and listed as a publicly traded company, with Constellation Software maintaining a 50.1% stake. In 2023, Lumine Group was spun out in connection with the acquisition of WideOrbit. According to Mark Leonard, the conventional wisdom with spin-offs is that they don't create excess shareholder value. A conventional CEO would embrace the conventional wisdom—but that doesn't describe Leonard. His ethos is to test old truths. Spinning out Lumine and Topicus does just that, and the results will form part of the future playbook of Constellation Software. It would not be surprising if several other large acquisitions are coupled with a spin-off over the coming years.

Constellation's six operating groups offer support and assistance to acquired companies without micro-managing them. The trust-based relationship is a beauty of the decentralized operating model. Navi Hehar, the former VP we heard from earlier, describes the power of maintaining autonomy post-transaction:

> "You sell to us. We won't ever change your name. We're not trying to integrate you. That's part of the sales pitch. These founders might have a business they could have sold for \$6m and they choose to sell for \$5m to Constellation because there's a certain amount of ego to it. Johnson & Sons software company will stay Johnson & Sons, and they'll stay Johnson & Sons for 50 years. … Most of the founders Constellation is buying from are 50. These are older guys. They're not going out to buy a Lambo or start their next company. They're retiring. They're not looking to have it integrated. They want Johnson & Sons to stay Johnson & Sons. There's an emotional aspect to it, just like when people sell to Berkshire Hathaway, like Van Tuyl Group sold their auto dealership to Berkshire Hathaway. They could have gotten more if they sold to another big auto dealer group, but they sure as hell wouldn't be called Van Tuyl anymore. They'd be called something else and for that family that is worth billions of dollars, they were like, 'No, we want to keep the name we built.' These things are worth it to people that have a fair bit of money…"

High-performance conglomerates

Despite Leonard's absence from the media, his investor letters have offered shareholders and outside observers a glimpse into his mindset and decision-making process. In one of the letters, he shares his thoughts on autonomy and decentralization. Comparing Constellation Software to other high-performance conglomerates

(HPCs) like Jack Henry and Danaher, he found that a decentralized model with entrepreneurial leaders requires an unusually trusting culture and a long-term outlook.

In 2016, Leonard shared his findings from studying other HPCs. The key takeaway was that all the HPCs he studied followed a "multi-decade pattern," starting with solid growth from attractively priced acquisitions through to paying higher multiples for more significant acquisitions as the HPCs became very large. This, in turn, led to diminishing returns on capital. At that point, Leonard realized that one way of maintaining a high return on capital was to expand the growth runway into areas outside software without sacrificing autonomy and decentralization. By doing that, according to Mark, Constellation Software should increase the odds of delaying diminishing returns on capital as they grow. It is hard to think of another CEO who would argue the case against his own original business model like this—and have a plan in advance to counteract it.

Leonard and his team are hungry learners, and we've seen it up close. The entire culture of Constellation is dedicated to learning from the success and failure of organizations. The goal is to become a little bit better each day. While many corporations become increasingly bureaucratic as they grow, Mark Leonard does everything in his power to empower entrepreneurship and defy the bureaucracy creep. He knows that it is not a winning game.

Compensation aligned with shareholders

While we give Mark Leonard a lot of credit in this book, it is important to emphasize that he has not built Constellation Software alone. The CFO, COO, and CIO have been instrumental to the company's success. Mark Miller, now executive chairman of Volaris and COO of Constellation Software, was originally the founder and president of the company that became Constellation's first acquisition. Rather than exit, he stayed on and transitioned into M&A, eventually building Volaris, now Constellation's largest operating group. As one of Mark Leonard's earliest and most influential protégés, Miller played a key role in shaping and scaling the model that would define Constellation's growth. Together they have cultivated a culture that values frugality, transparency, and prudent risk-taking at every level.

In one of Mark Leonard's letters to shareholders, he gave outsiders a vivid illustration of Constellation Software's frugality. Leonard, who stands 6'5" and weighs 280 pounds, described how he flew economy on a business trip to the UK despite the discomfort involved and his ability to afford business class. This choice wasn't simply personal frugality but a leadership standard, emphasizing that when spending shareholders' money, Constellation operates with even greater restraint than personal spending. Leonard's example sets a clear expectation for Constellation's hundreds of employees who travel each week on company business, reinforcing a culture of accountability and shareholder respect.

This emphasis on responsibility extends to Constellation Software's approach to compensation and ownership. Employees and managers are incentivized through shares that are held in escrow for multiple years, a structure designed to align their long-term focus with the company's growth. Leonard believes that without this type of alignment, employees are less likely to care about multi-year initiatives or to prioritize long-term profits over short-term gains. Constellation has intentionally avoided option plans, instead building a unique approach where 75% of senior managers' bonuses, after tax, must be used to purchase Constellation shares at market price, which are held for a minimum of four years—a structure that, according to Leonard, results in employees maintaining an even longer holding period.[46]

This disciplined, ownership-based structure aligns with Constellation Software's measurement and performance culture. Leonard has built an organization that prioritizes data-driven decision-making. Hypotheses are rigorously tested, and ideas are refined through empirical learning that draws on the company's decentralized structure of individually tracked business units. Each unit provides an opportunity to experiment and validate new business practices in a low-risk environment, enabling Constellation to determine swiftly and economically if a new process adds value.

Leonard describes Constellation's "open, collegial, and analytical culture" as a key differentiator. This culture empowers curious managers and skilled analysts to collaborate and experiment without requiring extensive corporate systems or rigid methodologies. When a business process proves successful, the company's extensive benchmarking systems enable rapid emulation across other business units, driving continuous improvement throughout the organization. This ad hoc experimentation and best-practice sharing is integral to Constellation's high-performance ethos, and it mirrors the successful models of a few other conglomerates that have similarly emphasized process refinement and swift learning curves in their acquired businesses.

Manager compensation is closely aligned with that of shareholders, with Mark Leonard among the company's largest shareholders. The management group and the six top managers collectively own approximately $4bn in shares, with over 100 equity millionaires within the company. Additionally, the CEO, CFO, COO, and CIO have served the company for 27, 19, 27, and 27 years, respectively.

What stands out from Leonard's communication is his frankness. He has put in place a system of compensation where senior managers who consistently generate high returns on capital are well incentivized financially, and where these managers also experience a challenging and entertaining workplace.

Rational decision-making and honest communication

It is rare to experience CEOs willing to talk down the share price. In a very unconventional move, Mark Leonard, in the annual report of 2011, argued that the share price of Constellation Software had appreciated too much ahead of intrinsic value:

> "Unfortunately, our stock price has increased at over twice that rate (of intrinsic value) during the last year, a differential that would seem difficult to be sustained in future years."

Previously, Mark Leonard believed that if the company focused on the fundamentals, the share price would take care of itself. Over time, he realized it would be unhelpful if the share price moved too far away from intrinsic value (either to the upside or downside). The company risks losing loyal shareholders and employees if the share price is too high compared to intrinsic value; the former are more likely to crystallize profits, and the latter are more likely to cash in their bonus shares and start competing businesses. If the share price is too low, on the other hand, the company could become a target for other companies.

For investors, nothing catches Constellation Software's cultural tone and ethos better than the annual letters to shareholders. In one of his letters, Mark Leonard shared his vision of leadership as a form of partnership rather than mere employment. Leonard detailed how he went through a shift in his compensation, asking to reduce his salary to zero and waive bonuses, aligning his interests even more closely with those of shareholders. For Leonard, true leadership isn't about perks or titles but genuine alignment with those he served. He doesn't only treat his employees as partners but also his shareholders. The legend goes that companies get the shareholders they deserve, and with its loyal shareholder base, it is no coincidence that Constellation Software's share price has never had a drawdown of more than -26% from highs.

Leonard famously remarked, "I like the feel of the partner relationship a whole lot better." This philosophy reflects what famed investor Philip Fisher described as a "sense of trusteeship"—where management runs the company for the benefit of shareholders, not themselves. In effect, Leonard's approach to stewardship represents a higher level of shareholder alignment, which is rarely seen in the corporate landscape.

The remuneration policy at Constellation reflects this philosophy. Leonard's official salary is just $1, with his compensation relying primarily on his 2% ownership stake in the company, ensuring that his personal success is directly tied to shareholder value. This equity-based compensation model extends to other senior executives, including Mark Miller, the company's COO, who also holds a 2% equity stake.

Leonard's influence permeates Constellation's broader culture, where 75% of senior managers are promoted internally,[47] a practice that emphasizes loyalty and reinforces the company's core values and decentralized structure. For Leonard, leadership developed from within embodies a continuity of values that strengthens Constellation's foundation.

With a guiding philosophy of "perpetual ownership," Leonard has built Constellation into a long-term holder of niche software businesses. In his view, this model requires skilled, ethical general managers who can drive both growth and profitability—a challenge he sees as central to Constellation's success.

An unconventional corporate governance policy

What sets Mark Leonard apart—not just from the companies featured in this book but in a broader sense—is his unique and distinctive perspective on corporate governance and how it should function to maximize long-term shareholder value. Where he diverges successfully is from conventional standards of how companies should be governed. In Mark Leonard's ideal world, boards should emphasize independence and diversity without setting limits for director tenures. He argues that these standard policies, while well-intentioned, may hinder high-performance companies. Rather than focusing solely on governance as a system of checks and balances, Leonard advocates for a board whose primary role is to build intrinsic value within the company. In this model, Leonard suggests that frequent replacement of board members can undermine continuity, a critical ingredient in sustaining a company's high performance over time.

Leonard believes that the board's role should not be confined to governance alone. Instead, he distinguishes between two functions: governance, which involves basic oversight, and a deeper "coaching" role, where directors contribute more than just oversight. He argues that limiting the tenure of skilled directors can hinder their ability to acquire the long-term industry expertise necessary for meaningful contributions to the company's growth and strategy. Leonard draws on the concept of "deliberate practice"—popularized as the "10,000-hour rule" by Malcolm Gladwell—to highlight that board members, like any experts, benefit from sustained, focused involvement. To him, true expertise in directing a company cannot be achieved through limited, short-term engagement; it requires years of dedicated, in-depth learning about the industry and the company.

Leonard critiques the standard practice in public companies, where boards are seen as governors rather than mentors. Simple math, he points out, makes it unlikely that directors from outside the industry or with limited tenure can contribute meaningfully as coaches. Leonard suggests that for a director to be effective in both governance and coaching roles, they need decades of immersion within the company and industry—ideally beginning in their 40s or 50s, and continuing until they can no longer serve effectively. By advocating for long-term board appointments, Leonard underscores his belief that director tenure should be preserved when governance is strong, not limited. He argues that imposing arbitrary limits on tenure is comparable to firing a high-performance employee simply for reaching an anniversary milestone—a practice that weakens the company by disrupting continuity.

Leonard's approach to board composition is a powerful stance against what he sees as a one-size-fits-all mentality in corporate governance. He believes that when governance is already robust, limiting the terms of experienced directors is counterproductive. Instead, Leonard promotes a governance model where directors can deeply embed themselves in the company's trajectory, delivering guidance and strategic insight far beyond basic oversight.

Conclusion

Constellation Software boasts an enviable recurring cash flow stream that has successfully been deployed in acquisitions over many years. The long-term mindset and the shareholder-aligned incentive structure of the owner-operator, Mark Leonard, and his senior management team are rare among public companies. In recent years, the strategy has expanded in anticipation of difficulties matching past bargains, with larger carve-out deals alongside spin-offs. Yet opportunities among small VMS companies remain significant, and recent initiatives to deploy larger amounts of capital should prove successful. Constellation Software will evolve and grow, and there are reasons to believe future growth will come from areas outside of software. Constellation Software is the kind of company that makes you wish you had a time machine—just so you could fast-forward a decade and marvel at the journey. One thing's certain: transformation is inevitable.

10

A Snowball of Cash Flow Compounding

Heico

IMAGINE YOU STUMBLED across a company in 1990 where a family had recently bought a controlling stake. You believed in their way of doing business, invested $100,000, and forgot about the stock. When you opened your account 35 years later, your account showed $100m. That is the history of Heico in a nutshell.

Heico is a star in the aerospace industry, supplying critical parts to the world's largest airlines, defense contractors, and space missions. This family-run conglomerate has become the largest non-OEM supplier of jet engine components in the world, thanks to its sharp focus on acquisitions, organic growth, and a relentless commitment to safety.

With over 75 million parts delivered without a single in-flight failure, Heico's reputation for quality is unmatched. Behind this success is a savvy business model that defies the typical corporate approach. Heico's culture is deeply rooted in chairman and CEO Laurans ("Larry") Mendelson's vision of the company as a "snowball of cash flow compounding." Over 35 years, he has transformed a small manufacturing company into an industry leader with global reach.

Products engineered for Mars

Heico is an industrial conglomerate that supplies sophisticated and complex products for various industrial niches, focusing mainly on the aerospace industry. As one of the most prominent parts manufacturers for airlines in the United States, Heico has established a significant market position in a highly fragmented sector through both acquisitions and organic growth.

Heico's customers include most of the world's airlines, overhaul shops, satellite manufacturers, medical equipment manufacturers, telecommunications equipment suppliers, and more. Most products Heico offers are used in "cannot fail" environments, where requirements for quality and durability are at their most demanding. The products are highly specialized and niche-engineered, and essential for customers. For example, the company supplied the mission-critical components on board the InSight landing vehicle that touched down on Mars on November 26, 2018.

A few years ago, in a meeting with the Mendelsons, we were asked to guess the price of a small bag of screws that Larry had brought into the meeting. The screws were used by the airline industry. It seemed like a simple product, but we still guessed $10,000. Imagine our surprise when the CEO responded: "$90,000." It was a striking reminder of just how specialized—and valuable—their products really are.

Heico's primary business model focuses on providing spare parts for commercial airlines through its Parts Manufacturer Approval (PMA) authorization, a program approved by the Federal Aviation Administration (FAA). This authorization ensures that the original equipment manufacturers (OEMs) do not gain a monopoly over the sale of replacement parts for airlines. Over 50% of Heico's sales are generated in this aftermarket business. Because every part of an airplane has to be inspected and replaced on a regular basis, it forms the background for a profitable business model with recurring revenues.

OEM and PMA—what does it mean?

The market for alternative parts—which function the same way as OEM parts, but cost much less to obtain—continues to grow due to the high prices of OEM parts. OEMs defend themselves by pointing to safety risks, even though decades of evidence show no difference in the reliability and quality of parts approved under the PMA system. The FAA ensures alternative parts meet the same safety and quality standards, and safety issues have not increased despite airline fleets' growing use of PMA parts. PMA parts offer an alternative for airlines in the aftermarket—the most lucrative market for suppliers, with high margins and contracts that often extend years into the future. Airlines that were previously resistant to PMA parts have become more open to using them, especially after supply chain issues following COVID-19.

Heico has built a market position in the highly fragmented U.S. airline industry through acquisitions and organic growth. Today, Heico sells products and services across 115 countries, with approximately 40% of sales outside the U.S.

Heico is the world leader in its niches, and the markets in which it operates are fragmented, providing ample opportunities for organic growth and acquisitions. Airlines continue to face pressure to reduce costs, and Heico is a crucial partner, offering more than 12,000 parts and developing about 300–500 new parts yearly. On its impressive customer list are more than 200 airlines worldwide—19 of the world's 20 largest airlines are customers.

The parts made by Heico offer a good value proposition for customers, and its long track record of producing FAA-approved products through advanced engineering capabilities is impeccable. Airlines usually save between 30% and 50% compared to going directly to OEMs. In addition, Heico offers further price discounts for those who sign long-term contracts. Meanwhile, recurring revenues are partly driven by mandatory replacement cycles, since certain parts of aircrafts are life-limited and must be removed after a designated number of allowable flight hours, take-offs, and landings. The rigorous approval process presents significant barriers to entry for would-be rivals. An applicant's ability to complete the PMA process is limited by several factors—notably the FAA's confidence level in the applicant.

Although Heico is best known for its products in the civil airline industry, it also manufactures specialty military electronics, such as sophisticated cooling systems for the U.S. Air Force's F-22 fighter aircraft. In response to the events of September 11, 2001, the company diversified its revenue base through a series of acquisitions, resulting in more than 35% of revenues coming from customers outside the commercial aviation industry, including medical, electronics, and other manufacturing markets.

Despite no patents, Heico has developed proprietary techniques, software, and manufacturing expertise to manufacture replacement parts. The company continuously improves its manufacturing methods and processes to ensure it stays ahead of the game in product development.

Figure 10.1: Heico share price performance since 1990

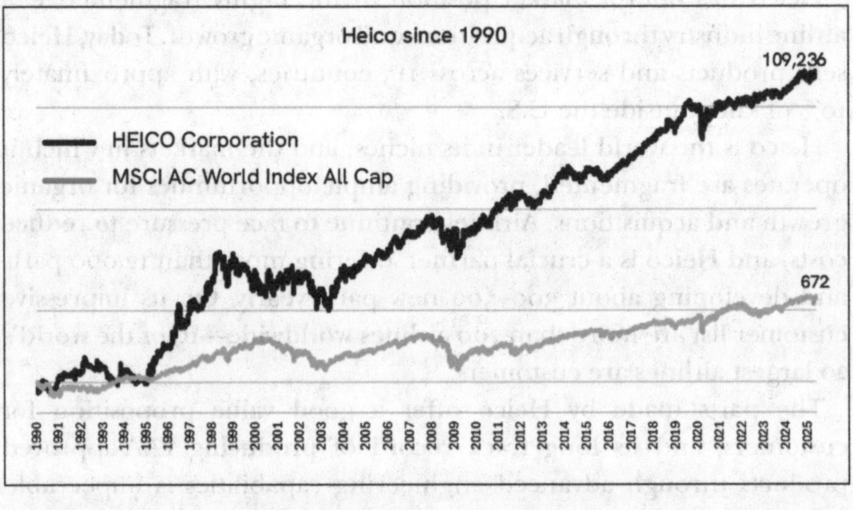

From $0.1m to $100m

Heico was founded in 1957 and listed in 1960, but its story truly began in 1990 when the Mendelson family took control of the company. The Mendelson family and employees today own around 23% of the company. They run the company as if it was a private firm, with an ultra-long-term perspective.

Since 1990, Heico's net sales have grown from $26.2m to $3.8bn in 2024, representing a compound annual growth rate of approximately 16%. During the same period, the company also improved its net income from $2m to $514m, a compound annual growth rate of approximately 18%. If you had invested $100,000 in Heico in 1990 and reinvested the dividends received, your investment result's total value would amount to that $100m we mentioned at the start of the chapter.

Interestingly, Larry Mendelson's background is far removed from the aviation industry. After earning his degree from Columbia Business School, Larry worked as an accountant at Arthur Andersen, a now-defunct American accounting firm. He later transitioned into real estate investing. Larry's two sons, Victor and Eric—who are heavily involved as co-CEOs of the business—also attended Columbia. According to Eric, the famous New York university provided them all with "the ability to think and process information," and schooled them in the process of applying "a beginner's mind"—approaching subjects without any preconceived ideas. Presenting at Columbia Business School has even become a family tradition for the Mendelsons.

A "cradle-to-grave" business model

When the Mendelsons acquired HEICO in the late 1980s, it was a small manufacturing company primarily focused on a single product: an engine combustor. This product served as a stepping stone for Heico's later success in PMA parts. At that time, the board members held few shares and had little skin in the game. However, Heico had a good position in the aerospace market. The Mendelson family was particularly drawn to the maintenance aspect of the combustor for engines, and the "cradle-to-grave" service requirements of engine parts; they saw the potential for gaining approval for other parts as well. The family purchased $3m in Heico shares and demanded a board seat. After winning a proxy fight, the family took control of the company, and assumed leadership positions.

The Mendelson family instilled an entrepreneurial culture within Heico. This translated to highly decentralized operations, with a high degree of autonomy granted to the people closest to customers. In Eric Mendelson's own words, "We decentralize where it makes sense." When all subsidiaries are granted autonomy and authority, each company can tailor products to the needs of clients. Heico does not enforce standardization of processes and products.

Today, the Mendelson family still runs the company, with Larry Mendelson serving as chairman of the board. His two sons, Eric and Victor, each run one of the company's two operating groups—the Flight Support Group and the Electronic Technologies Group, respectively—in addition to serving as Heico's co-CEOs. Victor Mendelson said that his dad, very early in their careers, would ask them for input on a lot of business topics like marketing and sales. This built the sons' confidence—and aptitude. As a seven-year-old, Eric even had a part-time job as a receptionist at one of his dad's real estate projects.

A 2018 article offers interesting insights into Larry's parenting style.[48] His two boys, just 13 and 15 years old, wanted to flip an apartment to buy a BMW with the profits. Unfortunately for the boys, the buyer backed out at the last minute, leaving them at risk of losing some capital. Larry refused to bail them out. In his words: "You study a book, but you don't get that feeling inside your bones when a deal does not work out." In the end the boys found another buyer at a lower price. They bought a car, but it was a Ford instead of a BMW.

Historically, General Electric, Pratt & Whitney, and Rolls-Royce were the only sources of jet engine replacement parts, and OEMs were the sole sources of replacements for their aircraft parts. As we will explore later, there were several milestones on Heico's journey to becoming the largest non-OEM jet engine and aircraft component replacement parts supplier in the world. The company had to convince large airlines to sign contracts and simultaneously fight OEM competitors in the courts.

OEM manufacturers have historically claimed that the parts made by suppliers like Heico are not up to their standards. Some have gone further than this. United Technologies took legal action against Heico, alleging misappropriation of trade secrets and unfair competition. However, in March 2000, 11 years after the initial complaint was filed, Heico received a permanent license to make and sell the parts in dispute.

This lawsuit was not anything new for the company. In the late 1990s, Travelers Casualty & Surety also filed a lawsuit against Heico. This was dismissed by a federal court due to a lack of jurisdiction. Despite lawsuits and similar challenges to its reputation, Heico has come out stronger every time. Its focus on quality has proven out; Heico has gained a reputation as a top supplier of non-OEM parts.

The breakthrough—onboarding top airline customers

During the 1990s, Larry Mendelson and his two sons expanded Heico's product portfolio, and the company received a significant investment from Lufthansa, the German flag carrier, which purchased a 20%

stake in Heico Aerospace, a subsidiary of Heico. As part of the deal, Heico agreed to manufacture parts for Lufthansa. It proved pivotal for the company. Having Lufthansa on board both as a customer and a minority owner gave Heico a significant stamp of credibility. The company was showing signs that it had something truly special coming.

The Lufthansa deal was not the only significant collaboration in Heico's history. In 2001, Heico announced two new joint ventures with AMR Corporation, the parent company of American Airlines, to develop, design, and sell FAA-approved jet engine and aircraft component replacement parts. The following year, Heico further strengthened its position by entering into a strategic relationship with United Airlines, which agreed to purchase FAA-approved parts from the company and collaborate on developing new components. Heico secured these deals after spending years proving that its products were reliable and good value for money. With its growing reputation in the industry, Heico took another critical step in 2003 by signing a parts supply and development agreement with two major airlines: Delta Air Lines and Air Canada. These agreements aimed to accelerate the development of aircraft and engine parts, further solidifying Heico's position in the market.

On the back of all this momentum, Heico made significant progress in China, signing a "Joint Cooperation Agreement" with China Aviation Import and Export Group Corporation (CASGC), a state-owned comprehensive service provider for aviation supplies. It was a breakthrough deal that also made Heico a respectable player in the international arena. The deal aimed to promote Heico's FAA-approved aircraft and engine replacement products in China, mainly focusing on aircraft engines, spares, ground support, and safety equipment. The deal also covered leasing maintenance, component repair and overhaul, consignment stores, manufacturing, and training. This was a telling example of how Heico embeds itself within its customers' operations.

A well-oiled acquisition machine

Heico's ability to allocate capital in a way that creates excess shareholder value has been outstanding. The core part of its capital allocation strategy has been to buy small niche manufacturing companies, preferably family-owned. Since 1990, Heico has completed over 100 acquisitions, with a 98% success rate—a nearly flawless track record that few companies can match. Interestingly, despite being one of the best-run aerospace parts companies, Heico does not view itself as such. Instead, it views itself as "a vehicle that generates strong cash flow, and we do it through aerospace parts and technology," as Larry Mendelson puts it. This is important, because it does not constrain Heico from only deploying capital into the aerospace parts industry. Instead, the company can put money at work where returns are the most attractive, something the company has already proven with ventures into other industries.

In the last decade Heico has accelerated its acquisition pace. It has acquired companies in the aviation, space, medical, defense, telecommunications, and electronics sectors. Despite the acquisitions being spread across various sectors, they share similar characteristics: good growth prospects, solid margins, and strong cash flow profiles. How wisely they have reinvested that strong cash flow is the real key to its success.

The company is flexible regarding where to allocate capital. But it is inflexible in the quality it seeks: it strongly prefers businesses with high margins, preferably above 20%. The Mendelson family has proved adept at identifying sectors with sustainable operating margins of 25%. Flight support and electronic components are two such areas.

The company uses the following example to illustrate why high margins are critical: "If you have 7% operating margins, like most industrial companies have, you have to invest $93 to earn $7, a ratio of 13:1. If you have 25% operating margins you have to invest $75 to earn $25, a ratio of 3:1. It is that simple!"[49]

Rather than spending heavily on large headquarters, Heico has always minimized overhead costs, and its family-driven and entrepreneurial mindset is attractive and deep-seated. Employees are encouraged to work as smart as they can with the tools and machines available rather than spending capital on expensive upgrades of machinery. When one of their subsidiaries in Fort Myers, Florida—an area prone to hurricanes and power outages—needed a backup generator, the team didn't spend $500,000 on a new one. Instead, they found a used generator on eBay for just 5% of the cost. It's one of hundreds of examples that illustrate Heico's deeply ingrained culture of frugality.

Heico's trust-based culture doesn't just guide how it operates—it gives the company a competitive edge. In many cases, sellers choose Heico before others even get a chance to bid. That's because the businesses Heico acquires are often niche, high-margin operations built by skilled, entrepreneurial founders who value independence. These are leaders who've built something that works—and they want a partner who values their success. Heico's philosophy of minimal interference makes it not just a buyer, but the *preferred* buyer.

Interestingly, Heico usually does not buy the entirety of a company. It views this as a way to maintain an entrepreneurial spirit, keeping private sellers incentivized through stock ownership. Instead, it typically seeks a majority stake, usually at least 80%. This approach allows subsidiaries to retain real ownership and benefit from future upside. Heico has found this a compelling proposition. As part of its deal structures, Heico often secures the right to purchase remaining non-controlling interests over time. In parallel, sellers are granted the option to sell their remaining shares back to Heico, typically based on a multiple of earnings.

Heico's long-term success is no accident. Beyond its entrepreneurial and family-driven culture, the company's disciplined approach to capital allocation has been crucial. Understanding that increasing shareholder value requires strong cash flow, Heico remains committed to prudent financial decisions—particularly when it comes to acquisitions. The company avoids overpaying, historically acquiring businesses at multiples of just 5–8× operating profit, even when those businesses boast healthy operating margins of 20% or more. A key part of Heico's strategy has been targeting smaller, entrepreneurial companies, typically with sales ranging from $10m to $100m. This brings lower competition, more reasonable valuations, and diversification without complexity. Another advantage of many of these small acquisitions is that the founder is still active as CEO, and wants to continue to run the company under the ownership of Heico. The entrepreneurial culture is kept alive and kicking.

When acquiring companies, the personal relationship between the subsidiary CEO and employees is hugely important for Heico. Heico wants management to remain in place, and it wants that to mean that employees will remain motivated and continue to work productively. In their book *The Titanium Economy*,[50] Asutosh Padhi, Gaurav Batra and Nick Santhanam explore the acquisition process of Thermal Structures, acquired by Heico from Vaughn Barnes in 1999. When Larry Mendelson was touring the factory floor of Thermal Structures for the first time, the authors note:

"As dazzled as he might have been by the fancy technology they were using, he was always far more interested in learning if employees were motivated and respected by the management for their skills and opinions."

Vaughan Barnes makes an interesting related point. Thermal Structures had multiple suitors, and Heico was notably different in one key respect. "In every meeting [with potential acquirers], I'd ask, 'What happens to my people?' And they would reply, 'Why do you care?' You'll have your money."[51] The one company that didn't have that attitude: Heico.

The Berkshire of aerospace

Heico's business model shares many similarities with Berkshire Hathaway's. Both companies attract business owners who want to stay involved in their companies even after selling a significant stake. Unsurprisingly, like-minded entrepreneurs and investors often gravitate toward each other. Therefore, it was not a surprise when Berkshire Hathaway began accumulating shares in Heico in 2024—a testament to the alignment between the two companies' philosophies.

Just like Berkshire, Heico tries to avoid bureaucracy and middle management. Corporate politics are not welcomed. Instead, the key is to get the 6,000+ "team members" to embrace an ownership mentality, treating the companies as their own. As Eric Mendelson says, "You want to develop talent, not chase talent away."[52] About 80% of all Heico's companies are standalone operations where the original owners have 10–30 years of experience in their niche.

A decentralized structure emphasizes accountability, leading to higher cost-consciousness among individual companies in the group. The companies Heico has acquired are already profitable and run by entrepreneurs who know how to preserve cash. The decentralized model means Heico has to be selective. As Larry Mendelson puts it: "[B]ecause our model is a decentralized model, we don't go in and clean house with acquisitions and throw people out of jobs and all that kind of stuff. So ... we have to be a little bit careful in how we do things." Nevertheless, being picky hasn't proved a problem: "[T]here are enough potential transactions out there that will enable us to close on our fair share of what's available."[53] The management team meets all subsidiary companies every year, and tries to be on top of each business, not just reviewing financials. Plans are not imposed top-down on all companies. Heico prefers to coach its subsidiaries through the daily grind.[54]

Factory workers and secretaries becoming multimillionaires

A company's greatest asset is its employees. This is especially true for Heico. The company places significant value on all of its workforce; they are "team members," not staff. It maintains a generous 401(k) retirement plan, and even during difficult times like the pandemic it fully funded all eligible employees' plans. Heico employees contribute 6% of their salaries as a tax-deferred contribution, and Heico matches it with 5% of the wage in Heico stock. Over the years, this has made several factory workers and secretaries multimillionaires.

The company also maintains good health and safety practices, resulting in an injury rate about half that of other U.S. manufacturing companies. The company has an open-door communication policy. All team members are able to communicate with Heico's senior management on any subject. There is no "we against them" you get in many companies.

Heico's employee-friendly philosophy also extends to its shareholders. Its dual-class share structure—where "A" shares carry enhanced voting rights—preserves the Mendelson family's control, while helping to mitigate long-term succession risk. The Mendelsons still manage Heico as a private business, prioritizing long-term decisions that benefit all shareholders.

Heico also displays frugality when it comes to executive compensation. For example, during downturns (like the COVID-19 pandemic), management reduced their own short-term compensation and favored substantial investment in R&D. Meanwhile, in challenging years, the company has always fully contributed to employees' retirement plans when many other companies reduced them.

Conclusion

The Mendelson family had the foresight to recognize the enduring value of recurring cash flow from aerospace parts—and the courage to act on that insight by going head-to-head with established OEMs. Since 1990, Heico's snowball of compounding cash flow has accelerated faster than most U.S. companies. The recent investment by Berkshire Hathaway stands as a testament to Heico's remarkable success.

A down-to-earth culture, combined with an entrepreneurial mindset and a knack for winning over founders, has been key to the company's outstanding performance. Heico often retains a minority stake for sellers in acquired businesses, ensuring they maintain skin in the game. The Mendelsons have built two powerful engines driving Heico's growth: a disciplined capital allocation strategy focused on acquiring niche suppliers in industries with favorable economics, and a commitment to invest in those businesses for organic growth. Larry Mendelson rightfully belongs in the company of great builders like Warren Buffett. Standing beside their highly successful father are his two sons, Victor and Eric, who have lived and breathed Heico for decades. Their continued leadership as co-CEOs ensures that the company's unique culture will endure well into the future.

11

From Vacuum Motors to NASA's X-Ray Monitor

AMETEK

FAILURE, THEY SAY, is the greatest teacher. For AMETEK, failure wasn't merely a chapter in its story—it was the prologue. It all started in 1930, following the aftermath of the 1929 stock market crash, a time when businesses toppled like dominoes. Among the wreckage was the Manhattan Electric Supply Company, a small business selling telegraph equipment and early electrical components. On paper, its bankruptcy marked the end of the line. For its undeterred stockholders, however, it was merely the beginning.

Rising from the ashes, they regrouped and formed a new, publicly traded company: American Machine and Metals, Inc. The restart was anything but grand, focused on practicality rather than prestige. Centrifuges for pharmaceuticals, laundry machine components, and electric motors for household appliances were its bread and butter. The products were utilitarian, not glamorous—water filtration systems, for instance—but they were also the lifeblood of industries.

Beneath this humble operation lay an unrelenting vision—a desire to grow, innovate, and redefine itself—and a determination never to suffer a 1929 scenario again. By the early 1960s, the company had shed its descriptive but uninspired name and rebranded itself to AMETEK. It marked the start of a move into products with high value and higher margins, transitioning from a producer of commodity industrial parts to a leader in cutting-edge instruments, precision components, and specialty materials. AMETEK wasn't content to power machines—it wanted to power progress.

This evolution spanned decades. For AMETEK, it was not just about transforming the business. It was also about making the choices that would position the company favorably: in structurally growing markets where it could earn high returns on capital. Initially, nearly 80% of the business consisted of commoditized electric motors. But by 2011, AMETEK's portfolio was almost unrecognizable, with 95% of its products now differentiated, mission-critical offerings. These products often represented a small fraction of their customers' costs but were indispensable to their operations. This unique positioning granted AMETEK a significant competitive advantage: pricing power. The result? Sales soared from $30 million in 1955 to nearly $7 billion in 2024, with operating margins climbing from 12% in the early 2000s to an impressive 26%.

A striking example of this transformation can be found in AMETEK's subsidiary, Amptek, a leader in X-ray technology. In 2016, Amptek played a critical role in NASA's Bennu mission, providing the solar X-ray monitor that enabled researchers to analyze the asteroid's surface composition. This wasn't just a milestone in space exploration—it was a testament to how far AMETEK had come from its early days manufacturing vacuum cleaner engines.

One of the key forces behind this transformation has been the AMETEK Growth Model, introduced in the early 1990s. This model formalized the company's approach to continuous improvement and disciplined growth: combining accretive acquisitions, operational excellence, global and market expansion, and product innovation into a repeatable formula. The growth model would become the backbone of AMETEK's strategy, guiding the company through its remarkable evolution into a leader in high-margin, mission-critical products.

Today, AMETEK is one of the world's premier multi-industry companies, boasting over 40 subsidiaries that operate with considerable autonomy while leveraging AMETEK's global scale, infrastructure and business systems. Its reach spans industries ranging from aerospace to healthcare, and from energy to advanced technology. AMETEK's products are no longer mere components—they are highly differentiated technology solutions that drive innovation and solve complex challenges across the globe.

Figure 11.1: AMETEK's share price performance since 1990

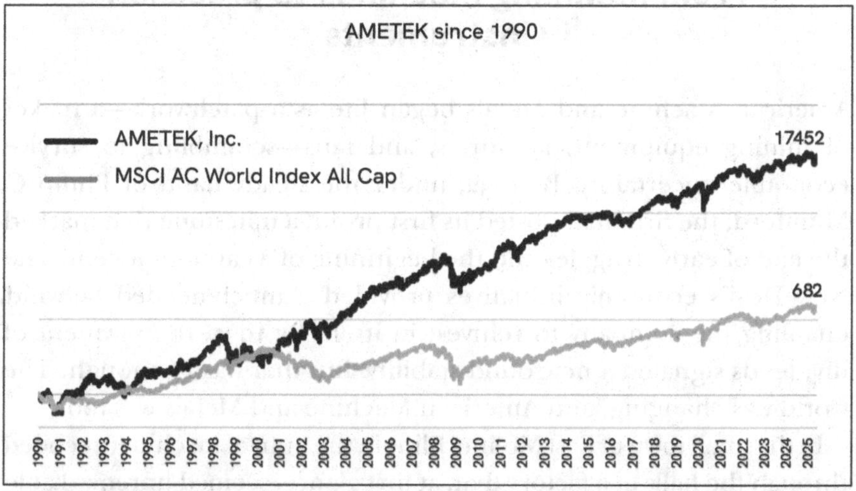

For investors, AMETEK's journey has been nothing short of extraordinary. Imagine traveling back to 1990 with $1m to invest in AMETEK stock. By March 2025, that investment would have grown to over $175m with dividends reinvested. AMETEK has been a 175-bagger. A CAGR of 16% in total shareholder returns over three decades has dwarfed the performance of the S&P 500 and the S&P 500 Industrials, its closest benchmark index. Over the same period, AMETEK generated a 13% CAGR in free cash flow per share, highlighting a recurring theme across all the companies featured in this book: long-term shareholder performance increasingly reflects a company's fundamental strengths as duration increases. Remarkably, this growth occurred with a shrinking share count due to stock repurchases and while operating with a conservative balance sheet. For those who understood AMETEK's model, this success was no surprise; it stemmed from a company firmly grounded in its principles and unwaveringly dedicated to enhancing per-share value. This is rare among all companies, but common among the compounders.

AMETEK's journey from bankruptcy to becoming a high-performing, global industrial technology company is a story of resilience, course correction, and meritocracy. Every extraordinary ascent has a starting point—often rooted in unassuming beginnings. To truly understand AMETEK's remarkable rise, we must go back to where it all started.

From humming machines to precision instruments

American Machine and Metals began life as a patchwork—a maker of mining equipment, laundries, and fans—scrambling to survive economic uncertainty. By 1932, under the steady hand of Philip G. Mumford, the firm had posted its first profit, a milestone that marked the end of early struggles and the beginning of a cautious ascent. The New Deal's economic initiatives provided a much-needed tailwind, enabling the company to reinvest in itself. By 1935, the payment of dividends signaled a newfound stability. But that wasn't enough. The world was changing, and American Machine and Metals was too.

In the small town of East Moline, Illinois, the hum of machinery echoed through the halls of a factory that, at first glance, seemed unremarkable. But in 1941, with much of the world at war, this factory was to become the center of a revolution. The U.S. government sought partners that could quickly shift into producing essentials should it enter the second world war. American Machine and Metals answered the call. The East Moline facility became a hub of innovation, producing laundries for naval ships, fans for armored tanks, and later centrifuges that would contribute to the manufacturing of life-saving penicillin and sulfa drugs.[55]

By the war's end, the company's ambitions were clear: it would no longer settle for being a commodity producer of mundane products. In 1944, the firm acquired the U.S. Gauge Company for $3m—an important acquisition that would cement its place in the precision instruments market. Specializing in pressure and temperature gauges, U.S. Gauge wasn't just another acquisition. It marked a pivot from basic machinery to advanced technology. Over the following decades, U.S. Gauge became a cornerstone of AMETEK's operations, solidifying its leadership in precision measurement—with customers including the U.S. military, railroad companies, oil and gas drillers and refiners, heavy machinery makers, and chemical and process plants. This leadership persists over 80 years later.

The Frankenstein's lab

This move from basic to advanced technology has not ceased. Today, AMETEK specializes in the extraordinary. Its researchers are dedicated to pushing boundaries through innovation, turning the impossible into reality.

Imagine stepping into a laboratory straight out of a sci-fi thriller—a place where technology allows scientists to measure and analyze individual atoms within a semiconductor chip. That's precisely what AMETEK's CAMECA Tomographic Atom Probe can do. This machine is so precise and advanced that it could easily be mistaken for an invention from Frankenstein's lab. It enables researchers to peer into the building blocks of technology, helping to design faster, more efficient semiconductors—the components that drive our modern world.

Through its subsidiary Vision Research, the company developed the Phantom v710 camera, capable of capturing an astonishing 1.3 million frames per second. Phantom high-speed cameras are used in several applications including product development, biomedicine, combustion research, atomization, microfluidics, particle image velocimetry and more. They have, for instance, been used to investigate the combustibility of liquid oxygen to ensure the safety of first responders.

AMETEK's ingenuity extends beyond the lab—it is found in the most extreme real-world environments. Take the F-35 Joint Strike Fighter, the advanced, stealth-capable fighter aircraft developed primarily by Lockheed Martin for the United States and its allies. Flying this engineering marvel is no small feat, and conditions inside the cockpit can be grueling. To help pilots perform at their peak, AMETEK designed a cutting-edge cooling unit that circulates chilled liquid through a vest worn by the pilot. This system ensures the pilot remains cool, focused, and responsive, even in the most intense combat scenarios.

Birth of a superinvestor

In the mid-1950s, a defining moment unfolded at AMETEK's small headquarters. The company acquired Lamb Electric Motors—a manufacturer of electric motors primarily for vacuum cleaners—from American Securities for $34m. But in doing so, it acquired more than a firm. American Securities had been founded by Julius Rosenwald, former president of Sears, Roebuck and Co, the 19th-century mail-order catalog business that had been transformed into America's largest retailer under Rosenwald's stewardship. Rosenwald hadn't merely been a financier—he was a pioneer in modern private equity, and a believer in blending profitability with purpose. He developed not just successful companies but ambitious philanthropic endeavors, building more than 5,000 schools for black children across the segregated American South through his Rosenwald Fund. When Rosenwald's grandson, William Rosenwald, joined AMETEK's board following the Lamb acquisition, the stage was set for a transformative era. The Rosenwald philosophy would go on to influence AMETEK's growth strategy and philanthropic efforts for decades.

The impact of American Securities' involvement was immediate yet understated. With two board seats and a 20% ownership stake, the firm began subtly steering AMETEK toward a new mindset—a private equity mindset—while ensuring AMETEK remained true to its industrial roots. The idea was simple but revolutionary: acquisitions weren't to be just one-off deals but a strategic engine for reinvestment and growth. Initially a quiet undercurrent, this way of thinking grew steadily over the years.

By the late 1980s, the influence of this private equity mindset became formalized by the board under then CEO Walt Blankley's leadership. Acquisitions evolved from opportunistic deals into one of the four core growth strategies of the AMETEK Growth Model. They were now a process, not events.

Elizabeth Varet, Julius Rosenwald's granddaughter, served on AMETEK's board for over 30 years, ensuring that the values her grandfather instilled remained integral to AMETEK's governance. Upon her retirement, AMETEK created the Elizabeth R. Varet Sustainability Award to recognize her many important contributions to AMETEK's sustained success.

Since the early 2000s, AMETEK has pursued a disciplined campaign of acquisitions, typically focusing on companies with between \$30m and \$100m in revenue, targeting niche-market leaders with specialized technologies. As AMETEK has grown in size, so has the size of its acquisition targets. Over the years, AMETEK has completed close to 150 acquisitions and these have expanded its product portfolio and opened doors to new markets. The company's business leaders work closely with an in-house team of acquisitions specialists to continuously identify new acquisition opportunities. The goal is to strengthen AMETEK's position as a provider of highly differentiated technologies for mission-critical applications.

What began with a single acquisition in the 1950s has become an important part of the AMETEK Growth Model, providing a disciplined capital allocation framework. This guiding principle—acquire for growth and reinvestment rather than mere scale—has weathered market cycles and industry shifts, making the shareholders who invested in AMETEK profoundly wealthy. Lamb Electric, though no longer operating under its original name, still remains a small part of AMETEK today. AMETEK's presence in the vacuum cleaner market has diminished over time—but its evolution has unlocked greater opportunities.

The engine behind AMETEK's growth

A carefully crafted and consistently executed formula lies at the heart of AMETEK's journey: the AMETEK Growth Model. Well understood and practiced by its employees, it has been the driving force behind the company's long-term success.

The foundation for this approach was laid by Dr. Jon Lux, AMETEK CEO from 1966 to 1990, who introduced modern management methods, encouraging deeper engagement of leaders within teams and prioritizing continuous improvement. Dr. Lux was replaced as CEO by Walter Blankley, an engineer with 30 years' experience at AMETEK. Armed with a deep technical background and a thorough understanding of the company, Blankley envisioned a path for AMETEK that was ambitious yet sustainable: achieving double-digit annual earnings growth and superior returns on invested capital while continuously reinvesting in the company's core capabilities.

The AMETEK Growth Model was formalized under Blankley's leadership, emphasizing four foundational pillars:

1. operational excellence
2. new product development
3. global and market expansion
4. strategic acquisitions.

Throughout the 1990s, under Walt's leadership, AMETEK instilled the various elements of the Growth Model throughout the company with great success. Those four foundational pillars remain the same today—showing impressive strategic stability.

Following Walt's retirement in 1999, Frank Hermance was named CEO. Frank had joined AMETEK in 1990 to lead its modest but fast-growing instrumentation businesses. During his tenure as CEO, AMETEK transformed from a small industrial supplier into a global leader of high-tech engineering solutions, as the AMETEK Growth Model matured, delivering exceptional growth and shareholder returns.

Today, under CEO David Zapico, the legacy of Lux, Blankley and Hermance thrives. Organic revenue growth continues to climb, acquisitions further expand the company's reach, while operating performance and cash flow generation remain best in class. AMETEK's position as a leader in mission-critical, niche markets is impressive.

What sets AMETEK apart from many of its peers—and indeed, from several companies profiled in this book—is its strong focus on organic growth. Unlike companies that emphasize acquisitions as their primary growth lever, AMETEK has crafted a strategy in which acquisitions complement a steadfast commitment to organic growth. Three of the four pillars of the AMETEK Growth Model—operational excellence, new product development, and global and market expansion—underscore the company's focus on building from within. This deliberate reinvestment in its capabilities supports a sustainable, long-term innovation strategy.

Since 1955, revenues have compounded annually at a high-single digit rate with a mix of organic growth and acquisition growth. While historically this has been driven more by acquisitions, since David Zapico became CEO in 2016, organic revenue growth has averaged approximately 4% per year (2017–24). A focus on new product development and technology innovation is essential for this. Each year, the company reinvests about 5% of sales into research, development, and engineering, a notable figure that keeps AMETEK at the forefront of innovation. This investment fuels a strong pipeline of new, innovative products and technologies that help solve their customers' most complex challenges, with these new products consistently contributing around 25% of AMETEK's annual sales. For example, Gatan, an AMETEK business focused on electron microscope technology, introduced the EDAX Elite Ultra system. This system improved how researchers identify and measure elements in very thin samples, offering faster, more accurate results. Its larger sensor, developed with another AMETEK business, AMPTEK, enhanced detection capabilities and sped up analysis. The Elite Ultra is an example of Gatan's advanced tools for scientific research.

This is what the company calls its Vitality Index: the percentage of sales derived from new products launched within the last three years. It serves as a barometer of innovation. Since 2008, the index has shown a strong upward trend, rising from 18% to a record 27% at the end of 2024. This steady increase reflects AMETEK's R&D efforts, the strength of its engineering teams, and its ability to bring high-margin, mission-critical products to market.

Earning a special place in the value chain

In the world of industrial technology, the smallest components can have the largest impact. Take, for example, a temperature sensor supplied by AMETEK to a facility producing advanced aerospace components. Though its cost is small in the context of the overall system, its role is anything but minor. A failure in such a component could disrupt operations, delay production, and lead to costly setbacks. AMETEK's ability to deliver products that ensure reliability and precision is at the core of its value to customers.

AMETEK stands out in the manufacturing and industrial sectors, where profitability is often hard to achieve. Its two main operating groups, the Electronic Instruments Group (EIG) and the Electromechanical Group (EMG), are central to its success. EIG contributes nearly two thirds of total sales, with a focus on advanced instrumentation and solutions for industries including medical, semiconductor, power, and aerospace, maintaining outstanding operating margins of 30%. EMG complements this with the remaining third of total sales. It offers specialized solutions for automation, medical technologies, defense, and industrial applications, and boasts 25% operating margins.

AMETEK's largest end markets reflect its diversity as well as its focus on critical industries. Medical and healthcare account for just over 20%, followed closely by aerospace and defense, which represent slightly under 20%. Other key markets include power, research and automation (10% each), further diversifying the company's exposure and ensuring stability across different economic cycles. As CEO David Zapico explains, "AMETEK has earned a special place on its customers' value chains by providing essential solutions to help solve their challenging problems."

The diversified nature of AMETEK's various end-markets is a recurring theme in its success. While individual end-markets can often be cyclical, AMETEK's collective portfolio has demonstrated robust performance throughout economic cycles. When energy markets are struggling, medical or aerospace markets may be thriving. Importantly, AMETEK's proven operational excellence, global production footprint, and flexible and asset-light business structure allows it to successfully navigate challenging market dynamics.

Each of AMETEK's businesses sell many unique parts, amounting to thousands across the company. These components, while often relatively low in cost compared to the final products they support, are indispensable. This fosters strong, long-lasting customer relationships and significant pricing power. This loyalty, in turn, underpins predictable cash flows, so that AMETEK's business model functions effectively with minimal risk—a characteristic highly valued by the top-tier acquisition-driven compounders in this book.

For this model to succeed, acquisitions must predominantly be funded through self-generated cash flows. This demands high predictability and robust cash conversion, which AMETEK's asset-light operations consistently deliver. The company ensures a steady foundation for its growth with free cash flow to net income (or free cash flow conversion) exceeding 110%. However, to fully realize the potential of this model, acquisitions require rigorous discipline—a principle that will be examined later.

The black belts of AMETEK

In a bright conference room, a team huddle around a whiteboard, dissecting every step of a production process with surgical precision. A Black Belt, one of AMETEK's Lean and Six Sigma experts—specialists in eliminating waste (Lean) and reducing variation and defects (Six Sigma)—leads the charge. He is steering a week-long *kaizen* event to uncover inefficiencies and implement solutions. By week's end, the team's work will have yielded tangible results, small changes that will ripple throughout the organization. This kaizen process—the Japanese business philosophy of always seeking ways to do things better, simpler, smarter—is consistently practiced across AMETEK's businesses, and it drives continuous improvement and meaningful impact at scale.

A commitment to operational excellence has defined AMETEK's remarkable evolution. Over the past two decades, the company's operating margins have grown from 12% to 26%, fueled not by bold gambles but by disciplined execution and a culture of efficiency.

AMETEK embeds Lean and Six Sigma methodologies into its operations, not as isolated tools but as a cohesive strategy. Six Sigma practices, like Design for Six Sigma (DFSS), enhance product reliability and innovation, accelerate the introduction of new products, and eliminate waste. Black Belts lead these initiatives and mentor teams. Lean principles help streamline operations, optimize material flow, and strategically relocate production to cost-efficient locations. These methodologies also have a critical role to play in acquisitions. AMETEK has built a model that seamlessly aligns newly acquired companies with its high standards, creating compounding advantages from incremental gains.

AMETEK's journey demonstrates the power of small, consistent improvements driven across a distributed operating structure. The company has sustained growth by systematically driving efficiency improvements, eliminating waste, reducing defects, and refining processes while expanding its margins.

Global and market expansion

AMETEK has diversified its market and geographic presence to balance risk and capture global growth opportunities. With 50% of its revenue now derived from international markets, AMETEK has expanded its reach beyond the U.S. through acquisitions and targeted organic growth investments. This expansion is not about chasing trends but identifying the niche markets and applications where AMETEK's differentiated technology can provide meaningful value to customers. It is about embedding AMETEK's mission-critical products into attractive sectors such as power generation, aerospace, and medical technology, where long product cycles and recurring aftermarket sales create predictable cash flow streams. Today, aftermarket sales make up around 20% of AMETEK's total revenue, illustrating the strength of this approach in driving sustainable, organic growth.

Turning businessmen into deal makers

So far, in this book, we've seen that most companies embrace decentralized operations but centralize acquisition responsibility (albeit with a few exceptions or tweaks). Acquisitions are typically handled by a small, specialized team at the top, removed from day-to-day operations. AMETEK, however, utilizes a hybrid approach. Its business unit managers, who are closest to their markets, technology and strategy, play an important role in identifying and driving acquisitions, working closely with a dedicated team of corporate development professionals, with AMETEK's senior management then having final approval.

Over the past decade, AMETEK has reinvested approximately 75% of its free cash flow into acquisitions, following a bottom-up deal-sourcing approach that originates at the business unit level. By acquiring businesses that complement its existing offerings, AMETEK can integrate new technologies, expand its product lines, and increase its reach within key markets. This approach minimizes integration risks and ensures that acquisitions align with AMETEK's long-term strategic and financial objectives, providing a balanced path to growth and solid returns on invested capital.

As a result of this process, the acquisition pipeline is rich with targets with complementary product lines or niche businesses that can strengthen customer relationships. Every acquisition is closely tied to existing strategic objectives.

Aligned incentives, shared success

This strategy works because incentives are perfectly aligned. Managers are deeply invested in the success of their acquisitions. A successful deal means improved performance for their unit, directly impacting their compensation. Deals are not just theoretically strategic—they're operationally essential. Business unit managers bring unmatched insight into their industries. They understand their customers' needs, competitive dynamics in their markets, and the gaps acquisitions can fill. This proximity to the market allows them to spot opportunities that an entirely centralized M&A team might miss. It's a tactical advantage that has consistently fueled AMETEK's growth.

AMETEK's Ultra Precision Technologies division over the last 20 years shows this advantage at work. The acquisition of Taylor Hobson in 2004 provided the foundation for what is now a sizable precision measurement and metrology portfolio. Through targeted acquisitions and organic investments, AMETEK has strategically built out a $1bn+ platform.

AMETEK's acquisition model is a proven formula for long-term value creation. The company compounds growth over time by combining autonomy, accountability, and market insight. Each acquisition strengthens its portfolio, reinforcing its position as a disciplined and effective operator.

Leading small markets

A key theme among all the companies featured in this book is the mantra "small is good," and AMETEK is no exception. Instead of chasing sizeable total addressable markets, AMETEK focuses on niche markets of $200m–$300m in size, capturing a meaningful share in each. While these individual markets may seem small, together they form a strong, decentralized portfolio built for resilience.

What makes this approach so effective is its inherent defenses. Small markets are typically unattractive to larger competitors. Regulatory barriers in sectors like med-tech, aerospace, and power make entry difficult. Products in these industries are often "spec-ed in"—officially included in the specifications for a project, system, or product design—ensuring long-term customer loyalty. This stability aligns with AMETEK's strategy of prioritizing predictable cash flows over volatile, high-growth opportunities. Why is this so important? Because the growth model thrives on stable, recurring cash flow streams. It's not necessarily the fastest-growing prospects that matter, but stability. This is a deliberate choice that protects against competition and allows AMETEK to acquire niche companies at favorable terms, as fewer bidders target these regulated markets.

In other words, AMETEK's playbook is simple: develop a leadership position in small, defensible markets where AMETEK's businesses win based on the strength of their differentiated technologies. Be the #1 or #2 player. This strategy provides exceptional resilience in regulated sectors, where the stakes are high and disruption is minimal. Their products—highly engineered, mission-critical, and essential—become cornerstones for their customers.

Seeking regulatory barriers

In 2003, AMETEK took a further step into one of the most challenging and impenetrable markets: defense. They acquired Airtechnology, a supplier whose precision-engineered motors, fans, and environmental control systems were critical to military applications. These weren't products you could simply replicate in a garage—they cooled sensors and electronics, stabilized temperatures in armored vehicles, and protected soldiers from nuclear, biological, and chemical threats. Their functionality was mission-critical, their quality non-negotiable, and the regulatory oversight surrounding their production was formidable.

This combination—stringent requirements, niche applications, and sky-high barriers to entry—made the acquisition so appealing. For AMETEK, the regulatory burden wasn't a deterrent; it was an opportunity.

Another common theme across AMETEK's business units is the focus on regulated markets. By their very nature, these markets repel the unprepared and the unproven. They demand meticulous compliance, specialized expertise, and financial patience—qualities AMETEK has perfected over decades. The allure of these markets lies not just in their exclusivity but in the competitive moat they naturally create.

Consider Airtechnology. Its products exist in small, demanding markets where failure isn't an option. Military vehicles must endure extremes. Avionics cooling systems must perform without exception. In such settings, "close enough" doesn't cut it. AMETEK subsidiaries embed themselves in regulatory frameworks others shy away from. Once inside, these frameworks favor incumbents like AMETEK, discouraging new entrants whose cost-to-comply often outweighs the potential reward.

This dynamic delivers two core advantages. Would-be rivals are often daunted by the cost, complexity, and regulatory rigor of entering the market. And stability means that relationships aren't fleeting; sales cycles are longer, but so are the partnerships they create.

Looking across AMETEK's biggest end markets, we find pockets of highly regulated markets like process and analytical instruments, automated and engineered systems, electromechanical and aerospace and defense, power, industrial, and healthcare. Complex, defensible, and indispensable markets remain core to AMETEK's focus and success.

The tyranny of the P&L

There is a term whispered in the hallways of companies like AMETEK: "The Tyranny of the P&L." This phrase captures more than a focus on profit and loss; it embodies a culture where decentralization lives side by side with full P&L responsibility. Managers can run their own business units, but that freedom carries a sharp edge—a relentless emphasis on financial performance.

One AMETEK manager put it bluntly: "expectations are always clear, and there's little room for excuses."[56] Only those who thrive under pressure stick around in this environment. The culture here doesn't just tolerate stress; it thrives on it, selecting for high performers who see accountability as fuel, not a burden.

The tone for AMETEK's decentralized culture was set over half a century ago, in the 1960s, and it has remained steadfast ever since. As far back as 1968, AMETEK's annual report captured this spirit:

> "AMETEK's organizational structure allows for a high degree of divisional autonomy while enabling corporate management to provide guidance and support when needed for overall corporate growth. Divisional and group executives are granted broad responsibility to manage their respective units. This approach allows operating management to focus on increasing productivity, sales, and earnings."

However, at first glance, AMETEK's organizational structure seems similar to the rest of the acquisition-driven compounders featured in this book. The company has four group presidents, internally labeled as "mini CEOs," who manage roughly a quarter of the company each, overseeing a total of ten divisions. Below these divisions, the company has 40 business units, led by a general manager who has full P&L responsibility. This layered setup allows each unit to operate with significant autonomy, acting almost as a standalone business with the freedom to make decisions directly impacting its bottom line. Local decision-making is balanced with centralized oversight to drive long-term growth.

Where AMETEK's structure stands apart is in the trust-based concept of "mini P&Ls." Within the 40 business units, AMETEK implements "mini P&Ls" to develop leadership talent. These mini P&Ls typically blend two vital functions—marketing and operations, say, or engineering and production—providing a real-world setting where future leaders can sharpen their skills. With a pro forma P&L in hand, aspiring leaders are given the chance to manage a tangible business, building their financial savvy and honing their decision-making skills. It's like a dynamic training ground—a simulated yet realistic business environment—where they can gain crucial experience without the full burden of a major business unit. This approach allows AMETEK to spot leadership potential early and cultivate high performers ready to take on bigger, more impactful roles across the company. This is one of many subtle cues that explain the high-performing culture running through the veins of AMETEK, but also why it has been able to mostly recruit internally over the decades.

The expectation is clear: *run your business like it's yours.* As one former employee aptly put it, "It really is up to me."[57]

The autonomy that AMETEK grants its business units could be challenging for some. While general managers have control over day-to-day operations, they are held to high standards for performance. The company's corporate leadership maintains a strong grip on financial metrics, with each business unit required to deliver rolling 12-month forecasts. Profitability targets are ambitious, often exceeding 15% annually. This duality, a balance between decentralized autonomy and centralized control, doesn't fit everyone. This culture naturally selects for certain types of individuals—those who thrive on responsibility, independence, and relentless financial discipline. For others, the focus on strict targets can overshadow the creative freedom they might expect in a decentralized model.

Plow horses and meritocracy

AMETEK values substance over style; in its own words, "plow horses rather than show horses." It has a deep-rooted preference for meaningful work and steady commitment over superficial display. The company has had only four CEOs over 58 years. Delivering on commitments is essential, as is quickly reacting to changing market dynamics. Underperformance is addressed directly, and performance drives recognition. This results-driven environment attracts people inspired by accountability and committed to delivering consistent outcomes, just as decentralized companies attract business heads who want to prove themselves with full P&L responsibility.

Much of AMETEK's success stems from internal talent development. Here its decentralized structure once more comes to the fore. Business unit leaders actively participate in hiring and development decisions. There are clear pathways for advancement and a meritocratic culture.

The AMETEK University is particularly important when it comes to instilling the firm's culture, vision and operating model across the company. This is a three-day program developed by AMETEK's senior leadership team, offering participants an intensive, hands-on deep dive into AMETEK's history and culture, with sessions focused on each of the elements of the AMETEK Growth Model. These annual programs have proven invaluable in supporting AMETEK's growth and in preparing a new generation of leadership.

Depth over breadth

AMETEK's acquisition strategy is focused on strategically scaling its existing businesses, not on creating a wide array of standalone operations. Hence, acquired companies are typically integrated into relevant parts of AMETEK's structure to build depth. This helps the company avoid over-fragmentation—something many peers have faced after expanding into too many business units and product categories, only to later restructure to regain focus. Whether acquiring a $50m or $100m company, AMETEK typically seeks to integrate that business into an existing platform. Even as AMETEK doubled its sales from roughly $3.5bn to $7bn—in which time it acquired nearly 50 businesses—the number of AMETEK business units increased by only eight. As the company looks to double revenue again, it expects to do so with only a modest increase in business units.

Central to AMETEK's growth model is its "strategic adjacency" approach. When entering a new market, the company looks beyond the initial acquisition—identifying opportunities up and down the value chain, across similar industries, and in adjacent geographies. Each acquisition is guided by a detailed adjacency map that outlines future pathways for growth and integration.

According to AMETEK's CEO, David Zapico,[58] this strategy was shaped by studying others who scaled too broadly, becoming "a mile wide and an inch deep." AMETEK learned from those examples and chose a platform-based approach instead: buying similar businesses and combining them to strengthen existing platforms rather than pursuing diversification for its own sake.

Merging similar businesses also unlocks synergies. With experience, AMETEK has refined a reliable integration playbook—generating efficiencies while maintaining a decentralized structure where entrepreneurial autonomy can still thrive. Each deal is backed by a synergy plan that targets cost savings through global sourcing, facility consolidation, and factory-floor efficiencies and streamlined back-office functions. AMETEK also looks for opportunities in cross-selling, shared sales channels, and growth kaizens. The result is an integration model that creates long-term value—for AMETEK, its shareholders, and the businesses it acquires.

Take the acquisition of Zygo, for instance, a company known for its expertise in non-contact metrology (the science of measurement) and precision optics. Zygo is part of the Ultra Precision Technologies division noted earlier. While Zygo's technology was a valuable addition to AMETEK's precision measurement and metrology portfolio, it had not consistently delivered strong results under previous management. AMETEK saw an opportunity to bring its operational acumen to Zygo, using its own capabilities in sourcing and international distribution to elevate Zygo's performance. By embedding Zygo within its decentralized structure and applying the AMETEK Growth Model, AMETEK was able to improve efficiency and profitability, bringing Zygo's margins first in line with its own and now well above, and accelerating new product development. This integration process, refined over years of acquisitions, is a cornerstone of AMETEK's approach. Each new business gains access to AMETEK's infrastructure and resources while retaining the autonomy that allows it to remain close to its customers.

While other companies might struggle to balance decentralization with synergy—and often outright ignore it—AMETEK has achieved a rare equilibrium. Its structure empowers business units to operate independently, yet seamlessly integrates new acquisitions, adding value at every step.

In many companies, decentralization comes with a cost: lost synergies and sacrificed efficiency gains. However, AMETEK has found ways to maintain synergy across its distributed network. A central piece of this strategy is shared infrastructure. For example, AMETEK's international sales and service offices handle back-office functions, freeing individual business units to focus solely on sales, customer relationships, technology development and operations. Its global shared service centers perform a similar function. By centralizing these services, AMETEK enables its business units to operate with the speed and responsiveness of smaller companies, all while benefiting from the resources of a much larger organization.

Sourcing is another area where AMETEK leverages its scale to support decentralization. The company excels at sourcing globally from low-cost regions. New businesses with limited experience in cost-efficient sourcing can immediately tap into AMETEK's expertise, reducing operational costs and improving profitability. Again, subsidiaries are able to operate with the agility of a small company while reaping the benefits of a larger organization's resources. In other words, growing big by staying small.

Brewed from within: 58 years of leadership through four CEOs

Corporate leadership is often described as a revolving door, with CEOs cycling in and out. At AMETEK, however, leadership has a different rhythm. Over the last 58 years, the company has had just four CEOs. This remarkable consistency reflects more than careful succession planning—it embodies a philosophy of internal growth and cultural continuity. AMETEK's leaders have all been deeply rooted in the company before stepping into the top role. Long tenures aren't just common; they're expected. Around 75% of business unit managers have been promoted from within, fostering a leadership culture that combines deep technical expertise with an understanding of AMETEK's long-term strategies.

However, the decentralized model that defines its structure truly sets AMETEK apart. Real decision-making happens across over 40 business units, each led by a general manager who acts as a "mini-CEO." These general managers oversee strategy, operations, technology innovation and sales and marketing for their individual units. These business units are further organized within ten operating divisions, each managed by a division vice president. Four group presidents oversee these divisions, reporting directly to the CEO. This layered yet decentralized structure allows AMETEK to operate with agility while maintaining alignment. While the group presidents act as cultural carriers, setting the tone and ensuring alignment with AMETEK's overarching mission, the day-to-day decisions that drive growth and innovation are largely in the hands of the business unit P&L managers.

During the pivotal 58 years since the mid-1960s, the company has evolved. AMETEK looks very different in terms of its products, capabilities, and scale. But if you think about the core underlying strategies and capabilities, they've just been adjusted. This could only have been achieved with such cultural consistency and long tenures.

Each leader inherited not just a title but a legacy of cultural alignment and operational expertise. It's a system that prioritizes continuity over disruption, building on what works rather than chasing the next big trend. This rhythm of leadership is central to AMETEK's success. While its products, markets, and scale have evolved significantly, its underlying strategies and values have remained remarkably consistent. This consistency is no accident; it results from deliberate choices to promote from within, cultivating leaders who deeply understand AMETEK's culture.

AMETEK's leadership model demonstrates that sometimes the best way to ensure success is to look inward. By promoting from within and fostering long tenures, the company has built a leadership tradition that is both stable and forward-looking. Four CEOs in 58 years isn't just a statistic; it reflects a culture that values expertise, alignment, and trust.

It all boils down to culture

In 1968, AMETEK's annual report introduced an idea that would quietly shape the company for decades to come: decentralization and the value of divisional autonomy. There were no flashy announcements or grand proclamations—just a clear and confident belief that giving individual business units responsibility and independence would lead to lasting success. And it did.

Looking back at AMETEK's history, it's clear that its success is driven by more than just leadership. The company has seen remarkable stability at the top. But this success isn't defined by any single leader. These leaders have been cultural carriers—stewards of principles that empower the company's decentralized structure, where individual business units operate with trust, independence, and accountability to deliver results. This is the beauty of the high-performing acquisition-driven compounders featured in this book: from the outside, they can look confusing and complex, but in practice, they are ruthlessly rational and efficient, forming self-sustaining, compounding vehicles.

AMETEK's journey proves that sustainable success doesn't come from top-down directives or a single visionary leader. Instead, it flourishes in a culture where individuals are empowered, businesses are trusted to perform, and a robust capital allocation framework supports innovation. From its humble beginnings to its position today as a diversified, high-performing industrial conglomerate, AMETEK's strength comes from a system designed to foster autonomy, accountability, and thoughtful execution while thoughtfully course-correcting along the way.

At its core, AMETEK's success isn't about personalities—it's about principles and shared values. It is the beneficiary of a virtuous cycle. People shape culture; culture drives capital allocation; capital allocation fuels innovation and per-share value creation, those results attract and empower exceptional people. This cycle, sustained over decades, is the hallmark of companies like AMETEK—quiet achievers whose strength lies not in spectacle but in substance.

12

Discipline and Precision

Judges Scientific

AROUND TEN YEARS ago, on a typical grey London day, we struggled to find our way to the offices of a little-known company. We began to wonder if the firm had given us the right address. A glance at the maps on our phones said that we were on the spot, but there was no obvious sign of any office. Having spent considerable time walking around, we finally found our way to an old residential apartment block. The building looked like it was in dire need of refurbishment. After using the back stairs to get inside, our confusion deepened. Instead of a large and lofty office, dressed with stylish furniture, we were met by a small and unpretentious apartment that seemed to have space for only four people. And there was the CEO, David Cicurel, welcoming us with coffee he had himself brewed.

Although our first reaction was bewilderment, we quickly realized that this was a company that simply had no need to show off. It was prepared to show its value by the numbers and not by looks.

UK-based Judges Scientific remains relatively under the radar due to its small size (with a market capitalization of £500m at the time of publication), but in terms of generating shareholder wealth it stands among the elite. Since floating in 2003 at 95p per share, the company has compounded shareholder value over 100 times including dividends, translating to a 24% CAGR. What makes Judges Scientific particularly compelling is that it remains small yet has built a strong foundation for years of continued compounding. Its disciplined approach and focus—in this case, on scientific instruments—highlights how precision and patience can drive considerable shareholder returns.

Judges Scientific's focus is on acquiring niche, highly profitable instrument companies. Since its listing, the company has executed 25 acquisitions, steadily expanding its customer base across top universities, major consumer brands, and leading research institutions. Its capital allocation strategy—targeting small, founder-led businesses—makes it a standout among acquisition-driven compounders. Judges Scientific has become a formidable cash-generating machine, compounding shareholder value one acquisition at a time. David Cicurel puts it best: "We are not interested in the speed of acquisitions, but in the speed of value creation."

Buy cheap, generate cash, repeat

Judges Scientific was listed in 2003. Since then, it has acquired slightly more than one business every year. The company's long-term growth drivers include process optimization, which generates demand for highly engineered scientific instruments, and investments in higher education facilities by universities. The company has four main customer groups:

- top-tier universities such as Princeton, Oxford, Cambridge, and Harvard
- consumer companies such as L'Oréal and P&G
- camera producers like Leica and Nikon
- scientific organizations like Allen Institute and Thermo Fisher.

As a result, market demand is driven by growth in education and increased industrial needs for optimization and measurement.

The group's acquisition strategy is to acquire small and medium-sized scientific instrument manufacturers while "paying a disciplined multiple of earnings and to finance any acquisition, ideally, through existing cash resources and/or bank borrowings."[59]

As we have seen throughout this book, thoughtful game selection is crucial for how well the compounders can execute their strategy. There were three main reasons that made David Cicurel pursue a buy-and build approach, despite limited exposure to the industry.

First, the growing demand for scientific equipment, driven by expanding university research and the constant need for more advanced instruments in research and development. This created a strong foundation for long-term, secular growth. As Cicurel explained, "If you're in 1900 and you do a buy-and-build of makers of horse carriages, you can do a lot of deals and pay reasonable multiples, but 15 years later, you're out of business because cars take over."[60] For Judges, the long-term driver in scientific instruments—growth in university education—offered a future-proof sector with lasting potential, ensuring sustainable success.

Second, the sector's fragmentation—characterized by a large pool of small, often family-owned, niche companies—provided abundant opportunities for acquisition candidates, fitting seamlessly with Judges' buy-and-build strategy.

Third, the sector's inherent business attributes, with high levels of predictability and low capital requirements, aligned well with Judges' model, enabling high cash conversion—the key currency that drives their business model.

While the UK, a global leader in scientific instrument development and manufacturing, has proved the perfect base for Judges' ambitions, its portfolio is highly diversified geographically, with nearly 90% of revenues generated outside the UK. After Judges Scientific gets its hands on a company, it continues to thrive. A testament to this is that organic revenue and profit growth has averaged around 7% and 9% annually, respectively. Acquisitions have also significantly contributed to overall growth.

The architect David Cicurel

David Cicurel, aged 75, is the founder of Judges Scientific and still serves as its CEO. Under his leadership, management has focused on creating shareholder value by prioritizing profitability, cash generation, and return on capital. David has a long background as a turnaround specialist and value investor. Family and friends of Cicurel seeded the company's funding, and it started in late 2002 with something of an activist approach, buying small stakes in public companies. Today's strategy is very different.

The change began when the public investments ran into a problem. In 2003, Cicurel pointed out that the "increased ratings applied at present to small quoted companies are affecting our ability to acquire significant blocks of shares in target companies at suitable prices. This investment climate invites us to be selective and prudent."[61] By 2004, acquiring stakes in undervalued publicly traded companies had become even more challenging. Investor enthusiasm for small caps had driven the FTSE Small Cap Index up by 80% from its low point two years earlier, eroding the arbitrage opportunities between public and private valuations and significantly impacting Judges' future returns. The company's portfolio, known as "Judges Capital," held 2–3% stakes in several small listed companies.

Instead of continuing to invest in companies on the public market, David changed course. Wouldn't it be better, Cicurel wondered, to buy great companies in the private market that could be improved and owned forever—and that also came with lower price tags? The seed of today's Judges Scientific had been sewn. The way forward required adaptability and open-mindness, and David was on a mission to deploy all of his skills to take advantage of the opportunities. Judges Scientific began to transform.

Figure 12.1: Share price performance of Judges Scientific since 2005

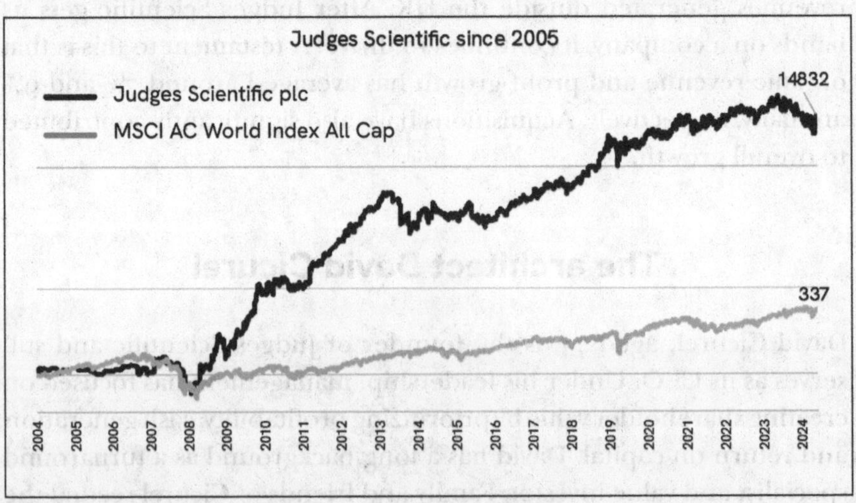

The pivot

The first signs of this new strategy emerged in 2005. Judges now began to acquire majority positions in small private companies instead of investing in public stocks. The first such acquisition was Fire Testing Technology Limited (FTT), a business manufacturing and servicing instruments that measure the reaction of different materials to fire and heat. Universities, technical institutes, and corporations like car and flight manufacturers were customers. These products must meet rigorous standards, as they are expected to perform reliably in extreme conditions. Such stringent requirements mean high regulatory barriers, and being able to meet them forms a strong competitive moat. As a result, the company enjoyed stable and predictable cash flows—ideal for reinvesting in similar businesses within the new Judges Scientific model.

Building on this, Cicurel decided to dispose of the quoted stock portfolio and focus on the instrument sector. He favored this sector as it was a large, global and fragmented market that consisted of small and highly niche manufacturers with attractive structural growth drivers. These companies often had monopoly-like positions in their respective niches, enjoyed generous margins, and boasted strong cash generation due to their asset-light nature. Thanks to the fragmented nature of the market, they often came with attractive price tags. For a value investor like David Cicurel, it was the ultimate opportunity.

The FTT team consisted of 19 employees and a founder who was 58 years of age and seeking a controlled succession for his company. With sales of $3m and 25% EBIT margins,[62] the acquisition ticked all the criteria Judges set. This acquisition not only established the tone for the company's shift in focus—it also revealed how Judges would come to approach its deals. David Cicurel saw these acquisitions as long-term partnerships. He personally went to meet the owner of FTT to introduce himself. The personal approach would come to win many deals for Judges in the future.

By late 2005, the company had begun to show what Judges Scientific would become, though it was still too soon to assess the new strategy's success. At this point, Judges had acquired two more companies, and its remaining public portfolio was being liquidated.

The same year, the company reported its first year of profit, and announced the acquisition of PE Fiberoptics, a leading provider of specialized equipment for testing the properties of fiber optic networks. Soon after, in 2006, the company acquired UHV Design, which designed and manufactured instruments capable of manipulating objects in ultra-high-vacuum chambers.

At the time, a potential investor in Judges would have had limited insight into the new strategy's success, and just one positive data point regarding underlying profits. In retrospect, it is easy to see the foundations of its success coming together—but for any potential investor looking at Judges Scientific in real-time, triumph was by no means obvious or inevitable.

In the following years, Judges Scientific finalized the phase out of its listed equity portfolio and made no new acquisitions. By 2008, the company had raised £479,000 through fresh equity at 110p per share in order to pursue acquisitions. However, a major acquisition was abruptly canceled late in the day due to the Global Financial Crisis. The impact was significant—£310,000 in acquisition-related costs, almost 25% of operating profit, had to be written off. For investors, those early days were doubtful. With just a handful of years of financial performance to assess, an unproven strategy, an equity issue, and a failed acquisition write-off, it was difficult to be sure of the direction in which Judges was heading.

Starting to execute

In 2009, things took a sharp turn. Judges Capital rebranded to Judges Scientific, marking the final shift in strategy, and David Cicurel seized the opportunity to acquire Quorum Technologies, a company specializing in sample preparation instruments for electron microscopes. The instruments were vital for disease research, food safety, and the development of advanced technologies and materials. The acquisition quickly proved successful. Two years after it was completed, operating profit had increased by 10%; three years later it had doubled. His confidence boosted by the Quorom acquisition, Cicurel went on to make additional acquisitions in 2010 and 2011. He targeted niche companies in gas purification and electron microscope production. Suddenly, the company's disciplined approach to acquisitions bore fruit. By 2010, return on total capital was a strong 45%. What had once been an unproven strategy was emerging as a powerful engine for growth. Though Judges was still early in its journey, investors started to recognize that it had unlocked the potential for significant future success.

A significant milestone for Judges Scientific came in 2012 when the company acquired Global Digital Systems Limited (GDS) for approximately six times its earnings. GDS specialized in selling instruments for testing the physical properties of soil and rocks, generating $1.3m in operating profit. This acquisition was substantial for Judges, accounting for nearly a third of the group's total earnings. Given the success of its previous acquisitions, David Cicurel approached the deal with confidence.

In the same year, the company launched its first Share Incentive Plan (SIP) to enable employees with a minimum of 12 months of service to acquire shares. The share incentive plan has successfully contributed to employees working in the best interests of both the company and shareholders. Today, almost a third of employees own shares in Judges.

Over the next two years, the company continued to execute both standalone and bolt-on acquisitions through its existing portfolio companies. The company developed growing confidence in not only the "buy" part of its buy-and-build model but also the "build" part. As the companies it acquires are already strong in their niches, Judges typically helps to amplify that strength by building a strong sales organization and putting more resources into R&D. Acquired companies have typically been founded and led by a scientist who has solved a problem by inventing a machine. Judges is able to help commercialize and expand their product range. A good example of this is Teer Coatings, which was acquired in 2021. Teer Coatings specializes in advanced coating systems for a range of sectors like motorsport, aerospace and medical devices. The coating systems enhance the properties of the underlying material. Judges has supported the company in expanding its product portfolio and establishing a stronger international presence. Bolstered by early success, in 2013 Judges went on to make its most significant acquisition yet, when it acquired Scientifica, a leading specialist in designing and manufacturing systems used in neuroscience research. Once again, Cicurel demonstrated his capacity for finding and acquiring companies at attractive returns: Scientifica was acquired for only six times operating profit.

Cicurel had always envisioned Judges Scientific as a self-funded company. However, it had yet to reach the scale necessary to rely solely on self-generated cash flow. To support its expansion, the company carried out an £8m equity issue in 2013 at 1625p per share, taking advantage of the attractions of its growing, diversified asset base and strong financial performance. Investor confidence in Judges' strategy was evident, and the share subscription was significantly oversubscribed. This successful capital raise marked a turning point. Ever since, Judges has not relied on external equity to fund acquisitions, thereby preventing the dilution of what David Cicurel refers to as "our precious shares," a sentiment shared by all the eight other compounders featured in this book, all of which emphasize a per-share value creation mindset.

While Judges had performed well for almost eight years, 2014 proved to be a challenging year. Tight public budgets and a slowdown in China, among other factors, reduced spending in key markets. With the majority of Judges' customers relying on public funding, this led to an 18% drop in earnings per share. Despite the challenges, Judges protected its cash flow and managed to increase operating cash flow by 55% by reducing working capital and capital expenditure. Thanks to generating such strong cash flow, despite a tough market environment, Judges was able to acquire two companies in 2015—Armfield and CoolLED. Both acquisitions were conducted at attractive multiples of around five times operating earnings, implying day one returns of 20%, way above the cost of capital of around 10%.

Even though David Cicurel has always been the architect of Judges, he has been supported by a strong team. One key figure has been Judges' initial group finance director, Ralph Cohen. After a decade of service, Cohen retired in 2015, leaving an impressive legacy. Under his financial leadership, Judges saw a 25-fold increase in market value—from £4m to £100m in just a decade. He was succeeded by Brad Ormsby, who has since played a vital role in the company's ongoing success.

In 2015, the company reached another milestone. Judges had now cumulatively distributed dividends greater than its original share price (113p cumulative dividends per share, versus a flotation price of 95p). This was a true validation of its strategy, dramatic proof it could grow profitably while also returning cash to its shareholders.

The holy grail: ROTIC (return on total invested capital)

When David Cicurel first laid out the plan for Judges' new strategy, there was one guiding principle that he put above all others: generating strong returns on capital. In David's mind, if he could borrow money between 3% and 6%, buy companies at 5× EBIT (yielding a 20% return), and make sure that most of that return was in the form of cash flow, he would have a great business model. To generate attractive returns on capital, disciplined capital allocation and strong cash flow generation were essential. By ensuring a large portion of profits was converted into cash, there was no need to issue shares. This approach aligned with his strongly held belief that shares were highly precious, particularly because he believed that Judges would produce very high returns on capital, making the opportunity cost of issuing shares exceptionally high. Central to the strategy was focusing on what Judges called "ROTIC" (return on total invested capital). ROTIC is calculated monthly at both the group and subsidiary levels, factoring in non-amortized intangible assets and goodwill. Cicurel rejected the use of traditional ROCE, arguing that returns should be measured against the actual capital invested, not against depreciated asset values.[63]

Cicurel views ROCE as primarily an accounting construct that doesn't accurately reflect economic reality. As he explains, you can't measure the return on something that is, in essence, an accounting fiction—particularly when assets have been amortized. For Cicurel, the key is ensuring a return on the actual money invested, rather than relying on a metric that doesn't capture the true economic performance of the business. Cicurel outlined a clear plan for achieving high returns, which included rigorous financial monitoring of each subsidiary: tracking sales trends, operating margins, and cash flow generation, and clear incentives for each company regarding growth in EBIT and use of working capital. The results of these initiatives were quickly evident, as cash generation continued to improve throughout the years—serving the company especially well when it struggled in 2014.

While many companies set financial targets, they rarely emphasize them during challenging times. Judges Scientific takes a different approach. In 2016, Judges Scientific's ROTIC dropped from 24% to

15% as a consequence both of acquisitions and three underperforming companies. Rather than downplaying the decline, David Cicurel candidly acknowledged it as "disappointing." Despite the setback, he reaffirmed his confidence in Judges' strategy:

> "[W]hilst we had a positive year for acquisitions but a disappointing year for performance, [Judges] remains well placed to continue with its enduring strategy of achieving growth in earnings via selective acquisitions of strong niche businesses in the scientific instruments sector, alongside the ongoing performance of its existing businesses."

In 2017, two of the struggling businesses recovered as demand returned. In the third struggling business, Judges Scientific had to undertake radical changes, including a change of management to cope with production and supply chain issues. This, in combination with good performance in most of the businesses, helped improve ROTIC to above 20% by the end of the year.

Cicurel's communication made it clear that ROTIC is the company's guiding star. Regardless of whether ROTIC rises or falls, he consistently highlights its importance in annual reports. Given Judges' acquisition-driven growth model, short-term dips in returns are not uncommon, and Cicurel ensures shareholders understand this dynamic through clear and transparent reporting.

Building, not just buying

An important part of Judges' value creation has been its "buy-and-build" program. Judges does not simply buy profitable companies, but selects acquisitions with the potential for attractive long-term growth—growth that Judges can help unlock.

To be interesting for Judges, a potential acquisition should demonstrate sustainable sales and profits, coupled with strong cash generation. Judges promotes a culture of creating "inventions that ship"—innovative products with strong commercial appeal. To maintain focus, subsidiaries are encouraged to prioritize only the top two or three projects at a time, rather than spreading resources too thin. Additionally, they should avoid single-client projects unless the product has broader market potential. Operating in the scientific instrument sector, it will also be in a resilient market that boasts long-term growth drivers, such as the global expansion of higher education and industrial need for greater optimization. More than two thirds of Judges' clients are public sector clients, who are less influenced by cyclicality and where the annual budgets set the tone for orders. Switching costs are high since it is a risk to start using a new instrument. Therefore, many of the products offered by Judges Scientific can be seen as non-discretionary items.

The need for a strong COO

As Judges grew, David Cicurel realized something was missing.[64] His epiphany came after reading *The Outsiders* by William Thorndike on a trip to Berkshire Hathaway's annual shareholder meeting in Omaha. One key lesson of Thorndike's study of great capital allocators is the importance of having a COO to oversee acquired businesses. Acquired companies need coaching and a speaking partner. A senior COO would free up time for David to continue to meet and acquire companies. But Judges didn't have one.

Cicurel looked for his experienced COO in the most logical place: within the most successful life science acquisition-driven compounder in the UK, a company called Halma. Halma had long been a role model for Cicurel, and in 2017 Cicurel persuaded its then COO, Mark Levelle, to join Judges in the same role. Levelle brought invaluable experience with him.

Most importantly, Lavelle instilled a mindset of constant improvement and operational excellence. While Judges does not micromanage its companies, the COO fills an important role as support to subsidiaries. To keep bureaucratic creep at bay, instead of interfering in daily work the COO has monthly meetings with managing directors. This frees up time for group management to focus on strategic priorities. Meanwhile, group management makes sure to stay informed by interacting with the subsidiaries every quarter. All managing directors have to take accountability and be the champions of their companies. A prime example of this is the budgeting process. Budgets are always set by the managing directors, not the parent company, and the MDs bear full responsibility for the targets set. Top management challenges the subsidiary companies on budgets and holds them accountable. The minimum commitment and expectation is to deliver on the budget. Excess cash flow from subsidiaries is sent to central headquarters. Therefore, any larger capex project must be funded by the central team. All in all, this creates an accountability culture and a cash focus among subsidiary companies.

The cash conversion of Judges is strong, partly due to a structural element of playing in the field of scientific instruments. Judges is more of an assembler of instruments than a manufacturer with big production lines. The products shipped by the company are typically low-volume and capital-efficient, requiring minimal capital expenditures. Additionally, the high cash conversion is partly due to the frugal mindset cultivated by the founders of the subsidiaries. These founders are accustomed to innovating with limited cash resources and maintaining low levels of working capital

Winning the hearts of entrepreneurs

Since its strategic pivot in 2005, Judges Scientific has created significant value for shareholders through a disciplined capital allocation strategy. Judges simply does not pursue acquisitions if their criteria of quality and price are not met. Acquisitions must have a sustainable profit growth and convert most of its profit to cash. When acquiring a new company Judges has the ambitious goal of doubling the size of the subsidiary within 3–5 years. Judges has successfully managed to only pay between three to six times operating profit for its acquisitions, depending on company size.

Equally crucial to Judges Scientific's acquisition strategy is ensuring a strong cultural fit between the group and the companies it acquires. One of Judges' true strengths lies in its ability to attract like-minded entrepreneurs ready to sell their businesses. Interestingly, Judges Scientific is often not the highest bidder. However, winning an acquisition is about more than just offering the highest price—it is about mutual understanding and trust. David Cicurel has mastered the art of speaking the entrepreneur's language, and making sure the entrepreneur understands that Judges wants to keep its name, brand, employees and culture. Judges does not buy companies in order to change or flip them, and this gives them an edge in securing deals.

When David Cicurel founded Judges Scientific, he firmly believed that earning the trust of entrepreneurs looking to sell their life's work required a confident and respectful approach to deals. To him, a handshake agreement held as much value as a signed contract. To gain an edge over competitors, he always secured financing before initiating negotiations. This allowed him to uphold agreed terms with sellers, vendors, and employees, earning him respect and a reputation as a preferred buyer. Similar to Warren Buffett, he reassured sellers that he would not interfere with the companies post-acquisition, as long as they continued to perform well.

Never bet the farm

Judges Scientific's approach to risk mirrors David Cicurel's frugal and risk-averse personality. He only takes decisions that will benefit shareholders in the long term. As a result, leverage is modest, with net debt to EBITDA usually below 2.5×. By growing the free cash flow per share by annually 22%, he has proven that long-term value creation is not equivalent to maximizing short-term profits and taking high financial risk.

David Cicurel is building Judges as a long-term industrial owner. He is not interested in playing financial games to exploit a short-term arbitrage between private and public market multiples. Cicurel points out that Judges does not seek a private/public arbitrage since the company does not like to issue shares—even though it did raise capital as a young company. Instead, Cicurel puts a high value on attracting long-term shareholders and not diluting them with additional equity raises. He seeks the arbitrage of being able to do good deals at attractive returns that exceed the cost of capital. As he puts it:

> "If we pay 2.7% to the bank and we get 25% return on our money and almost 100% cash return from cash conversion, the numbers are quite easy."[65]

As the group has expanded and profits have increased, it has efficiently paid down acquisition debt, creating room for future investments. This disciplined cycle of acquiring, generating returns, and reinvesting—always with a cautious eye on debt—has allowed

Judges to grow steadily while keeping shareholder interests at the heart of its strategy.

The primary use of capital has been directed towards acquisitions, which have been highly accretive for the shareholders, while a limited part has been towards organic investments in its companies (net working capital and capital expenditure). The first dividend was paid in 2006, and dividends have since grown at a compound annual rate of 22.9%. The cash flow generation in Judges Scientific has been so strong that the dividends distributed have aggregated to six times the initial market capitalization at the time of its initial public offering.

Like many other successful acquisition-driven compounders featured in this book, Judges Scientific has been able to grow its profits and generate significant shareholder value despite paying dividends. The focus on strong cash flow and a mostly self-funded approach to acquisitions makes for a low-risk growth strategy. Could they have expanded more quickly by forgoing dividends, using more debt, and directing more funds into an accelerated acquisition program? Certainly—but its chosen disciplined approach has made sense from a risk perspective.

Trusting local knowledge

The model is simple. Do not interfere daily with local managing directors. These managers know their niches, and group management's role is not to dictate direction. Every acquisition should provide a return without Judges Scientific exploiting synergies between companies. David Cicurel often says that Judges Scientific only owns "a fleet of companies" while his managing directors are the captains of their ships. "We do not tell the companies what to do."[66]

A company's true strength is revealed when it faces a real test. For Judges Scientific, the ultimate test of its decentralized culture came during the COVID-19 pandemic. While many corporations responded with top-down directives and rigid guidelines, Judges took a different approach. Rather than interfering, the company trusted its local leadership to make the best decisions for their teams, offering support instead of control. Despite profits declining by 17% in 2020, from £17.4m to £14.4m, they quickly rebounded by 34% in 2021 to £18.8m. But more importantly than emerging as a financially stronger company, the pandemic strengthened internal bonds and built personal connections that set a solid foundation for future growth prospects. In the short run Judges has been hit by weak order intake due to more uncertainty among funding at universities, reductions in orders from China and weak activity within one of its recent acquisitions, the Geotek coring business. This has led to falling profits and pressure on the share price. In similar weak periods for the company a pattern emerges: the company generates strong cash flow which is used to acquire companies. In 2024 the company took advantage of weak end markets and acquired a record number of three companies: Luicol, Rockwash and Teer Coatings.

In a culture that empowers and promotes local champions, leaders feel valued. This has been one of the key factors behind Judges' ability to find and nurture leaders who flourish under accountability and a high degree of managerial responsibility. Its leadership program has also been key. Being a niche player in the scientific instrumental space means that many of the companies Judges acquires have roots in the industry. Such companies are usually run by managers with deep technical knowledge, often with an engineering background. However, over the years Judges Scientific has realized that the most effective leaders are not necessarily those with the most technical expertise. Leadership skills and an entrepreneurial mindset are more important. Because the individual companies are often very entrepreneurial and frugal in their approach, it is crucial to maintain the same culture. Leaders of each company need the ability to develop people and products and bring new insights to the group as a whole.

For local autonomy to work in practice, Judges has had to sacrifice synergies for entrepreneurship. Instead of driving synergies, Judges encourages collaboration between companies, offering them a suite of possible opportunities. This can include market expansion plans, setting up of common locations, or simple administrative functions like common accounting services. As a perpetual owner, Judges provides a favorable environment for its businesses. The only requirement is that the subsidiaries regularly report to the head office on progress. In addition to tracking profit and loss, the balance sheet, and cash flows, the senior management team at Judges Scientific places the highest priority on closely monitoring order intake. They consider this metric the most reliable indicator of how their companies are performing and progressing.

This decentralized approach encourages agility. Each business can adapt to market conditions without waiting for approval from a central authority. It also helps subsidiaries remain competitive in niche markets where innovation and speed are crucial. Lastly, it allows the subsidiaries to retain their unique culture and specialized knowledge, which are often integral to their success. Instead of enforcing a uniform corporate identity, Judges preserves the individuality of each company, helping them maintain strong customer relationships and industry reputation.

Capital allocation at the center

While Judges Scientific operates with a fully decentralized approach to day-to-day operations, it maintains centralized control over capital allocation. This choice is deliberate, allowing the company to leverage the operational expertise of its managing directors while ensuring disciplined financial decision-making. Judges Scientific believes that, for the best results, managing directors should focus on what they do best: growing their businesses. Therefore, big capex projects are removed from the scope of the subsidiaries.

Judges sets its subsidiaries the ambitious goal of growing their companies organically by 10% annually, while generating strong cash flow. This is no easy task. To achieve this, managing directors need to focus all of their efforts on this target. Meanwhile, Judges Scientific encourages its leadership to remain alert to acquisition opportunities. Occasionally, a lead will come from its directors (though most acquisitions are handled centrally by senior management).

Avoid change for the sake of change

David Cicurel has built a truly unique culture at Judges. It is marked by passion for the company; people don't quit, they retire. Three of the original four board members of Judges Scientific are still active on the board. Among them is Ralph Cohen, who was finance director until he retired in 2015. The board at Judges is unlike any other board—it is the "guardian of our culture that does not police us."[67]

David has no official plan for retirement. The broad management team of Judges today makes it possible for David to do only what he does best—dealmaking. David has managed to keep the atmosphere of a small company despite of having more than 800 people in the group. When describing the culture with one word, David chooses "respect."

The most significant risk to Judges is change for the sake of change. Chairman Alexander Hambro, active in the private equity and venture capital sectors for over 30 years, has served as chairman since 2003. The CFO, Brad Ormsby, joined Judges Scientific in 2015, and Mark Lavelle, the COO, joined Judges Scientific in 2017, having spent almost 15 years at Halma. The management team's seniority, experience, and track record are invaluable.

David Cicurel has always believed that a company thrives when its people feel like true owners. From the beginning, Judges was built on a premise that embraced both shared success and shared setbacks. If employees and management were to treat the company as their own, they needed to have real ownership. Today, the management team owns 15% of Judges Scientific, with David himself holding 12%. Judges Scientific actively encourages its staff to invest, believing that when people have a stake in the business, they think and act differently. They take pride in their work, celebrate victories more passionately, and tackle challenges with a greater sense of responsibility.

For Judges, ownership isn't just about shares—it's about mindset. It's about creating an environment where every employee feels empowered to contribute to the company's long-term success.

Key lessons for investors

Judges Scientific is a successful example of a company that changed its strategy to become a highly successful acquisition-driven compounder. The recipe for success has been a disciplined acquisition strategy, a clear focus on return on capital, a decentralized business model, and an ownership mentality. Despite its success, the company is still small and has a long runway of growth opportunities.

Early on, Judges Scientific identified scientific instruments as an ideal market—capitalizing on structural growth in university education, abundant acquisition opportunities, and strong cash flow dynamics. These characteristics are crucial for executing a low-risk, value-accretive growth strategy. Additionally, many businesses in this subsector have untapped potential in commercialization and product expansion, aligning perfectly with Judges' strategy to acquire, develop, and enhance companies. David Cicurel chose to play in a field with structural tailwinds, a large deal pool, and low capital intensity—and where opportunity for growth abounds.

Another key insight for investors is the distinct capital allocation framework of the company. Cicurel's approach to value creation, where he compares the cash return on capital to the interest rates on loans, is both straightforward and impactful

A recurring theme throughout the book, shared by Judges, is a growth model that emphasizes disciplined pacing in acquisitions and focuses on genuine value creation rather than financial engineering. The emphasis is on real cash returns, not just growing earnings for growth's sake. This mindset aligns with the ethos of other companies in the book, all of which understand that without sufficient cash generation and paying sensible prices for targets, the model will lose momentum and rely on excessive leverage, share issues and financial engineering. Together, these principles create a low-risk cushion in the growth model, contributing to long-term growth and the compounding effects we've seen across the companies in this book.

Lastly, a further important consideration for long-term investors is that there's no need to rush into buying a stock immediately—there's time to observe how a company's strategy unfolds. Even if you had waited seven or eight years after the early days of Judges Scientific in 2005, investing in 2012 or 2013 would still have resulted in significant returns. An investor can buy "late" and still achieve strong shareholder returns. In fact, such "late" investors would have seen their capital grow nearly tenfold.

13

The Price Question

What should you pay for exceptional companies?

ALL OF THE compounders featured in this book are exceptional in terms of creating shareholder value. This prompts the question of what constitutes a fair price for a high-quality business that can reinvest its cash flows and generate strong incremental returns on capital over the long term.

Shareholder value is created when a company grows with a return on capital that exceeds its cost of capital. In essence, a company creates real value when it generates more dollars on its investments than the cost of capital for that investment. The compounders discussed in this book stand out because they can reinvest capital at rates well above their cost of capital. By contrast, companies that grow at 0% or fail to earn returns above their cost of capital do not create value. With that principle in mind, let's explore what an investor can justify paying for businesses that are able to deploy incremental capital at varying rates of return—provided those returns meet or exceed the cost of capital.

The table below illustrates the premium—over the market multiple—that an investor should be willing to pay for a company with varying returns on capital and growth prospects, relative to a baseline company with no growth opportunities or one earning exactly its cost of capital (assumed here to be 9.5%). For practical purposes, this baseline represents "the market."

Figure 13.1: The premium to pay

		Return on Capital				
		9.5%	**12%**	**16%**	**18%**	**22%**
	5%	0%	24%	46%	52%	64%
Growth	**6%**	0%	36%	70%	81%	98%
	8%	0%	111%	217%	252%	304%

When a company grows at an incremental return on capital equal to its cost of capital (9.5%), that growth creates no additional value—this is reflected in the first column of the table. However, if a company earns a 16% return on incremental capital and grows at 5% per year, an investor could justify paying a 46% premium over a no-growth business. At the higher end, a company generating a 22% return on capital and growing at 8% annually could be worth four times as much as a company with no growth.

What's striking is how powerful growth becomes when returns on capital are high. For example, increasing the growth rate from 5% to 8% in a business with strong returns can multiply its intrinsic value significantly. In such cases, a CEO overseeing a company with an 18% return on capital should prioritize finding opportunities to reinvest and grow, rather than focusing solely on further improving profitability.

Short run vs. long run

Exceptional companies are often worth far more than they initially appear. As a long-term investor in high-quality businesses, you must become comfortable holding stocks that may not seem cheap based on short-term valuation multiples. The power of compounding reveals itself only over time—and often, only after many years. While the businesses profiled in this book may have appeared overvalued in the short run, they have frequently been undervalued when viewed through a long-term lens.

Valuation multiples certainly influence long-term returns, but the primary focus should be on assessing a company's ability to reinvest capital at high rates of return. The next chart illustrates what price-to-earnings (P/E) multiples can be justified while still achieving a solid long-term return of 8% per year. It factors in varying reinvestment rates, return on equity (ROE), and a 20-year investment horizon.

As the data shows, the market often underestimates the true long-term value of companies capable of reinvesting 80% of their earnings at ROEs above 20% over long periods, These are the kinds of businesses where paying optically expensive multiples today can still lead to extraordinary outcomes over time.

Figure 13.2: Fair P/E for various investment rates and returns on equity

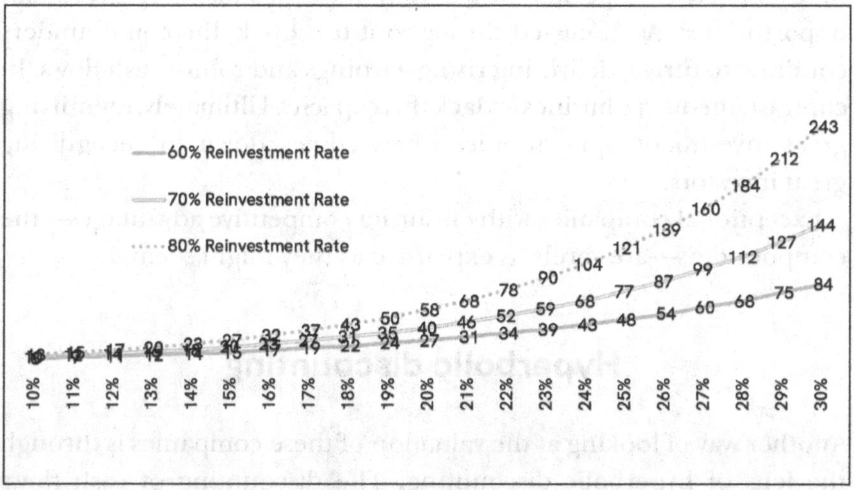

Successful long-term investing ultimately hinges on a few key factors: the durability of reinvestment opportunities, consistently high returns on capital, and strong confidence that those reinvestments can continue for many years. The analysis presented here demonstrates that when these elements align, the price one can reasonably pay for a stock is often much higher than conventional thinking would suggest.

What truly matters is investing in companies that are not only strong today but are positioned to become even stronger over the next 10 to 15 years. In such cases, traditional valuation models can appear almost irrelevant. Instead, the focus should shift toward identifying businesses with durable competitive advantages, sustainable reinvestment potential, and the capacity to strengthen their market position over time. When these qualities are present, the long-term power of compounding far outweighs short-term valuation concerns.

These calculations underscore an important principle: it is better to make a mistake in valuing a business than in judging its quality. Another critical insight is that selling shares solely on the basis of valuation is often a mistake. Investors frequently overestimate the value of short-term growth while underappreciating the significance of long-term durability. It is far wiser to own a business that can compound earnings at a steady 6% annually for decades than one experiencing rapid but short-lived growth followed by significant troubles.

The fair value of truly exceptional businesses may be higher than expected—especially when they have profitable reinvestment opportunities. As discussed throughout this book, the compounders continue to thrive, delivering rising earnings and robust cash flows. In contrast, mediocre businesses lack this capacity. Ultimately, identifying great investment opportunities often comes down to recognizing great investors.

Exceptional companies with enduring competitive advantages—the compounders—are rarely as expensive as they might seem.

Hyperbolic discounting

Another way of looking at the valuation of these companies is through the lens of hyperbolic discounting. The discounting of cash flows in the dividend discount model is discounted using exponential discounting. This discounting method is the standard method for discounting cash flows. Many know it by heart from business school exams. Most investors have only learned about this model. But what does this way of discounting cash flows mean, and is it the right way to discount them?

Exponential discounting is "time-insensitive," meaning that you have the same relative decline in the discount factor as time passes. It is the rational way to look at finance and valuation. Consequently, cash flows that are far in the future are not worth much under exponential discounting.

Behavioral studies however show that humans do not act as

traditional economic theory claims. We are not rational. Our way of discounting as humans is very much time-sensitive. In other words, we use different discount rates depending on how long it takes to get a payoff.

Consider the following two examples.

1. You can choose between receiving $100 today or $110 in one year. In experiments, people strongly tend to choose $100 today to get instant gratification.
2. You can choose between receiving $100 in ten years or $110 in 11 years. In this situation, people tend to be willing to wait an extra year to get $110. Since instant gratification is not there anyway, we act more rationally and think we can wait until year 11 instead of receiving the payout in year 10. It is so far into the future.

The challenge in example 2, in which you decided to wait 11 years, is that when you approach year 10, you would rather get the instant gratification of $100 than wait another year. In other words, people avoid waiting the closer they get to the end of the waiting period.

In the short term, people are irrational, but in the longer term, people choose the rational option.

The basis for the hyperbolic discounting model is human behavior. The pattern of how people choose as time goes on follows a "hyperbola." People do not appear to use a constant discount rate as exponential discounting purports to do. In economics, hyperbolic discounting is a time-inconsistent model of discounting. People make decisions much more similar to hyperbolic discounting than exponential discounting.

In hyperbolic discounting, valuations fall very quickly for periods close to the present because we want instant gratification, but they fall slowly for longer deferred periods. The hyperbolic model discounts more than the exponential model at the beginning and less than the exponential model for very long-term events.

Hyperbolic discounting states that discount rates are greater in the short term than in the long term. What does all this have to do with finance and the valuation of companies?

In the hyperbolic formula, the present value of short-term cash flows is lower than in the exponential model. However, the present value of longer-term cash flows is higher than in the exponential model. Consequently, the terminal value in hyperbolic discounting for companies with durable competitive advantages, like the companies in this book, will be higher than in the model we know from business school.

There are several mathematical forms of the hyperbolic discounting function, but we won't delve into them here. Instead, we'll simplify the concept using a practical example: a 20-year cash flow in which the discount factor declines over time. The falling discount factor reflects how experiments point to how humans make tradeoffs, represented by the hyperbola. The resulting chart shows the discount rates using the exponential function and a hyperbolic assumption.

Figure 13.3: Hyperbolic vs exponential discounting in action

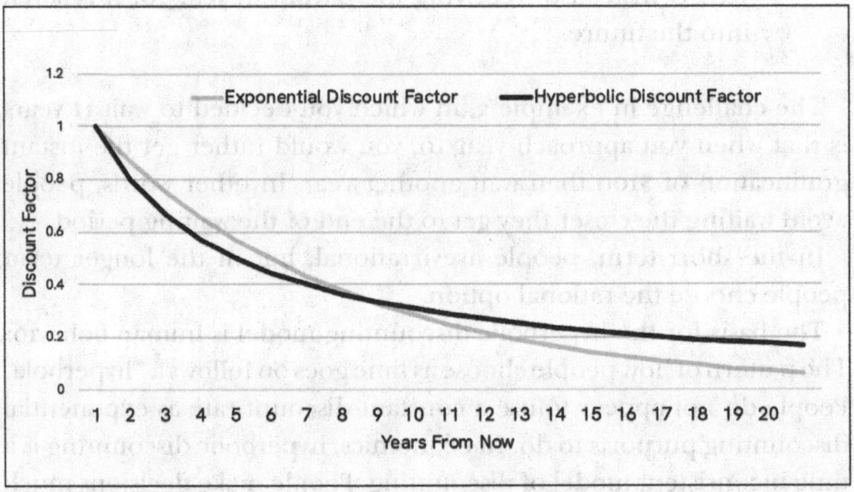

When cash flows are discounted using a hyperbolic function, the present value of a firm—especially one with long-term competitive advantages—tends to be higher than under exponential discounting. In our example, the hyperbolic method yields a present value nearly 40% greater than that produced by the exponential approach.

We are not advocating that you flip all your discounted cash flow models in favor of hyperbolic discounting. Rather, we highlight this concept because it may help explain why companies with strong, predictable long-term cash flows often trade at premium valuations. It's possible that the market, whether consciously or not, prices these businesses using a discounting approach that more closely resembles hyperbolic rather than exponential discounting. Relying solely on exponential discounting to value long-term compounders could lead to a significant undervaluation of their true worth.

Minimizing the odds of mistakes

An investor in a single-exposure company—one that relies on a narrow market and grows only organically—must consistently get multiple variables right to achieve strong returns. The success depends on the cumulative probability of correctly assessing all these factors.

Selling also introduces reinvestment risk. Each time an investor decides to exit an investment in a single-exposure company and reinvest in a new one, it introduces another opportunity to be wrong.

Investing in companies without the two engines characteristic of the nine compounders in this book means an investor must not only evaluate the management team effectively, but also predict industry outcomes with great precision. Additionally, understanding the probability distribution of capital allocation at the company level is crucial: How will management deploy cash? How will they raise capital? Will a new growth phase emerge? The more variables you need to get right, the lower your chances of a favorable outcome.

In contrast, high-performing acquisition-driven compounders—equipped with two engines and a programmatic approach to acquisitions—mitigate these risks. Their dual-engine approach extends the investment runway and reduces the number of variables an investor must navigate. This ability to stay invested is essential for reaching the second half of the chessboard, where exponential growth accelerates and meaningful compounding occurs.

That is why it's easier to stay the course with these types of companies—not only in strong markets but also in downturns. During down markets, these companies often find better opportunities to execute highly accretive acquisitions. Additionally, it is psychologically easier to remain invested when knowing that great investing and capital allocation skills are structural parts of their DNA.

Endnotes

1 Possibly apocryphally: www.snopes.com/fact-check/compound-interest. The insight still stands.

2 The inspiration for using this metaphor came from blogger LibertyRPF: www.libertyrpf.com/p/401-stock-indices-and-the-ship-of

3 From the book *Man säljer inga julgranar på annandagen*, by Carl Uggla, 2008.

4 According to Rune Andersson in the podcast *Stormens Öga*, 22 February 2024.

5 In an interview with Alf Zetterström at www.merger.nu/carl-bennet-koper-zetterstroms-rostfria

6 According to *Dagens Industri, an interview with Gunnar Tindberg*, 24 October 1992.

7 Historical reports from Industrivärden.

8 According to *Dagens Industri*, interview with Johnny Alvarsson 16 December 2010.

9 Definition of "best" by *Forbes* magazine: revenue <US$500m, an average return on equity and growth >10% for the last five years, and a growth of 15% the last year.

10 Based on discussions with former colleagues and Indutrade employees.

11 According to former and current employees in Indutrade

12 Indutrade Annual Report 2014.

13 Interview with Johnny Alvarsson, www.acquirers.com

14 According to our discussions with Gunnar Tindberg.

15 Indutrade Capital Market Day 2022

16 Lundbersföretagen Annual Report 2023.

17 www8.gsb.columbia.edu/sites/valueinvesting/files/files/Buffett1984.pdf

18 *Tisenhult: Grundaren, familjen och företagen* (Ronald Fagerfjäll)

19 According to an interview with Pär Stenberg, ex CEO Bergman & Beving in *Dagens Industri*, 25 January 1988.

20 B&B Tools 2002 annual report.

21 1983 letter to shareholders.

22 "Bergman & Beving to Addtech, a best-in-class serial acquirer", Acquirers.

com (www.acquirers.com/post/bergman-beving-to-addtech), and the book: *Tisenhult: Grundaren, familjen och foretagen* (Ronald Fagerfjäll)

23 From presentation material by Momentum Group AB.

24 www.lagercrantz.com/en/history

25 lagercrantz.com

26 Original images © 2025 Lagercrantz Group AB (www.lagercrantz.com/en/history)

27 According to the CEO, Jörgen Wigh

28 www.lagercrantz.com/en/strategy

29 www.lagercrantz.com/en/strategy

30 Extracted from investor presentation by Lagercrantz held at RedEye seminar in 2023.

31 Interview with Niklas Stenberg, Addtech CEO in Dagens Industri 28 August 2023

32 Addtech Annual Report 2003/04

33 A story shared by the former CEO Johan Sjö.

34 Addtech Annual Report 2008/09

35 Addtech Capital Markets Day 2019

36 opmwire.com/steve-scotchmer-mark-leonard-constellation-software

37 www.csisoftware.com/category/press-releases/2021/11/23/change-of-directors-at-constellation-software

38 Constellation Software shareholder letter 2Q 2009.

39 Constellation Software shareholder letter 2018.

40 Constellation Software shareholder letter 2015.

41 Interview with Navi Hehar, former VP and Head of Americas Corporate Development, Modaxo Division at Constellation Software. Third Bridge Forum, 30 September 2022.

42 From the conversation between Mark Leonard and Jeff Bender on the *#WeAreHarris* podcast.

43 aqfd.docsend.com/view/edfgtvz5zqa5w6f8

44 Constellation Software shareholder letter 2014.

45 REQ Capital.

46 While the 75% criterion is generally in place, senior executives are allowed to take their entire bonus in cash once every five years.

47 Roi Lipovetzky: aqfd.docsend.com/view/edfgtvz5zqa5w6f8

48 www.investors.com/news/management/leaders-and-success/family-ties-help-this-ceo-take-small-aerospace-firm-into-orbit

49 Conversation with Larry Mendelson on 2 November 2022.

50 *The Titanium Economy: How Industrial Technology Can Create a Better, Faster, Stronger America* by Asutosh Padhi, Gaurav Batra and Nick Santhanam
51 *The Titanium Economy.*
52 Conversation with Eric Mendelson on 2 November 2022.
53 Heico Q3 2021 conference call.
54 From our discussions with Eric Mendelson.
55 Large parts of this section are from meetings with management and from www.encyclopedia.com/books/politics-and-business-magazines/AMETEK-inc
56 From an interview with a former employee at AMETEK, used with permission from In Practise: inpractise.com/articles/ametek-manda-strategy-and-incentives
57 From an interview with a former employee at AMETEK, used with permission from In Practise: inpractise.com/articles/ametek-manda-strategy-and-incentives
58 Conversation with David Zapico, March 25, 2025
59 Judges Scientific website.
60 Conversation with David Cicurel on March 22, 2025
61 Judges Scientific annual report 2003.
62 Information from David Cicurel.
63 Discussions with David Cicurel on March 21, 2025. ROTIC is calculated by comparing attributable EBITA with the investment in fixed and net current assets (excluding surplus cash), before considering central costs and properties, and the effect of R&D capitalization.
64 Discussion with David Cicurel on 2 October 2022.
65 seekingalpha.com/article/4298533-judges-scientific-plc-collection-of-global-niche-leaders-in-scientific-instrument-sector
66 Conversation with David Cicurel on 2 October 2022.
67 Conversation with David Cicurel on 2 October 2022.

About the Authors

ODDBJØRN DYBVAD has almost 20 years of experience within portfolio management. He is the co-founder of REQ and currently serves as one of three equity portfolio managers, co-managing the REQ Global Compounders fund. Prior to founding REQ he worked for 15 years at ODIN Fund Management. For the last 11 years he was responsible for the Global Mandate at ODIN Fund Management, which won the best global fund 2020 award at the Morningstar Fund Awards for its historical track record at generating alpha. Oddbjørn holds a master's degree in economics with a specialization in finance from the Norwegian School of Economics and Business Management (NHH).

KJETIL NYLAND has over 15 years of experience in the financial industry, spanning equity portfolio management and buy-side equity and credit research. He is currently one of three equity portfolio managers at REQ and co-manages the REQ Global Compounders fund. Before joining REQ, he was a partner at Borea Asset Management, where he managed Borea Global Equities, a EuroHedge-awarded equity fund. He also has operational experience at Stacc Escali, a company specializing in vertical market software for financial services. Kjetil holds a master's degree in economics and administration with a finance specialization from the Norwegian School of Economics (NHH).

ADNAN HADŽIEFENDIĆ has over 15 years of experience in the financial industry in different roles as credit analyst and senior analyst for Danske Bank and Swedbank. He is currently one of three equity portfolio managers at REQ, managing the REQ Nordic Compounders fund. In his prior role as a senior analyst, he was the author of Sweden's most extensive study on acquisition-driven compounders, titled 'What Drives Shareholder Value for an Acquisition-driven Compounder?', presenting his findings to over 100 companies' executives and boards of directors. Adnan holds a master's degree in business and economics with a specialization in finance from Linköping University (LiU) in Sweden.

About REQ

REQ manages two equity funds—REQ Global Compounders and REQ Nordic Compounders—focused on ultra-long-term, high-conviction investing. REQ invests in publicly traded, acquisition-driven compounders—companies that generate strong cash flows and reinvest capital at high returns through programmatic bolt-on acquisitions in private markets, alongside organic growth.

The cornerstone of REQ's investment philosophy is capital allocation, decentralization, and people. REQ backs exceptional capital allocators who operate with an ownership mindset and embrace decentralized structures. Strong corporate governance is fundamental to REQ's approach, ensuring sustainable business practices and long-term shareholder value. As a partner-owned firm, REQ designs its funds to maximize enduring returns for its investors.

Disclaimer: At the time of publication, funds managed by REQ had ownership stakes in the companies profiled within this book. This information is for informational purposes only and does not constitute investment advice or an endorsement of any specific company.

www.ingramcontent.com/pod-product-compliance
Lightning Source LLC
LaVergne TN
LVHW040518210926
848480LV00007BA/1499
9781917943031